MEMBERSHIP OF THE PUBLIC SCHOOLS COMMISSION
(SECOND REPORT)

Chairman   *Professor David Donnison, B.A.,
    Director, Centre for Environmental Studies.

Vice-Chairman   *Lord Annan, O.B.E., D.Litt., D.U.,
    Provost of University College, London.

Members   C. R. Allison, M.A.,
    former Headmaster, Brentwood School.

    *Kathleen Bliss, M.A., D.D.,
    Lecturer in Religious Studies, University of Sussex.

    *T. Ewan Faulkner, M.A., Ph.D.,
    former Convener, City of Dundee Education Committee.

    Mark Arnold-Forster,
    Senior Leader Writer, *The Guardian,* London.

    *Dame Anne Godwin, D.B.E.,
    former General Secretary, Clerical and Administrative
    Workers Union.

    *W. S. Hill, M.Ed., B.Sc. (Econ.),
    Headmaster, Myers Grove Comprehensive School,
    Sheffield.

    Alderman F. H. Hutty, J.P., B.Com.,
    former President, Association of Education Committees.

    *H. G. Judge, M.A., Ph.D.,
    Principal, Banbury School.

    R. M. Marsh, M.A.,
    County Education Officer, Hampshire.

    B. H. McGowan, M.A.,
    Headmaster, Solihull School.

    Reverend Mother Angela Mary Reidy, O.S.U., B.Sc.,
    Prioress, Ursuline Convent, Wimbledon.

    Councillor T. Taylor, O.B.E., J.P.,
    former Chairman, Blackburn Education Committee.

    Lewis E. Waddilove,
    Director, Joseph Rowntree Memorial Trust.

    Miss Jean Wilks, M.A.,
    Headmistress, King Edward VI High School for Girls,
    Birmingham.

    *Professor Bernard Williams, M.A.,
    Knightbridge Professor of Philosophy, University of
    Cambridge.

    The Very Reverend Robin Woods, M.A.,
    Dean of Windsor.

* Members of the Commission for the First Report.

Roger W. Young, M.A., S.Th., F.R.S.E.,
Headmaster, George Watson's College, Edinburgh.

Assessors   D. Evan Morgan,
Department of Education and Science.

G. S. V. Petter, H.M.I.

Secretary   G. Etheridge
Mr. D. Neylan was Secretary to the Commission until his death in February, 1969.

Assistant Secretary R. D. Horne from March, 1969 to November, 1969

The Public Schools Commission

SECOND REPORT

VOLUME I: REPORT ON INDEPENDENT DAY SCHOOLS
AND DIRECT GRANT GRAMMAR SCHOOLS

LONDON
HER MAJESTY'S STATIONERY OFFICE
1970

The estimated cost of preparation of the Report is £64,500, of which £9,500 represents the estimated cost of printing and publishing the Report and £42,000 represents the approximate costs of services provided by the Department of Education and Science and the Scottish Education Department.

SBN 11 270170 1

MEMBERSHIP OF THE PUBLIC SCHOOLS COMMISSION
(SCOTTISH COMMITTEE)

Chairman   T. Ewan Faulkner, M.A., Ph.D.,
       former Convener, City of Dundee Education Committee.

Vice-Chairman Roger W. Young, M.A., S.Th., F.R.S.E.,
       Headmaster, George Watson's College, Edinburgh.

       James M. Gardner, M.A., F.E.I.S.,
       former Headmaster, Glenwood Secondary School, Glasgow.

       Thomas Henderson, M.A., B.Sc.(Econ.),
       Director of Education, Midlothian.

       Mrs. Elizabeth C. F. Leggat, M.A., Dip.Ed.,
       Principal, Callendar Park College of Education, Falkirk.

       Francis McCormick, S.S.C.,
       Solicitor, Glasgow.

       Alan E. Thompson, M.A., Ph.D.,
       Economics Department, Edinburgh University, ex-member of Parliament for Dunfermline Burgh.

Assessor   †J. F. McClellan,
       Scottish Education Department.

Secretary   J. W. Sinclair

       † Succeeded W. I. McIndoe in October, 1969.

29th January, 1970

Dear Secretary of State,

After presenting its First Report, on independent boarding schools, the Public Schools Commission was reconstituted to consider the independent day schools and the direct grant and grant-aided schools. We now present our Report on these schools. Our terms of reference are set out overleaf.

The situation in Scotland has been considered by the Commission's Scottish Committee. We present the Scottish Committee's findings as Volume III of our Report and we are also sending a copy of the Report to the Secretary of State for Scotland. We endorse their analysis, and commend their conclusions to the attention of all concerned with education in Scotland.

Yours sincerely,

DAVID DONNISON,

(*Chairman*)

The Rt. Hon. Edward Short, M.P.,
Secretary of State for Education and Science.

PUBLIC SCHOOLS COMMISSION—TERMS OF REFERENCE
(December 1965)

The main function of the Commission will be to advise on the best way of integrating the public schools with the State system of education. For the immediate purpose of the Commission public schools are defined as those independent schools now in membership of the Headmasters' Conference, Governing Bodies' Association or Governing Bodies of Girls' Schools Association.

The Commission will be expected to carry out the following tasks:

(a) To collect and assess information about the public schools and about the need and existing provision for boarding education; forms of collaboration between the schools (in the first instance the boarding schools) and the maintained system.

(b) To work out the role which individual schools might play in national and local schemes of integration.

(c) If it so wishes, and subject to the approval of the Secretary of State, to initiate experimental schemes matching existing provision with different types of need.

(d) To recommend a national plan for integrating the schools with the maintained sector of education.

(e) To recommend whether any action is needed in respect of other independent schools, whether secondary or primary.

In carrying out its tasks the Commission will be expected (while respecting the denominational character of the schools), to pay special attention to the following objectives:

(a) To ensure that the public schools should make their maximum contribution to meeting national educational needs, and in the first instance any unsatisfied need for boarding education in the light of the Martin[1] and Newsom[2] reports.

(b) To create a socially mixed entry into the schools in order both to achieve (a) above and to reduce the divisive influence which they now exert.

(c) To move towards a progressively wider range of academic attainment amongst public school pupils, so that the public school sector may increasingly conform with the national policy for the maintained sector.

(d) To co-operate closely with local education authorities in seeking to match provision with need for boarding education.

(e) To ensure the progressive application of the principle that the public school, like other parts of the educational system, should be open to boys and girls irrespective of the income of their parents.

---

[1] Report of the Working Party on Assistance with the Cost of Boarding Education, H.M.S.O., 1960.
[2] Half Our Future—A report of the Central Advisory Council for Education (England), H.M.S.O., 1963.

Additional terms of reference (October, 1967)

To advise on the most effective method or methods by which direct grant grammar schools in England and Wales and the grant-aided schools in Scotland can participate in the movement towards comprehensive reorganisation, and to review the principle of central government grant to these schools.

Table of Contents

VOLUME I

PART I–INTRODUCTION

PART II–THE BACKGROUND

Lists of Tables and Figures in this Volume

Part One

Introduction

CHAPTER 1

Introduction and Recommendations

1. Although our enquiry deals only with a small part of the nation's system of education—the direct grant, grant-aided and independent day schools which educate 5 per cent of the school children in Great Britain—it touches on many of the most hotly debated educational problems of the day. Some of these problems pose questions of policy on which schools and local education authorities are urgently seeking decisions. Many of them pose questions on which there is no consensus of opinion—least of all among the experts who have devoted their lives to teaching and educational administration. We therefore interpreted our terms of reference broadly, examining the whole development of secondary education and taking nothing for granted. We also worked as fast as we could, drawing on all the research available to us but launching no major new study of our own.

2. The Scottish system of education has many distinctive features, so a separate Committee, consisting of two of our members and five others from Scotland, studied the Scottish grant-aided and independent day schools with the help of their own Secretariat. They made their own enquiries and at our request have produced a report which can be read without reference to this Volume. We met with the Scottish Committee from time to time, and some of our members took part in visits to Scottish schools and in discussions with Scottish education authorities. We have studied the report they made to us; we endorse their analysis, and we hope that all who are concerned with education in Scotland will consider their conclusions. We reproduce this report as Volume III of the Commission's Second Report. Later in this Introduction we outline the Scottish Committee's main proposals and summarise their recommendations. Thereafter in this Volume we confine our discussion to England and Wales.

England and Wales

3. This Introduction explains the questions we considered, and the main conclusions reached at each stage of our enquiry. It is not a summary of our Report, for we do not discuss all our proposals, nor do we explain the evidence which led us to them. It is a guide to the argument of the chapters that follow.

4. Most of the schools whose future we discuss are day schools. Their work must therefore be considered in the context of local systems of day education. We were asked to show how these schools can "participate in the movement towards comprehensive reorganisation". Thus we had to start by studying the aims and character of this movement at the local level. We visited maintained, direct grant and independent schools, and colleges of further education. We talked with the governors, heads, teaching staff and pupils of schools, and with the elected members and officers of local education authorities. We learnt what we could about the recent development of secondary education in other countries. We studied the evolution of our own Government's policies for

secondary education, but we did not take these policies for granted or accept them uncritically.

5. The most striking feature which distinguishes this country's schools from those of most of our neighbours and economic competitors is the large proportion of our pupils who abandon full-time education at the earliest opportunity. Many of our schools are very good indeed. Nevertheless, on average, our children leave school sooner than children in comparable urban, industrial societies; and, despite the reorganisation now under way, most of them are still divided at a younger age into different types of school, distinguished by the apparent abilities of pupils, the work they do, and the academic expectations their teachers have of them. During the last twenty-five years this country has extended and reorganised a pattern of schools which originally grew up to meet the needs and aspirations of different social classes. All children now get a fairer (though not a fair) chance of competing for academic opportunities which are still available only to a minority of them. During the next twenty-five years we must enable all children to take their education to a point at which they are equipped to go on learning and adapting throughout their lives. This is the aim of the movement towards comprehensive education, a task in which many other countries are also engaged.

6. Those working on this task are finding there are more ways of tackling it, involving more types of school, than they first envisaged. We have explained the aims of comprehensive education as clearly as we can, and specified the roles we envisage for schools participating in a comprehensive system. And it is a system, not just a new kind of school, which is being created: each school within it must collaborate with others in ways that strengthen the varying local patterns in which they play their part and enlarge the opportunities of all children.

7. Good teaching making rigorous intellectual demands and producing high academic achievement—all that is best in grammar *schooling*—will be needed more urgently than ever. But once we have decided to enable all children to take their education as far as they can go, we cannot accept early selection and segregation of a minority deemed fit for opportunities of advanced education— the traditional grammar *school.* It would be illogical and self-defeating if central and local government were to bend their efforts towards creating a comprehensive educational system while simultaneously supporting schools outside that system which frustrate its development. We concluded that schools which intend to secure continuing support from public funds, for themselves or their pupils, must participate in the movement towards comprehensive education.

8. All but two of us are also convinced that the aims of this movement cannot be attained if the selection of children for particular schools depends on their parents' willingness to pay fees. Thus places in day schools participating in comprehensive systems should be free. The arguments leading to this conclusion are set out in paragraphs 244 to 254.

9. We turned next to consider the direct grant schools. Independent secondary schools were first given direct grants by the central government under the Education Act of 1902, and for a time such schools provided virtually the only opportunities for more advanced education open to children from the local elementary schools. But direct grant schools, as they later came to be called, gradually assumed a distinctive—and some would say anomalous—status as many of the original schools came to be maintained by local authorities, as earmarked

central grants for maintained secondary schools ceased, as more maintained grammar schools with stronger sixth forms developed, as fees for education in maintained schools were abolished, and as secondary education began to be reorganised on comprehensive lines. What was once the norm has become an exception. The arrangements the direct grant schools made with the central government and the local authorities no longer meet the needs of the times, and these schools are now exposed to growing and destructive uncertainties as some local education authorities change their policies in different phases of their reorganisation schemes and following successive elections. The schools need a new settlement which will enable them to play an important and continuing part in the national system of education. Their help will certainly be needed. Resources for various branches of sixth form teaching, for example, will be scarce for many years to come.

10. The direct grant schools are an exceedingly varied group. A few of them are famous, large and highly selective regional grammar schools; more are well-established local grammar schools, much like the maintained grammar schools; some are boarding schools, often resembling the independent boarding schools; many are Roman Catholic schools providing an academic education for Catholic children of a fairly wide range of abilities and drawing from fairly wide areas; and there are others which do not fit any of these descriptions. Taking direct grant grammar schools as a whole, their curriculum, teachers, equipment and costs are much the same as those of the maintained grammar schools. The achievements of their pupils appear to be similar to those of pupils with comparable ability coming from the same kinds of social backgrounds in other grammar schools. Since the work, resources and achievements of this group cannot for the most part be distinguished from those of the maintained grammar schools, a case for treating them differently from the maintained grammar schools must be argued on other grounds.

11. The schools have been praised for their diverse social composition and criticised for their exclusiveness. In fact they educate a broader mixture of social classes than the wholly independent schools, but have few children of unskilled and semi-skilled workers, and are therefore more exclusive than the average maintained school. Their combination of free and fee-paying pupils is said by some to result in savings to public funds (on the grounds that the fee-payers would otherwise be educated wholly at public expense) and by others to constitute an unjustified subsidy (on the grounds that parents who would otherwise pay full fees are securing a free or subsidised education for their children). We discussed these arguments at length and concluded that both parties to this debate tend to contradict themselves. The claim that the schools are socially divisive rests on the assumption that their middle class parents would otherwise use the socially more heterogeneous maintained schools. In that case it must be recognised that many of them are saving public funds by paying fees. The counter claim that the schools promote social mix depends on the assumption that parents would otherwise be using the socially more exclusive independent schools. In that case there is a cost to public funds since their children get an education free or at a subsidised price. Either way, the costs or savings to public funds are very small in relation to the whole system of secondary education.

12. Nevertheless the direct grant schools are, for most purposes, independent foundations. Their governors have produced the capital that has been invested in

them, building up good schools in response to national needs and in accordance with the past educational policies of the nation. The schools are entitled by law to become wholly independent if they wish, and are rightly concerned about their freedom of action and naturally apprehensive of any step that might curtail it. It is this independence which distinguishes them, as a group, from maintained grammar schools.

13. We therefore studied the rights and duties of governors, heads and staffs of schools, and their relationships with central and local government. We concluded that a clearer statement of their respective responsibilities is required for schools of *all* kinds. We believe our recommendations on this subject will help to assure direct grant schools working under the new arrangements we propose for them the degree of independence they would expect—an independence which the best local education authorities already accord to their own schools.

14. The Secretary of State asked us how the direct grant day schools could participate in the movement towards comprehensive reorganisation. We present two schemes for this purpose—Scheme A in paragraphs 264 to 282, and Scheme B in paragraphs 283 to 293. Under both schemes the schools would work out with the education authorities what contribution they can best make to local systems of comprehensive education. The Secretary of State would approve the agreements made, and arbitrate if agreement could not be reached. Since they would take no more fee-payers once they entered comprehensive schemes, both their capital debts and their current expenditure must be met from public funds. Other proposals—for the junior schools attached to direct grant schools, for safeguarding the position of free place holders in schools going independent, and so on—will be found in our Report. Thus far we are agreed (but see paragraphs 229-233). Thereafter we differ over important features of these schemes.

15. Some of us propose that the current and capital expenditure of the schools (to be known as "full grant" schools) should henceforth be largely met from public funds through a School Grants Committee appointed to supervise and assist in the negotiations, and to advise all parties concerned. This Committee, on which the schools, the education authorities and others would be represented, would also assume the responsibilities proposed in the Commission's First Report for the Boarding Schools Corporation.

16. Some of us would invite the schools to apply for voluntary aided or controlled status, and bring direct grants from the central government to an end as soon as negotiations about participation can be concluded and the position of existing pupils safeguarded.

17. The first of these proposals—Scheme A— is designed to preserve the schools' financial and administrative links with central government which many of them see as an assurance of their continuing independence. The second—Scheme B—lays greater stress on the responsibility of local education authorities for planning and co-ordinating their schemes of reorganisation.

18. Some of us believe that either Scheme A or Scheme B could achieve their agreed common objectives, and that the choice between them should be made when the Government has responded to our main proposals, and the schools and the local authorities have considered the terms on which they could best collaborate.

19. Next we had to consider the direct grant boarding schools (all of which have some day pupils). The Commission's First Report suggested two ways in which

boarding public schools might be integrated with the State system. The first proposal was that an integrated school should make at least half its places available to children who needed boarding education and who came from a wide range of abilities and social backgrounds. If this scheme is set up, direct grant boarding schools choosing to go independent could take part in it. Most of them already have substantial proportions of pupils who for a variety of reasons need boarding education.

20. A second proposal, more briefly sketched in the First Report, would create a form of nationally aided status. Our centrally financed scheme for direct grant schools—Scheme A—is the natural development of this proposal. If Scheme A is adopted it will meet the needs of boarding schools as well as day schools. Those of us who would invite day schools to apply for a locally maintained status, under Scheme B, would similarly ask direct grant boarding schools to participate in reorganisation as locally maintained schools.

21. We all agree that boarding schools, and boarding wings of day schools, are likely to be more successful if some of their pupils—say, between half and one third—are there simply by choice of their parents, rather than because they need a boarding education. Parents of these boarders would be liable to pay fees, although in full grant or maintained boarding schools the fees would be scaled according to parental income and would at most only cover the costs of boarding, tuition being free. Day pupils in boarding schools should, so far as possible, have a range of ability and social background similar to the boarders. In full grant or maintained schools they would pay no fees. The arrangements for the admission of day pupils paid for by local education authorities at the integrated independent boarding schools would be part of the scheme of integration for the school concerned. The Boarding Schools Corporation (or School Grants Committee) would therefore consider the arrangements to be made for day pupils before recommending such schemes of integration to the Secretary of State for approval.

22. The independent day schools are an even more varied group than the direct grant schools. We hope some of them—and particularly that important minority which already offer many of their places to the local authorities—will participate in the movement towards comprehensive education under the schemes we propose for direct grant schools. Independent schools would not normally receive any help from the Government in settling their debts, but in other respects their position would be similar to that of the participating direct grant schools.

23. Schools remaining or becoming wholly independent will be able to offer help to the maintained system of education if they provide particular services not available in local maintained schools. But authorities relying on independent schools to meet more general needs, such as the education of academically gifted children, which they ought to provide for in their own schools, should be asked to make their own provision as soon as they can. We hope that the best independent denominational schools will become full grant or locally maintained schools. Until then, the present arrangements whereby authorities pay for or assist pupils at independent denominational schools should continue.

24. If they are adopted, our proposals would enable direct grant and independent day schools to participate fully in comprehensive education. But they cannot be expected to participate—and comprehensive reorganisation cannot

succeed—if local authorities continue unnecessarily to take up places at academically selective independent schools. It follows that education authorities must make declining use of places in any independent school which is only willing to collaborate on academically selective terms.

25. Throughout our Report we have tried to bear in mind the needs of all children and the contribution that all schools can make to their education. The schools we have been asked to study deserve to be considered in this national context, for together they exert a national influence. But we have also been concerned with the education of specially gifted children. We postpone our discussion of this important subject to the end of our Report because specially gifted children are found in schools of all kinds and the discussion cannot be confined to chapters dealing with particular segments of secondary education.

26. In our final chapter we consider the evidence we have assembled about the definition, selection and education of gifted children, and the opportunities which different educational policies and systems offer to gifted children and to others. Every system, comprehensive or selective, has its advantages and disadvantages, but none offers a complete solution to these difficult problems.

27. We are agreed that the conventional grammar school, selecting about twenty per cent of children at about the age of eleven, will not provide what the country or its most gifted children need. Children with outstanding gifts in ballet or music should have opportunities of going to secondary schools which specialise in developing their talents. But most of us are convinced that we shall do best for children with more academic gifts if we concentrate on finding and developing their talents, whenever and wherever they emerge, within comprehensive systems of education, although more research and carefully planned experiment must be devoted to discovering how best to meet their needs in this context. A minority of us believe that it would be dangerously premature to reach this conclusion when the evidence for it is still uncertain: they therefore recommend that a small number of the larger selective schools, capable of educating the most gifted children, should become "super-selective schools" recruiting children from the top two per cent of the ability range. Such schools may be found in the independent, direct grant or maintained sectors of secondary education. They would be financed in the future as full grant schools through the School Grants Committee to which advocates of this proposal would give responsibility for central government grants to direct grant schools participating in comprehensive reorganisation. These super-selective schools could not perform their task of offering a special education to all academically gifted children unless all places in them were free. In due course their achievements would be assessed to determine whether this experiment should be developed into a national system or not.

28. The costs of all our recommendations cannot be precisely estimated because they depend upon the response that schools, local education authorities and parents make to any initiative taken by the Government. If all the direct grant schools and all independent day schools in which at least fifty per cent of places are already taken by local authorities were to participate in comprehensive reorganisation, and if the pupils in maintained schools increased by an equivalent number as a result, then the additional current cost to the taxpayer would be approximately £6·5 million a year. That amounts to less than 0·5 per cent of present current expenditure on education. If, on the other hand, all the direct

grant schools were to become independent and the independent sector was enlarged by the number of places available in them, then the State would save £15·7 million a year, amounting to about one per cent of its current expenditure on education. The outcome cannot be predicted with any certainty but it will lie somewhere between these two extremes. The net cost or saving is unlikely to be large enough to make this a decisive factor in determining policy.

29. In conclusion, we ask that our proposals be considered as a matter of urgency by the Government, the local education authorities, the schools, and all concerned with education in this country. We found in the course of our enquiries that the direct grant schools were already beset by uncertainties about their future before our investigations began; some local authorities repeatedly change their demands upon these schools, and it is increasingly difficult for the schools to make firm plans for the future. Education authorities need the help of good schools, but are uncertain what part to ask these schools to play in their changing educational systems; too often, as reorganisation proceeds, it becomes harder to make constructive use of the important contribution the direct grant schools could offer. We found that the proportion of children who enter independent schools has been falling for many years. With the rapid growth now taking place in the sixth forms of maintained schools, the proportion of the nation's sixth formers in independent schools is falling even more quickly. These schools will never again be able to make so valuable and influential a contribution to the development of secondary education. In short, time is on no-one's side: the longer decisions are delayed, the less constructive they will be for all concerned.

Scotland

30. The Scottish Committee's conclusions—their agreements and their disagreements—closely match our own. Before we summarise them, some distinctive features of the Scottish system of education must be noted. It varies from one place to another, as the Scottish Report explains, and the comparisons that follow cannot do justice to this variety.

31. Comprehensive secondary education in neighbourhood schools, taking pupils at the age of twelve, has long been established in many parts of Scotland. All the education authorities have now adopted the policy of comprehensive reorganisation and are putting it into practice. The Scottish examination system means that pupils staying on beyond the minimum leaving age do not specialise quite so severely as their English contemporaries, and there is no clear break in the content and character of their work, such as occurs in England and Wales when pupils enter the sixth form. These differences mean that the forms of comprehensive organisation which can be envisaged in Scotland, and the roles open to schools participating in them, are different from those in England and Wales, and less varied in character.

32. In Scotland the denominational schools have been wholly maintained by the education authorities since 1918, and there is no equivalent to voluntary aided status. This status is therefore not open to grant-aided or independent schools as it is to their counterparts south of the Border. Maintained schools are directly administered by the education authorities without the intermediary of boards of governors or managers. The future status and rights of governors of independent and grant-aided schools collaborating with the education authorities are thus of special importance in Scotland.

33. The grant-aided schools all have primary departments recruiting pupils at various stages from the age of five onwards. Their grants are paid by the central authority on terms which do not require the offer of free places, do not call for uniform selection policies, and do not produce so uniform a level of fees as is found in direct grant schools in England and Wales. Except at a few schools, public contributions to the grant-aided schools are made from central government funds entirely. Thus these schools are academically less selective than the direct grant schools, and are less closely linked to the education authorities and the maintained schools. Participation in comprehensive systems is therefore likely to be easier for grant-aided schools in some ways, but harder in others.

34. The proportion of children who go to independent schools is smaller in Scotland than in England, and the independent schools of consequence are few in number though some are distinguished. Education authorities in Scotland pay or assist with the fees of very few pupils at independent schools.

35. The Scottish Committee came to the conclusion, as we did, that schools expecting continuing support from public funds must be prepared to participate in the movement towards comprehensive education. The Report on Scotland explains the aims of this movement, lists the potential roles which schools may play within it, and concludes that all places in participating schools must be free. It recommends that schools and education authorities should negotiate agreements about participation with each other, subject to the approval, and if necessary the arbitration, of the Secretary of State for Scotland.

36. The Scottish Committee were divided, on much the same lines as we were, about the principles and procedures for enabling schools to participate in comprehensive reorganisation. Some members favour inviting grant-aided schools to participate with education authorities in the provision of education by becoming locally maintained. Grants direct from the central government would be brought to an end as soon as negotiations about participation were concluded and the position of existing pupils would be safeguarded. The full costs of participating schools would be met by the education authorities concerned. Others propose that the current and capital expenditure of the schools (to be known as "full grant" schools) should be met by the central government and "user" education authorities through a Scottish School Grants Committee, which would also supervise and assist in the negotiations and would advise all the parties concerned. This Committee, on which the schools, the education authorities and others would be represented, would assume in addition the responsibilities proposed in the Commission's First Report for the Boarding Schools Corporation.

37. The Scottish Committee gave particularly careful attention to the government of schools and their relationship with education authorities. They recommend that participating schools should retain their present freedom and responsibility, so far as they are compatible with playing a part in comprehensive reorganisation, and that for their own schools education authorities should set up school committees which in the longer term should be allowed to develop into boards of governors.

38. It is proposed that independent day schools should be invited to participate in the movement towards comprehensive reorganisation on exactly the same principles as grant-aided schools.

39. Only one grant-aided school has a majority of boarders; the other twelve which have boarding places are primarily day schools. The Committee thinks

that if the recommendations of the First Report for integrated schools are adopted they offer an appropriate option for the first school. Proposals for boarding in the others would be related to their status as locally maintained or full grant schools. In either case tuition would be free for all pupils and the boarding costs of pupils in need of boarding would be met in full. While all the members regard it as desirable for the schools to have some boarders also who are there by the choice of their parents, some think that such parents should pay full boarding but no tuition fees, while others propose that the boarding contribution should be according to an income scale.

40. The Scottish Committee considered the needs of the gifted child, as we have done, and reached the unanimous conclusion that selective schools catering only for the gifted—other than a small number of the artistically or musically talented—would not make a useful contribution in Scotland. They call for more research on the gifted and further experiment in meeting their needs, within the comprehensive system, but are opposed to the creation of "super-selective" schools.

41. If all the grant-aided schools were to participate in comprehensive reorganis-ation, with the same numbers of pupils, then the additional current cost to public funds would be approximately £1·5 million a year, which is 0·78 per cent of current expenditure on education in Scotland (excluding universities) or 1·3 per cent of present current expenditure on schools in Scotland. If on the other hand all the grant-aided schools were to become independent and the indepen-dent sector was enlarged by the number of places available in them, then the State would save £1·55 million a year, that is just under 1·4 per cent of current expenditure on schools. The outcome cannot be predicted with any certainty, but it will lie somewhere between those two extremes.

SUMMARY OF MAIN RECOMMENDATIONS—
ENGLAND AND WALES

Our main recommendations are as follows. References to paragraphs in the Report are shown in brackets.

I Participation in a Comprehensive System

1. Day schools receiving grants from central or local authorities should partici-pate in the movement towards comprehensive reorganisation in ways that accord with local needs and plans. We explain what we mean by the movement towards comprehensive reorganisation in paragraphs 187 to 199. Arrangements for participation should be worked out between schools and the local education authorities and be approved by the Secretary of State for Education and Science. (201 and 202)

2. Schools participating in a comprehensive system should become one of the following:

> *(i) an all-through comprehensive school (providing for the age range from 11 or 12 to 18);*
> *(ii) one component of a tiered system, within which some schools will provide for the lower secondary stage (to the age of 13 or 14) and others for the upper secondary stage;*

(iii) a "mushroom" type of school, receiving pupils at the lower secondary stage (i.e. at the age of 11, 12, 13 or 14) on a non-selective basis, and further pupils at the age of about 16;

(iv) a junior or sixth form college receiving pupils at the age of about 16;

(v) a comprehensive school for the age range 11 or 12 to 16;

(vi) a school providing for special needs—for example, a choir school or a music school;

(vii) a school meeting boarding needs.[1]

The time required to enable schools to adopt one of these roles will depend on the resources available and the pace at which local authorities reorganise the maintained schools. Schools may therefore have to be reorganised gradually and by stages. (208 to 215)

II Finance and Status

3. Day schools taking part in the comprehensive system should no longer charge fees, and the present direct grant arrangements should therefore be discontinued.[2] (244 to 254)

4. Children already in the schools at the time of the change should be entitled to continue their education undisturbed. If schools decide to become independent, the present direct grant should be phased out in such a way as to protect the interests of the existing pupils and parents. (278 and 288)

5. The salaries and status of staff in schools participating in reorganisation should be protected on the same terms that are applied to staff in maintained schools undergoing reorganisation. (295)

6. Seven of us recommend the introduction of a new "full grant" status for former direct grant and independent day secondary schools willing to participate in comprehensive reorganisation. Full grant schools would receive grants from public funds to cover up to 100 per cent of their approved debts and future capital expenditure. Foundation income and capital resources should be taken into account when these grants are determined. Current expenditure should be financed similarly, according to the principle that the staffing ratios, equipment and other resources of the schools should be no better and no worse than the general level for maintained schools with similar functions. Grants to the schools should be administered by a central body—a "School Grants Committee"—which would also take over the functions of the Boarding Schools Corporation proposed in the Commission's First Report. The Committee should derive its funds from local authorities and the Department of Education and Science in such a way that authorities neither gain nor lose financially by having day pupils in their area attend these schools instead of locally maintained schools. (264 to 282)

---

[1] Two of us recommend that another role should be added to this list, namely, that of a school catering for pupils aged 14-18 whose intake would represent that proportion of the total ability range agreed between the governors and one or more local education authorities. (227-228)

[2] Two of us recommend that former direct grant schools and day independent schools participating in the movement towards comprehensive reorganisation should charge fees on the basis that all pupils shall be assisted according to an agreed scale of parental income. (229-232)

7. *Eight of us consider that participating schools should adopt one of the forms of locally maintained status already available. The approved debts of these schools would be met from public funds. If those becoming voluntary aided schools need additional capital grants to enable them to participate in comprehensive reorganisation, the possibility should be considered of making grants for this purpose to them and to other voluntary aided schools with similar needs. (283 to 293)*

8. *Four of us find either of these two proposals acceptable in principle and think that the choice between them should be taken by the Government of the day in the light of the response made by schools and local authorities to our proposals. (297)*

9. *All of us agree that direct grant schools unwilling or unable to participate in comprehensive reorganisation should retain the right to become independent schools if they wish. (278 and 288)*

10. *Junior or lower schools under either scheme will have three options: (a) to close, making their buildings available for any expansion required to enable the secondary school to participate in reorganisation; or (b) to become an independent primary school; or (c) to become a maintained primary school. If they choose (b) or (c) their pupils should not have privileged rights of entry to the secondary school. (294)*

III Government of Schools

11. *Governors, heads and staff at direct grant schools which choose to become full grant or locally maintained schools should retain the essential freedoms they already have, subject to prior agreement about the role of the school within the comprehensive system and about the arrangements for the admission of pupils. (303 to 311)*

12. *Maintained secondary schools should have the same essential freedoms as former direct grant schools, and we urge the Secretary of State to issue to local education authorities a memorandum of guidance on the government of schools setting out the principles we recommend. Such a memorandum should be issued promptly as a helpful preliminary to negotiations with the direct grant schools. (316)*

IV Independent Day Schools

13. *The legal right of voluntary bodies to provide efficient private education paid for by parents should not be curtailed. (319)*

14. *Independent secondary day schools should be encouraged to participate in a comprehensive system on terms similar to those we propose for direct grant schools, except that their capital debts should not normally be met from public funds. If a school becomes a voluntary controlled school the local education authority will meet loan charges as part of the running costs. (325)*

15. *The interpretation of local education authorities' powers and duties to assist with or pay the fees of pupils at independent schools should be more nearly uniform. The Secretary of State should issue guidance setting out the principles to be followed. If authorities wish to depart from these principles they should submit their proposed arrangements to him for his approval. (328 and 329)*

16. *The principles which should be observed are:*

(i) *The fees of pupils attending schools not recognised as efficient should not be paid in full or in part by local education authorities.*

(ii) *Where a child requires a particular kind of educational provision not available in an accessible maintained school or college of further education the local education authority should pay the full fee.*

(iii) *Where there are not enough places in full grant or maintained schools to meet the needs of children whose parents want them to go to these schools, the local education authority should pay the full fees for these children at independent schools. But this expedient should be brought to an end as soon as sufficient places can be provided in maintained schools, or sufficient direct grant or independent schools become full grant or locally maintained schools.*

(iv) *Local education authorities should retain their present powers to enable pupils to attend independent denominational schools, provided places are not available in accessible maintained denominational schools, and provided the progress of comprehensive reorganisation is not hindered.*

(v) *Local education authorities should continue to have discretion to assist with the fees of children at independent schools whose fees have in the past been paid by parents whose financial circumstances have so changed that their children's education would be disrupted unless assistance is given.*

(vi) *Local education authorities should continue to have discretion to assist with the fees of pupils who, though not classed as requiring special educational treatment, would for physical or psychological reasons especially benefit from education at particular independent schools.*

These principles should apply to future admissions of pupils assisted by local education authorities; pupils who already have free or assisted places should be entitled to retain them. (330 and 331)

V Direct Grant Boarding Schools

17. *If the Government accepts the recommendation in the Commission's First Report that integrated independent boarding schools should be established, it will be open to the direct grant boarding schools to become independent and participate in this form of integration. (347)*

18. *If the Government accepts the proposal made by some of us to establish a new full grant status, the direct grant boarding schools will be able to apply for this status. We regard this proposal as equivalent to that made in the Commission's First Report for a scheme for national voluntary aided status. (349)*

19. *Whether or not the Government accepts any of these proposals, it will be open to the direct grant boarding schools to apply for locally maintained status. (352)*

20. *Local authorities should be encouraged to take up day places in boarding schools becoming integrated on the terms proposed in the Commission's First Report, provided such arrangements contribute to the educational and social objectives of integration schemes. (348)*

21. *The procedure for determining boarding fees at maintained schools, the income scale used for parental contributions and the criteria for distinguishing pupils for whom no contribution is required should be standardised. (353)*

VI Costs

22. *We estimate the costs or savings attributable to our proposals on various assumptions. Whether the outcome will result in costs or savings will depend on the numbers of schools becoming, or remaining, independent and the choices of school made by parents. (Chapter 13)*

VII Gifted Children

23. *More research and experiment should be devoted to discovering how best to find and develop exceptional talents. (398)*

24. *Fourteen of us think that academically gifted children should be educated within comprehensive schools. There they will need special attention and opportunities. (390 to 393)*

25. *Five of us wish to preserve and develop a small number of highly selective schools on an experimental basis taking pupils from within the top two per cent of the ability range. Such schools could be drawn from schools that are at present maintained, direct grant or independent. They should no longer charge fees. (394 to 397)*

SUMMARY OF RECOMMENDATIONS AND CONCLUSIONS FOR SCOTLAND

The main recommendations of the Scottish Report (Volume III) are as follows. References to paragraphs in that Report are shown in brackets.

Schools in a Comprehensive System

1. *All schools in the public system of education should fulfil comprehensive roles in local schemes of reorganisation (paragraph 7.25). What is understood by "the movement towards comprehensive reorganisation" is explained in Chapter 7.*

2. *No schools in a comprehensive system should charge fees, since fee-paying is inconsistent with the objectives of comprehensive education (paragraph 7.12).*

3. *Education authorities should, wherever this is practicable, make their zoning arrangements flexible enough to allow freedom of choice of school, and they should make efforts to involve parents in the whole process of education. Exercise of choice should not, however, be permitted either to upset the balance of such social and academic mix as exists in particular schools, or to depress standards in schools that are already in under-privileged areas (paragraph 7.22).*

4. *Education authorities should take positive action to assist neighbourhood comprehensive schools in under-privileged communities in three ways:*

    (a) by paying more attention to drawing up catchment areas in such a way that they represent a wider range of social classes;

    (b) by devoting additional resources to schools attended by large proportions of children from under-privileged groups; and

    (c) by giving more publicity to the advantages and achievements of neighbourhood schools (paragraph 7.17).

Grant-Aided Schools

5. *If grant-aided schools are to receive support from public funds they should fulfil one of the following possible roles in a comprehensive system:*

> (a) *All-through (12-18) comprehensive schools, either singly or in groups of two or more as parts of "consortia";*
>
> (b) *One or more components of a "three-tier" system, comprising primary (5-10), middle (10-14) and upper (14-18) schools;*
>
> (c) *Components of "two-tier" organisations including 6 year comprehensive schools, each associated with one or more 4 year schools, from which potential S.C.E. Higher grade pupils transfer at the age of 14 or 16—an arrangement more likely to be related to short-term plans for reorganisation;*
>
> (d) *Parts of "two-tier" organisations comprising junior and senior high school complexes—like (c) more related to shorter term schemes;*
>
> (e) *Schools catering for special needs, e.g. music (paragraph 7.26).*

6. *A participating school should not be entitled to choose unilaterally the comprehensive role it will fulfil, but should negotiate with its local education authority its future place in the local system of education (paragraphs 7.26 and 9.1).*

7. *Participating schools should retain their governing bodies to be responsible for the general administration of the schools, and should retain the essential freedoms and responsibilities which their managers, heads, and staffs presently enjoy, so far as is consistent with central and local supervision of the whole public system of education (paragraphs 9.1, 10.5 and 10.7).*

8. *The governing bodies of participating schools should be constituted to allow due representation of the different interests concerned with the schools, e.g. the foundation, the education authority and the public interest (paragraph 10.6).*

9. *When proposals for participation have been approved, grant-aid should cease and fee-paying should be stopped forthwith, since a comprehensive role cannot be reconciled with fee-paying (see recommendation 2) (paragraph 9.18).*

10. *A new system of public support is required for schools participating in comprehensive reorganisation. Alternative schemes of finance and control are proposed by different members of the Committee:*

> Locally maintained status *is recommended by one group, under which the current and capital expenditure of participating schools would be met by the appropriate education authorities, which would be partly reimbursed through the Rate Support Grant; under these arrangements managers of schools would negotiate with education authorities the future of such matters as endowment schemes, the use of the schools' own resources of income and the powers, responsibilities and composition of governing bodies.*
>
> A new full grant status *is recommended by the second group, under which a Scottish School Grants Committee would finance the schools according to approved annual estimates from revenue derived from central government grants and contributions from "user" authorities; the Committee would also assist in negotiations about future roles between education authorities and schools and would reach agreement with the schools on matters relating to governing bodies and the schools' own sources of finance (paragraphs 9.4 to 9.11).*

11. *The capital costs of converting schools to participating roles should be serviced through annual expenditure whether under the locally maintained or under the full grant scheme (paragraph 9.13).*

12. *Debts incurred by participating schools should be taken over. They should be serviced either through annual expenditure to meet interest payments, or in special circumstances paid off by* ad hoc *grants from public sources (paragraph 9.14).*

13. *The new building projects required to put schemes of participation into effect should be submitted to the Secretary of State by education authorities as part of the programme for their areas or directly by the School Grants Committee. These should be considered by the Scottish Education Department as part of the overall school building programme for Scotland (paragraph 9.15).*

14. *The proposals for secondary departments of grant-aided schools should equally apply to their primary departments. The latter should be considered in the negotiations between boards of managers and education authorities. Depending on the outcome of these negotiations they should be operated either as part of participating schools or as buildings for the improvement or expansion of their secondary departments or as separate primary schools, whether independent or wholly maintained by the education authorities (paragraph 9.16).*

15. *Schools and education authorities should be given two to three years from a date named by the Secretary of State to complete discussions about the future roles of grant-aided schools, their part in the educational provision for their areas and their admission procedures; during this period grants to the schools should continue at existing levels; the period of negotiations should be subject to extension by the Secretary of State. Schools and education authorities should submit for the Secretary of State's approval proposals for the form of participation agreed between them, relating to interim and long-term arrangements; in the event of the parties concerned failing to agree on a future role for a grant-aided school it should be open to one or the other to appeal to his arbitration (paragraph 9.17).*

16. *The salaries and status of staff affected by the participation of their schools should be protected on the same terms as those applying to teachers in education authority schools (paragraph 9.19).*

17. *Schools which are unable or unwilling to participate in comprehensive reorganisation should be free to become independent. Grant to these schools should be gradually reduced over, say, 5 years from the end of the period of negotiation or from a date to be named by the Secretary of State, to safeguard the interest of the pupils already in the secondary departments (paragraph 9.20).*

Government of Schools

18. *Participating schools should retain their present freedoms and responsibilities, so far as they are compatible with playing a part in comprehensive reorganisation. For their own existing schools education authorities should set up school committees which should be progressively enabled to assume functions and powers comparable to those retained by the governors of participating schools.*

Independent Schools

19. *Independent day schools should be invited to participate in the movement*

3

towards comprehensive reorganisation on exactly the same principles as grant-aided schools (paragraph 11.4).

Boarding Provision

20. Quite apart from the opportunity of participation, St. Joseph's College should be given the choice of becoming an "integrated" school, if the Government accept the recommendations of the First Report (paragraph 12.10).

21. Of the other twelve grant-aided schools which have a minority of boarding places, those which eventually participate in comprehensive reorganisation should have their boarding places filled by a mixture of pupils with a special need for boarding education and children whose parents choose a boarding education for them. Under the locally maintained scheme education authorities should adopt common policies for establishing categories of need; under the full grant scheme the School Grants Committee should lay down a common policy for establishing such categories (paragraphs 12.11 and 12.13).

22. Tuition should be free for all pupils; no boarding fees should be charged for cases of "need". Some of us recommend that boarders who have no recognised boarding need should be assisted on a scale related to the income of their parents; others recommend that parents who choose a boarding education for their children should meet the full boarding cost (paragraph 12.13).

Part Two

The Background

CHAPTER 2

Secondary Education

42. In this second Part of our Report we describe the changing system of education to which our own proposals, presented in the third Part, must be applied. This Chapter and the next deal with secondary education in England and Wales, pointing out some of the main changes at work within this system, and tracing the new patterns of comprehensive education now taking shape. Then, in two chapters on the direct grant schools and the independent day schools, we describe the sectors we have been asked to study.

International Comparisons

43. Schools in different countries have developed in different ways from different origins. But the educational systems of the urban, industrial economies are now on the move in response to increasingly similar pressures and in pursuit of increasingly similar goals. Before examining our own system we should look abroad, note this country's peculiar strengths and weaknesses, and see what can be learnt from the experience of other countries. It is to Europe, North America, Australia and Japan that we shall look. Such comparisons, if they are to be presented briefly, must be painted with a broad brush in generalisations which obliterate the finer points and omit the many reservations and qualifications which a longer account would include. A more thorough study of the evidence about other countries can be found in Appendix 5.

44. Compulsory education begins about a year earlier in Britain than in most urban, industrial countries. But elsewhere substantial proportions of children go to nursery schools of some kind before the compulsory age: that is a pattern which tends to favour children who already have most advantages, for it is they who are more likely to start early.

45. At the age of eleven most of our children enter a school in which they will remain until the end of their school days. In most other countries the transfer to secondary education comes later; and in many there is a break at age 15 or 16 when children go to upper secondary schools of some kind. In this country the pupils who stay on to complete their course normally take public examinations at 16 and 18, and they specialise earlier and more severely than children in other countries. Elsewhere there is usually only one public examination, taken at the end of secondary education, and pupils over the age of 16 will usually be studying 5, 6 or more subjects. Here they are studying only 2, 3 or (more rarely) 4 subjects for examination purposes, although they do study others as a matter of general education.

46. Heads of schools in this country probably have greater freedom to shape the character of their schools than they would have in most other countries. But this independence is limited in practice by the system of public examinations. Not only do these examinations at present come twice in the school career, but they are in the main conducted by external examiners, whereas in many other

21

countries they are conducted mainly by the children's own teachers. Thus in British schools entering pupils for public examinations there is less variety in the curriculum than might be expected. In primary schools, now that eleven-plus selection tests are disappearing, there is more genuine freedom and greater variety.

47. In this country there is little explicitly vocational education for children of school age, apart from shorthand, typing and commercial classes for girls in their last years at school. In many other European countries there are more frankly vocational courses alongside the academic streams in the later stages of secondary education, sometimes starting with children as young as thirteen. Many of our young school leavers complain about the lack of vocational content in their studies and the apparent irrelevance of their work to life outside school.[1] Yet a narrow, vocational education is clearly to be avoided at school. It may be that the raising of the school leaving age will eventually lead us to the right balance.

48. Although most countries have what could be termed independent schools—often catering for larger proportions of children than our own independent sector—in no other country have they the prestige and influence that the English independent schools have. The more famous of our independent schools are more closely linked to the upper income groups in society and play a more significant role in the country's class and power structures than the independent schools of other countries. One result is that many of the most influential parents in this country do not rely on the schools maintained by the State and are not personally involved in them.

49. The most striking feature of the British system, when compared with those of other countries, is the heavy loss of pupils at the minimum leaving age. Comparisons between the proportions of pupils staying on at school in different countries, with different educational systems and presenting statistics in different ways, must be hazardous. Figure 1 offers only a rough guide. Nevertheless one conclusion can reasonably be drawn from the figures—that smaller proportions of our children are still at school between the ages of 16 and 18 than would be found in almost any comparable economy. Comparison of such figures is complicated by the fact that many young people in these age groups are in this country and in Scotland educated in colleges of further education for which comparable figures are not available from other countries. But the effect of any errors arising from this gap in the statistics is small. Even if full-time students in colleges of further education are added to this country's figures, and their counterparts in other countries ignored, our place in the rank order shown in Figure 1 is scarcely altered. The proportion of children remaining at school in Britain has risen considerably since 1965-66, the year adopted for Figure 1. Data for later years are not available for all the other countries appearing in this comparison, but it is clear that staying-on rates are rising fast in most places. Thus, if data for more recent years are used for all countries, our place in the rank order shown in the Figure is unlikely to change greatly.

50. Since they start a year earlier, pupils in this country who stay on at school will generally have had one more year of education by the time they reach the age of 16 or 17 than their counterparts elsewhere. It is tempting to assume that

---

[1] See "Young School Leavers", paragraphs 107 and 126, Schools Council Enquiry, H.M.S.O. 1968.

BOYS AND GIRLS AT SCHOOL AS A PERCENTAGE OF AGE GROUP IN TOTAL POPULATION IN DEVELOPED COUNTRIES

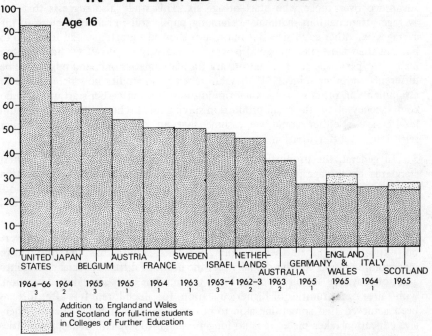

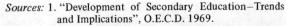

Addition to England and Wales and Scotland for full-time students in Colleges of Further Education

Sources: 1. "Development of Secondary Education—Trends and Implications", O.E.C.D. 1969.

2. "International Study of Achievement in Mathematics", Volume I Torsten Husén.

3. Statistics provided by overseas Education Departments. England and Wales from 1965 Statistics of Education Part I. Scotland from Scottish Educational Statistics 1965 and the Scottish Education Department.

Figure 1

they will therefore be a year ahead of children in other countries in their general intellectual development. We have found no evidence to support this view. A study of mathematical attainments at the ages of 13 and 17-18 in twelve countries[1] suggests, for this subject, that children who start at age five have no advantage over those who start at age six. This study also suggests that our average attainment in mathematics among pupils still in school is close to the averages for other countries. But our results showed a greater spread from top to bottom than most; i.e. our good performers are very good but we have far too many bad performers. These results are for mathematics only and might well be different for other subjects. If they are repeated in studies now being made of attainments in other subjects, they would show that our earlier start warrants no complacency about the small proportion staying on at school after the minimum leaving age. Neither could we assume that an earlier start justifies earlier selection and differentiation.

51. In general, the proportion of a country's age group attaining the highest standards by the age of 17 or 18 appears to depend heavily on the proportion who continue their education to this age. Early selection and early specialisation, if they are achieved at the cost of high wastage from school at ages 15-16, tend to *reduce* the numbers attaining these high standards.

52. When European education first took shape the majority of children were not expected to pursue their schooling far. Each country has therefore had to incorporate schools which originally met the needs of different social classes into a national system for all children. First, the aim has been secondary education, with fairer opportunities of higher education, for all children. It is after this has been achieved that something akin to our own movement towards comprehensive education takes place. It is no longer enough to give children opportunities to compete for entry to the more academic forms of secondary education: they must be enabled and persuaded to take their education as far as they can. The United States of America, Australia, Japan, Sweden, Norway, France and the East European countries all have or will shortly have largely comprehensive educational systems, up to age 15 or 16 at least. Other countries (Denmark and Italy, for example) have introduced, or are introducing, common schooling up to the age of 14. Other countries (Germany and Israel, for example) are experimenting with forms of comprehensive schooling or (as in Austria) with ways of making parallel systems more flexible and facilitating transfer between schools after the age of selection. All are engaged in the movement towards comprehensive education.

53. We examine the experience of other countries again in Chapter 14 where we discuss the education of the most gifted children. We now turn to the system of secondary education in England and Wales. It is a system in movement, and our description therefore concentrates on the main changes that must be borne in mind by those formulating policies for the schools in our terms of reference.

Pupils

54. The numbers of children at school are increasing. In 1947 there were about 5·6 million: in 1968 there were 8·1 million and in 1980, the Department of Education and Science estimates, the number will have gone up to 10·2 million.

---

[1] "International Study of Achievement in Mathematics" edited by Torsten Husén: John Wiley and Sons, 1967.

If past trends continue, independent schools as a whole will take both a declining proportion of these pupils and a declining number, though the number in schools recognised as efficient remains steady. The maintained primary and secondary schools must therefore take the increase in numbers, as they have done in the past. The Department estimates that, in 1980, maintained schools will have 9·6 million pupils. Of these, 4·2 million are expected to be in maintained secondary schools (unless some transfer to further education establishments) compared with 2·9 million in 1968. Thus in the twelve years from 1968 to 1980 the Department expects that there will be two million more pupils in maintained schools, 1·3 million of them in secondary schools. It is against this background that we have considered the future of the 100,000 pupils in direct grant upper schools and the 79,500 secondary day pupils in independent schools which are recognised as efficient.

The Growth of Sixth Forms

55. It is in the sixth forms that the most dramatic growth is taking place. In twenty years, the numbers of pupils aged sixteen or more who are still at school have risen from about 115,000 to 373,000. Taking those in maintained[1] schools only, the rise has been even steeper, from 75,000 to 297,000—an increase of nearly 300 per cent. Part of this growth can be explained by increasing numbers in the age groups concerned, and part by the growing proportion of pupils who go to maintained schools. But most of the growth is due to the rising proportion staying on at school. In maintained grammar schools, where the opportunity of staying beyond the minimum leaving age has been more generally available compared with other maintained schools, the proportion staying until the age of 17 or over has grown from less than a third to nearly two-thirds. Figure 2 traces the growth in numbers of pupils aged 16 and over in maintained schools, and gives comparable figures for direct grant and independent recognised efficient schools. The figures are for January of the year concerned, and most of the pupils will be six months older by the time they leave school. Figure 3 shows how the percentage of seventeen-year-olds in maintained schools has grown, alongside comparable data for direct grant schools and independent recognised efficient schools (see also Table 11).

56. Most striking of all has been the expansion in the numbers of full-time students under 18 in colleges of further education. In 1947 there were about 21,000; in 1968 there were 97,000. Gone is the dominance of evening classes which characterised these colleges twenty years ago. Alongside the 18 per cent of the 16-18 age group who were at school in 1968, there were another 5 per cent attending further education colleges full-time. In the same year some 16 per cent of the 16-18 age group attended part-time day courses and some 6 per cent attended evening classes at the colleges. A further 7·4 per cent attended classes at evening institutes. (Some pupils attending both day and evening classes will be counted twice in these percentages.) The numbers of sixteen and seventeen-year-olds and the percentages of seventeen-year-olds in colleges of further education are shown in Figures 2 and 3 for the purpose of comparison.

57. Figures 2 and 3 use a normal arithmetical scale. They show how the numbers of pupils over 16 in school have increased. What they do not reveal is the *rate of increase*. This can be demonstrated by plotting the figures on a graph using a

---

[1] i.e. county, voluntary aided, voluntary controlled and special agreement schools.

Figure 2

PUPILS AGED 16 AND OVER IN DIFFERENT TYPES OF EDUCATIONAL ESTABLISHMENT

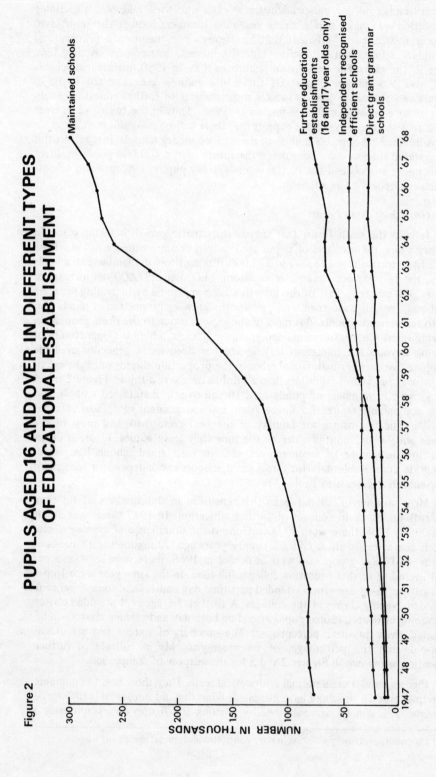

Source: Department of Education and Science returns.

Note: The figures for further education establishments are in respect of full-time students only. Students in national colleges and colleges of advanced technology and those on short full-time courses have been excluded.

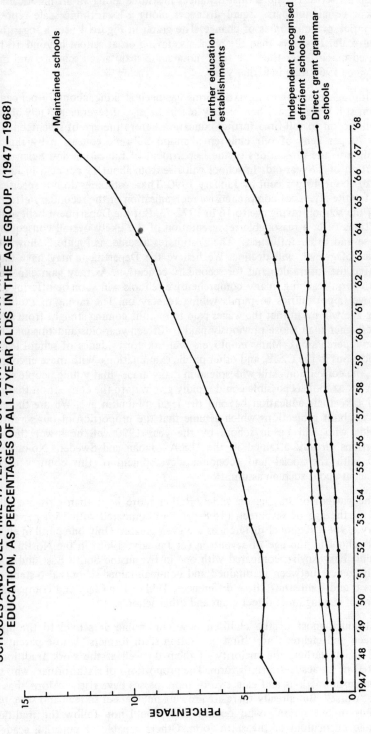

Figure 3 17 YEAR OLD PUPILS IN MAINTAINED, DIRECT GRANT AND RECOGNISED EFFICIENT INDEPENDENT SCHOOLS AND FULL-TIME 17 YEAR OLD STUDENTS IN GRANT-AIDED ESTABLISHMENTS OF FURTHER EDUCATION, AS PERCENTAGES OF ALL 17 YEAR OLDS IN THE AGE GROUP. (1947–1968)

Source: Department of Education and Science Statistics.

Note: The figures for further education establishments are in respect of full-time students only. Students in national colleges and colleges of advanced technology and those on short full-time courses have been excluded.

logarithmic vertical scale. Equal distances measured along an arithmetical scale represent equal numbers. Equal distances along a logarithmic scale represent equal ratios or equal rates of change. The graph in Figure 4 uses a logarithmic vertical scale. It shows that the numbers staying on at school beyond 16 have increased much faster than the total numbers in maintained schools, and much faster since 1960 than in earlier years.

58. Although the growth in sixth forms has been striking, about 77 per cent of children still leave school before they reach the age of seventeen. Only about 8 per cent go on to full-time further education before the age of seventeen. Thus about 70 per cent of our children abandon full-time education by this age. According to the projections of the Department of Education and Science, the proportion of 17-year-olds in school will rise from about 19 per cent in January 1969 to about 40 per cent by January 1990. These estimates do not specifically allow for the effects of comprehensive reorganisation or the secondary effects of raising the school leaving age to 16 in 1972-73. But the Department believe their projections offer a reasonable representation of the likely overall consequences of these and other influences. Their estimates assume, as Figure 5 shows, that the rate of growth will decline. We believe the Department may have under-estimated the future demand for secondary education. As they gain experience in sixth form teaching, many comprehensive schools will soon be offering more attractive opportunities to pupils willing to stay on. The raising of the school leaving age will mean that the wages paid to recruits coming straight from school will be higher than those previously paid to fifteen-year-olds and this may have further repercussions. Many employers will ask for evidence of school leavers' qualifications in the C.S.E. and other public examinations. With these encourage-ments, the convention—still widespread in many areas—that young people should start work as soon as possible could rapidly give way to the convention that they should take their education beyond the legal minimum age. We are therefore sceptical about projections which assume that the proportion of our seventeen-year-olds who will be in school by the year 1990 will be lower than the proportions *already* attained in the U.S.A., Japan and Sweden. No-one con-cerned with the social and economic development of this country can be complacent about such an assumption.

59. The pattern of staying on varies. Rather more boys than girls are still in school at the age of seventeen (16·8 per cent compared with 15·4 per cent at January, 1968). Regional differences are even greater. Only one pupil in eight is still at school at the age of seventeen (at January, 1968) in the North, North West and East Anglia, compared with one in five in the South East and Wales. The differences between maintained and non-maintained schools also stand out. Figures 6 and 7 illustrate these differences. Table 11 in Chapter 4 compares the patterns of staying on at direct grant and other schools.

60. Although most of the children now continuing at school to the age of seventeen and eighteen are "first generation sixth formers" whose parents left school much earlier, the majority of them do well at the work traditionally expected of an academic sixth form. The proportions of sixth formers who take 'A' level examinations and gain two or more passes have risen. "More" has not meant "worse". But already there are growing numbers of sixteen and seventeen-year-olds in our schools who do not—and should not—follow the traditional academic curriculum of the sixth form. Others capable of pursuing academic

**ALL PUPILS AND THOSE AGED 16 AND OVER IN MAINTAINED SCHOOLS
AND STUDENTS AGED 16 AND 17 IN GRANT-AIDED ESTABLISHMENTS
OF FURTHER EDUCATION**

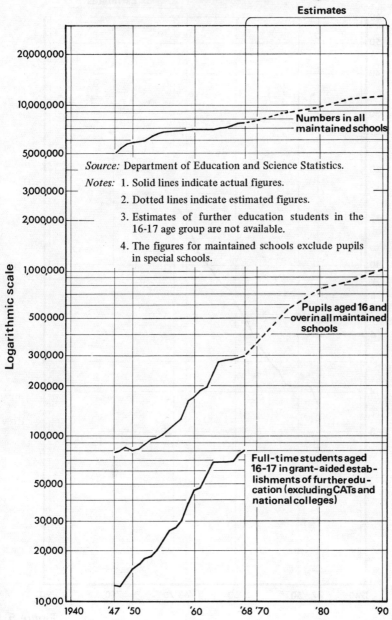

Estimates

Logarithmic scale

20,000,000

10,000,000

Numbers in all
maintained schools

5,000,000

Source: Department of Education and Science Statistics.

Notes: 1. Solid lines indicate actual figures.

3,000,000

2. Dotted lines indicate estimated figures.

2,000,000

3. Estimates of further education students in the
16-17 age group are not available.

4. The figures for maintained schools exclude pupils
in special schools.

1,000,000

500,000

Pupils aged 16 and
over in all maintained
schools

300,000

200,000

100,000

Full-time students aged
16-17 in grant-aided establishments of further edu-
cation (excluding CATs and
national colleges)

50,000

30,000

20,000

10,000

1940   '47 '50   '60   '68 '70   '80   '90

Figure 4

17 YEAROLDS IN MAINTAINED SCHOOLS AS A PERCENTAGE OF ALL 17 YEAROLDS

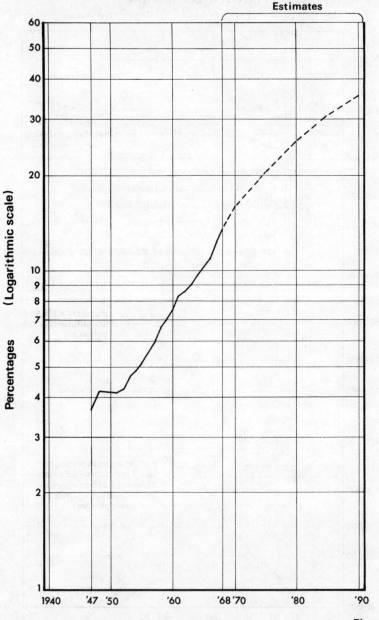

Figure 5

Notes: 1. Solid line indicates actual figures.

2. Dotted line indicates estimated figures.

Source: Department of Education and Science Statistics (1947-68), estimated figures
Statistics 1968, Volume 1, Table 45.

PERCENTAGE OF THE 16, 17 & 18 AGE GROUPS AT
SCHOOL & FURTHER EDUCATION ESTABLISHMENTS

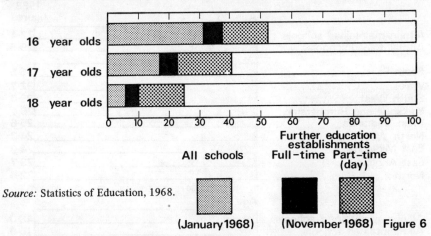

Source: Statistics of Education, 1968.

All schools

Further education
establishments
Full-time   Part-time
(day)

(January 1968)   (November 1968)   Figure 6

courses successfully will need more help and encouragement than their prede-
cessors in the sixth forms if they are to realise their full potential. Among school
children's families in which parents have unskilled or semi-skilled occupations,
one third have less than six books in the home and over four-fifths of parents
ceased full-time education at age fourteen.[1] Such children may not give of their
best if schools assume that academic teaching has the support and understanding
of well-educated parents.

61. The expectations of teachers are as important as the morale of their pupils.
Some recent research on primary school children suggests that the confidence
teachers have in their pupils' abilities can have exceedingly important effects on
their progress.[2] "Boys and girls", as the Plowden Report said, "tend to live up
to, or down to, their reputations."[3] Teachers who are to work successfully
amidst the sixth form explosion must be capable of stimulating the interest,
drive and confidence of pupils who would not feel at home in the more
traditional sixth form.

The Work of the Schools

62. The revolution in teaching methods which began in the primary schools is
now spreading into the secondary schools. Pilot schemes for "Nuffield Science",
the various New Mathematics Projects and the Humanities Curriculum Project
are examples of more widespread trends. The Schools Council provides a focus
for these new ideas and a framework for testing them and publicising the results.
We have not attempted to evaluate these experiments, but it is clear that
teaching in secondary schools could be changed out of all recognition in the next
decade.

---

[1] "Young School Leavers", pages 191 and 192, Schools Council Enquiry 1, H.M.S.O.
1968.
[2] See for example, Professor Rosenthal's and Dr. Jacobson's work on "Teacher
Expectations for the Disadvantaged", "Scientific American", April 1968, and "French from
Eight", a National Experiment, by Clare Burstall, N.F.E.R., 1968.
[3] "Children and their Primary Schools", paragraph 413.

PERCENTAGE OF PUPILS REMAINING AT SCHOOL TO VARIOUS AGES IN EACH REGION

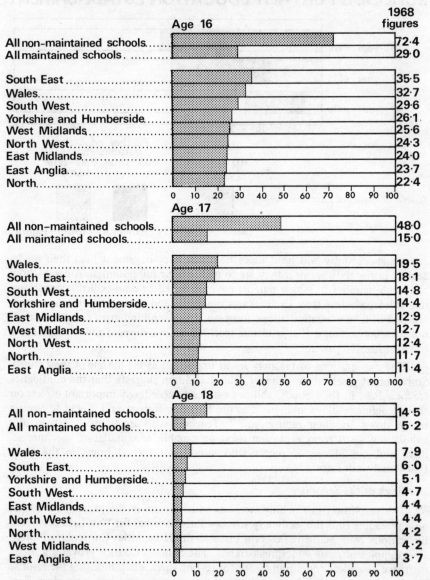

1968 figures

Age 16

All non-maintained schools......	72·4
All maintained schools.	29·0
South East.............................	35·5
Wales...................................	32·7
South West............................	29·6
Yorkshire and Humberside.......	26·1
West Midlands.......................	25·6
North West............................	24·3
East Midlands........................	24·0
East Anglia............................	23·7
North...................................	22·4

0 10 20 30 40 50 60 70 80 90 100

Age 17

All non-maintained schools....	48·0
All maintained schools...........	15·0
Wales...................................	19·5
South East.............................	18·1
South West............................	14·8
Yorkshire and Humberside......	14·4
East Midlands........................	12·9
West Midlands.......................	12·7
North West............................	12·4
North...................................	11·7
East Anglia............................	11·4

0 10 20 30 40 50 60 70 80 90 100

Age 18

All non-maintained schools....	14·5
All maintained schools...........	5·2
Wales...................................	7·9
South East.............................	6·0
Yorkshire and Humberside......	5·1
South West............................	4·7
East Midlands........................	4·4
North West............................	4·4
North...................................	4·2
West Midlands.......................	4·2
East Anglia............................	3·7

0 10 20 30 40 50 60 70 80 90 100

Source: Statistics of Education 1968 Volume I, Table 9.

Notes: 1. Figures for regions are for maintained schools only.

2. Percentages represent the number of pupils aged 16, 17 or 18 in January, 1968 expressed as percentages of the number of pupils aged 13 years, 3, 4 or 5 years earlier respectively.

Figure 7

63. It must be recognised that too many pupils regard much of their secondary school work as irrelevant or boring. The Schools Council's enquiry we have quoted showed that young people who left school early were particularly dissatisfied. The whole structure of secondary education and the systems of further and higher education to which it is related must be fundamentally reappraised if more of these young people are to make good use of a longer formal education.

64. The Dainton Committee showed that the proportion of sixth formers studying science has been falling.[1] More critical questions are being asked about the degree of specialisation needed in secondary education and the age when specialisation should begin. New forms of public examinations are being proposed. The work of colleges of further education can no longer develop in isolation from that of the schools: in many places there is a large measure of overlap between the two sectors, and some pupils of an age to work in schools feel more at home and work more successfully in the colleges.

65. New technologies are developing in the classroom. Audio-visual aids have been common for many years—models, projectors and radio, for example—but more recent developments have come too fast for full assessment or full use in schools. Tape recorders, language laboratories, programmed learning, closed circuit television, computerised teaching machines—all are becoming available. Video-tape recorders will soon be widely used. These and other devices will enormously increase the scope, flexibility and costs of secondary education. Equipment budgets and the supply of skilled and enthusiastic practitioners are not as yet keeping pace. Thus far, there is no evidence that mechanical aids will reduce the number of teachers needed, but they will make a growing impact on teaching methods; and the teaching unit—at present almost uniformly the class or set—will become more flexible, ranging from large groups to individuals working independently on their own, sometimes at school, sometimes in public libraries or "scarce resources centres", and sometimes at home.

Resources

66. In 1946-47 public expenditure on education amounted to £194 million. By 1956-57 it had grown to £626 million, and by 1966-67 to £1,694 million. The growth in these figures is due in part to a fall in money value, and they include large increases in expenditure on higher and further education; but they also reflect a large increase in the call which the maintained system is making on national resources. "The share of national resources used by the education service in the United Kingdom in the mid-sixties was $5\frac{1}{2}$ per cent compared with $3\frac{1}{2}$ per cent of considerably smaller resources ten years earlier."[2]

67. The increases in the numbers of pupils in the next decade or so will call for further large increases in expenditure. To provide the new places required for secondary pupils alone will cost at least £615 million at present day prices, without making any allowances for the new places required through shifts of population and replacement of old and unsatisfactory buildings. Current costs for secondary pupils were over £400 million in 1967-68 and could well double

---

[1] "Enquiry into the Flow of Candidates in Science and Technology into Higher Education", H.M.S.O. 1968 Figure 5.

[2] Quoted from the 1966 Annual Report of the Department of Education and Science, paragraph 2, page 9.

by 1980. In her paper "Education and Finance" (I.M.T.A. 1969), Dr. Kathleen Ollerenshaw predicted that public expenditure on education as a whole would rise so that by 1980 it would be equivalent to about 8 per cent of the Gross National Product; today it is about 6 per cent. Working on a rather different basis we would also conclude that if present policies are sustained, and recommendations like those of the Plowden Committee were carried through, over 8 per cent of the nation's productive capacity would be devoted to education by 1980. This assumes a 3 per cent growth rate in productivity and in salaries in the education system. On top of that it would be necessary to finance transfer items such as student grants.

68. While expenditure on secondary education has risen, its share in the total educational budget has fallen as the following table shows:

Table 1

Percentage Breakdown of Total Educational Expenditure

	1959/1960	1967/1968
Nursery schools	0·3	0·2
Primary schools	26·9	24·0
Secondary schools	34·8	29·3
Special schools	2·1	2·2
Further and adult education	10·2	12·5
Training of teachers; tuition costs	1·1	2·4
Universities[1]	6·8	11·3
Other expenditure	17·8	18·2
	100·0	100·0

Source: Statistics of Education 1968.

The country's recent economic difficulties have led to a check on the rate of growth of educational expenditure. Rate Support Grant for 1969-70 has been fixed by the Government on the basis that local authority expenditure as a whole is not expected to exceed a figure in the region of 3 per cent in real terms above what was agreed for 1968-69. Within this total increase, education expenditure is expected to increase by about 3¾ per cent in real terms. A similar increase in expenditure on education has been allowed for between 1970 and 1971. The education authorities are unlikely to be able to allow educational expenditure to rise much above this level. Clearly anyone making recommendations which would call for a substantial increase in public expenditure must not expect to see them implemented in the immediate future.

69. The post-war years have been a period of great activity in school building, but much of this work has had to be devoted to providing new places for the growing school population and to meeting needs arising from internal migration to new centres of housing. Meanwhile many schools are overdue for replacement: the School Building Survey carried out in 1962 showed that at that time three out of every eight secondary schools were in buildings erected before 1918. Because of this pressure on limited resources, the construction of large,

---

[1] Including colleges of advanced technology from 1965-66 formerly included in further and adult education.

purpose-built, all-through comprehensives will often be impossible, and the scope for organising comprehensive education through tiering schemes which link schools catering for different parts of the secondary age range is already being more carefully considered. If reorganisation is to proceed as quickly as possible and the best use is to be made of scarce teachers and expensive equipment, there will have to be many different patterns of comprehensive education, and this diversity is already appearing.

Teachers

70. Although the number of pupils at maintained schools has grown from 5 million in January 1947 to nearly 8 million in January 1968, the supply of teachers has risen even faster. The ratio of full-time teachers to pupils has improved from 1:27·0 in 1947 to 1:24·6 in 1968 and in addition part-time teachers are making a growing contribution. The proportion of secondary classes with more than 30 pupils has been reduced from about a half to just over a third. What is more, new non-graduate teachers now have at least three years training instead of the one or two years which was usual in 1947.

71. What about the future? Forecasting the numbers of teachers is even harder than forecasting the numbers to be taught. There were 316,000 qualified teachers in maintained schools in 1968. Estimates of future numbers depend on assumptions about the proportions of school leavers and graduates who will enter the profession, about the numbers who will leave teaching and return to it, and about the financial ability of authorities to employ the teachers needed. We cannot be confident about any of these assumptions. The Department, in the least optimistic of its forecasts, concludes that by 1980 the supply of qualified teachers will improve sufficiently to reduce the overall qualified teacher ratio from 1:23·9 in 1968 to below 1:20·0. This forecast, though pessimistic about the supply of teachers, may underestimate the number of pupils to be taught, as we explained in paragraph 58.

72. As schools are at present organised, sixth form teaching requires more staff than the teaching of younger pupils. The growth in sixth form numbers has not so far produced economies in cost per pupil because the range of subjects which pupils can take has extended and in general the size of teaching groups has not risen. Sixth form teaching calls for a high proportion of graduate teachers. In 1968, there were about 62,000 full-time graduate teachers in maintained primary and secondary schools. The total full-time qualified teaching force in those schools is about 297,000. On the more conservative of two hypotheses examined by the Department, the numbers of graduates will increase to about 132,000 by 1980—including 35,000 Bachelors of Education—out of 456,000 full-time qualified teachers.[1] The proportion of graduates in the total teaching force of maintained schools will increase from just over 20 per cent in 1968 to very nearly 29 per cent in 1980. It must not, of course, be assumed that all the extra graduates will go into secondary education. Indeed, the Plowden Committee called for more graduates in primary schools.

73, The number of graduates could increase generally yet still leave shortages in certain subjects and for certain aspects of school life. Mathematics and Science graduates are those most often mentioned in this connection. The Department

---

[1] See Statistics of Education, 1967, Volume 4, Table 45.

estimates that the numbers of graduate teachers in these subjects will rise from 16,600 in 1968 to over 24,000 in 1980, an increase of 45 per cent. Although this is less than the increase in graduate teachers from other disciplines, it could still be sufficient to keep pace with increasing numbers of pupils. But a greater proportion of their time may have to be devoted to teaching sixth formers taking these subjects since it is numbers in this age group which will rise most rapidly.

74. One of the fears frequently expressed to us has been that despite expected improvements in overall staffing ratios, comprehensive reorganisation will lead to smaller and less economic sixth forms without enough graduate teachers. There are many patterns of comprehensive organisation, involving schools which deal with different age ranges. But whatever the pattern, we think that by 1980 sixth forms will very seldom be fed from less than six forms of entry. An all-through comprehensive school with six forms of entry would today have about 1,000 pupils. By 1980 such a school would be larger because more pupils will stay on into the sixth. Moreover many schools will be based on more than six forms of entry. Therefore if there are 4·2 million secondary age pupils in maintained schools in 1980, there will probably not be more than about 4,000 sixth forms. If nine out of ten full-time graduate teachers are in secondary schools (as in 1967) and five out of six of them spend some of their time in sixth form teaching (as was the case in grammar schools in 1965) then there would be an average of 25 to each sixth form and about five of them would have degrees in science or mathematics. If sixth forms were fed from an average of eight forms of entry, there would be an average of 32 graduates per sixth form, six of them having science or mathematics degrees. Grammar schools in 1968 had an average of 20 full-time graduates, spending some of their time teaching sixth formers, nine of them having degrees in science or mathematics. Thus sixth forms of the 1980's could have more graduates, in total, than the grammar school sixth forms have at present—and appreciably more than those now available to the 29 per cent of 'A' level candidates who work in maintained schools other than grammar schools. But the proportions of mathematicians and scientists among sixth form teachers may decline. Special steps may be required to ensure that teachers with the scarcest skills concentrate their efforts on the pupils who need their help most.

75. The expansion of sixth form numbers and studies is putting, and will continue to put, a tremendous strain on the profession. It calls for more teachers with advanced academic qualifications in a wider variety of subjects, and more counselling and careers guidance among pupils. Meanwhile teachers of some subjects too often work with classes of no more than five or six pupils. There will be increasing pressures on schools to make more economical use of their skills. Critical questions will be asked about small sixth forms, and the barriers between separate schools may have to be broken down. Other countries contending with the same problems have had to reorganise the staffing and structure of schools, giving greater responsibilities and higher pay to some of those at the top of the profession, introducing more aides and technical assistants, and building more closely integrated systems of secondary education linking the work of different schools.

Administration and Organisation

76. Much of the 1944 Act was taken up with the problem of denominational

differences, and little attention was given to what proved to be one of the dominant educational controversies of the last twenty years, namely the *kind* of school which should be provided for secondary pupils. The central government is now seldom concerned with mediating between the denominations: they generally take a common line in pursuit of common aims. It has, however, been much involved in differences between parents and local education authorities over choice of secondary schools. Thus far, it has been sparing in its use of the powers of direct action given by the Act: co-operation has been the keynote in relations between the Department of Education and Science and the local education authorities as shown by the variety of provision and policies in different areas. But the tensions inherent in relationships between central and local authorities have been sharpened by comprehensive reorganisation. An Education Bill which would exert growing pressure on local authorities to reorganise their secondary schools in accordance with central government policies is now being prepared.[1]

77. There have been slight changes in the numbers of local education authorities in the last few years and some boundaries have been altered, but the system remains substantially as it was left by the 1944 Act. The report of the Royal Commission on Local Government seems likely to change all that. If acted upon by the Government, it will lead to a drastic reduction in the number of local education authorities, and a great increase in the numbers of schools that most of them administer.

78. Such a reform is bound to have repercussions on the government of schools. The governing bodies of secondary schools, which the 1944 Act requires local education authorities to set up, vary enormously in their composition, in the powers they wield and in their effectiveness. The study made by the London University Institute of Education Research Unit[2] detected a major difference between county boroughs and counties. The former tend to favour closer control of schools by officers acting for elected representatives. The latter, covering larger areas, are more apt to delegate responsibility. The Royal Commission recommended that, in the main, the education authorities should be larger units, and that school governing bodies should have more powers and represent people in their locality more effectively. We hope this will enhance the quality and standing of school governors. That, in turn, will affect governors' relationships with the heads and teaching staff of schools and with local education authorities.

Conclusion

79. A few of the points made in this brief survey must be re-emphasised before we go further. First, the most striking feature of sixth form education in this country is that the great majority of our children do not have it: to give them, and the country, a fair chance in a competitive world, we must enable far more young people to take their education much further. To do that we must contend with scarcities of staff in some of the specialisations in which advanced teaching will be needed, scarcities of buildings suitable for use as all-through comprehensive schools, and the growing complexity and cost of the equipment required for

---

[1] Presented to Parliament on 4th February, 1970.

[2] "Research Studies 6—School Management and Government", by G. Baron, Ph.D. and D. A. Howell, M.A., D.P.A., H.M.S.O. 1968.

secondary education. We must also inspire the interest and motivation of growing numbers of young people who have not been accustomed to a traditional academic curriculum from the age of eleven and do not share the aspirations or the social advantages of the traditional sixth former. These pressures will compel us to reappraise many of our assumptions, both about comprehensive schools and about grammar schools. Within a comprehensive system we shall need the help of good schools of every kind if we are to attain our aims.

80. The cost of any proposals we make must be carefully weighed: the objectives to which the Government is already committed will call for the diversion to education of a growing proportion of the national product. Although the supply of teachers will improve, there are likely to be shortages in particular subjects. For this reason, and in order to make efficient use of the money available, the scarcer and more highly qualified teachers must be deployed to the best advantage. Unless the standards demanded for sixth form study change completely, the days of small, isolated sixth forms are numbered. Sixth formers will have to be concentrated in larger units, either in large comprehensive schools starting at ages 11 to 13, or in schools starting at 14, 15 or 16. Alternatively, or in addition, education from 15 or 16 onwards may be more closely linked with further education.

81. The administration of education and the organisation of schools must be sufficiently flexible to cope with new developments and needs. They must ensure that scarce resources are used to the full and not duplicated wastefully at several institutions. This may call for the establishment of "scarce resources centres" serving several schools and containing, for example, language laboratories and computer units. Alternatively these scarce resources may have to become more mobile. The barriers between schools (and colleges of further education) must be broken down. In future, areas served by several schools will constitute the basic unit for the more closely co-ordinated planning of secondary education. Yet the independence and vitality of teaching within these groups of schools must somehow be preserved.

CHAPTER 3

Comprehensive Reorganisation

82. We have been asked to consider how schools "can participate in the movement towards comprehensive reorganisation". In this Chapter we describe the progress of the movement and the forms it is taking. Our own views about its aims and significance are presented in Chapter 7.

83. The idea of the comprehensive school is not a new one. As long ago as 1947 the Ministry of Education found it necessary to define it (in Circular 144). It was described as a school "intended to cater for all the secondary education of all the children in a given area without an organisation in three sides" (that is to say without separate grammar, secondary modern and technical departments). In 1950 the Ministry of Education's statistics showed 10 comprehensive secondary schools. By January 1965 there were 262. These schools had developed from initiatives taken by local education authorities. Under a Conservative administration, the Ministry of Education accepted proposals for comprehensive schools in country districts and in areas of extensive new housing but generally resisted proposals to establish new comprehensive schools which involved the closure of existing grammar schools.[1]

84. At the 1964 general election the Labour Party was returned to power pledged "to reorganise the State secondary schools on comprehensive lines, in order to end the segregation by the eleven-plus examination."[2] The Labour Government accordingly, on the 21st January, 1965, moved a motion, which by virtue of its majority in the House of Commons was agreed:

"That this House, conscious of the need to raise educational standards at all levels, and regretting that the realisation of this objective is impeded by the separation of children into different types of secondary schools, notes with approval the efforts of local authorities to reorganise secondary education on comprehensive lines which will preserve all that is valuable in grammar school education for those children who now receive it and make it available to more children; recognises that the method and timing of such reorganisation should vary to meet local needs; and believes that the time is now ripe for a declaration of national policy."

Circular 10/65

85. The next step was the appearance in July, 1965, of Circular 10/65 which asked local education authorities to send in plans for reorganising secondary education in their areas on comprehensive lines and gave guidance about the methods for achieving reorganisation. The Circular stated that the Government's objective was to end selection at 11+ and to eliminate segregation in secondary education. While progress was to be as rapid as possible it was not to be achieved

---

[1] See "Secondary Education for All", H.M.S.O., 1958.
[2] See "Signposts for the Sixties", the Labour Party, 1961.

by the adoption of plans whose educational disadvantages more than outweighed the benefits expected from comprehensive schooling.

86. The forms of comprehensive reorganisation to be adopted should depend on local circumstances and a local authority could propose more than one form in its area. Six main forms were identified:

(i) The all-through comprehensive school with an age range of 11-18.

(ii) A two-tier system whereby *all* pupils transfer at 11 to a junior comprehensive school and *all* go on at 13 or 14 to a senior comprehensive school.

(iii) A two-tier system under which *all* pupils on leaving primary school transfer to a junior comprehensive school, but at the age of 13 or 14 *some* pupils move on to a senior school while *the remainder* stay on in the same school. Most of these systems fall into two groups: in one, the comprehensive school which all pupils enter after leaving primary school provides no course terminating in a public examination, and normally keeps pupils only until 15; in the other, this school provides G.C.E. and C.S.E. courses, keeps pupils at least until 16, and encourages transfer at the appropriate stage to the sixth form of a senior school.

(iv) A two-tier system in which *all* pupils on leaving primary school transfer to a junior comprehensive school. At the age of 13 or 14 *all* pupils have a choice between a senior school catering for those who expect to stay at school well beyond the compulsory age, and a senior school catering for those who do not.

(v) Comprehensive schools with an age range of 11 to 16 combined with sixth form colleges for pupils over 16.

(vi) A system of middle schools which straddle the primary/secondary age ranges. Under this system pupils transfer from a primary school at the age of 8 or 9 to a comprehensive school with an age range of 8 to 12 or 9 to 13. From this middle school they move on to a comprehensive school with an age range of 12 or 13 to 18.

87. The Circular said that plans based on alternatives (iii) or (iv) would only be acceptable as a temporary stage of reorganisation because they separated children into different schools according to their different aims and aptitudes. The first proposal, for all-through schools, should be adopted wherever possible. Sixth form colleges were viewed with caution and middle school arrangements were to be approved only in a few experimental schemes. But the following year the Secretary of State issued a new Circular (13/66) in which he stated that proposals for reorganisation based on a middle school system were fully acceptable and would be considered on their merits along with the other types. The various long-term solutions recommended are shown in Figure 8.

88. Circular 10/65 stated that comprehensive schools should create communities in which pupils of all abilities and with differing interests and backgrounds would be encouraged to mix with each other, gaining stimulus from their contacts, and learning tolerance and understanding in the process. Some neighbourhoods, it was recognised, would produce too few pupils with high attainments and aspirations, and the authorities were urged to ensure, when determining catchment areas, that schools serve as broad a mixture of abilities and social classes as possible.

89. Local authorities were urged to start discussions with the governors of voluntary and direct grant schools. It was hoped that the governors of the direct

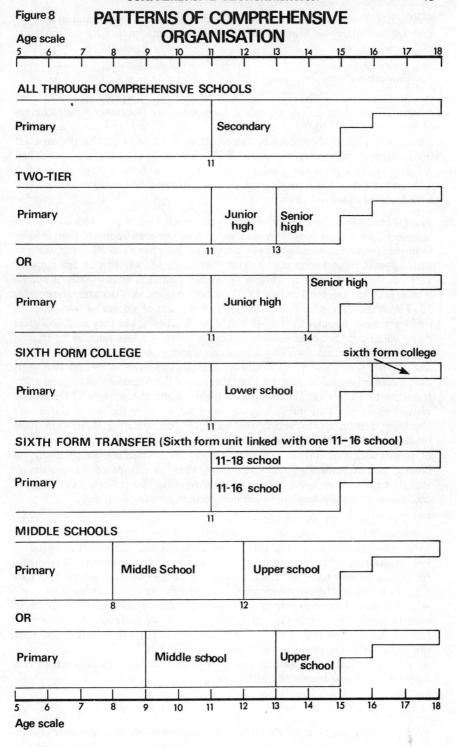

Figure 8

Age scale

PATTERNS OF COMPREHENSIVE ORGANISATION

grant schools would be ready to consider changes in curriculum and in method and age of entry to enable their schools to participate fully in the local authority's scheme.

Reorganisation Plans

90. In response to the Circular most authorities prepared plans for the reorganisation of secondary schools in their areas. By December 1969, schemes of reorganisation had been approved for 129 out of 163 local education authorities; 108 of these covered the whole or the greater part of the area. Of the remaining authorities, the plans of 12 were under consideration and 6 had yet to produce a plan. The plans of 11 authorities had been rejected, of whom 8 had not yet submitted revised proposals and 3 had declined to do so. A further 5 have declined to submit any scheme.

91. Table 2 shows the number of authorities which have chosen various types of organisation for their long-term plan where this has been approved (where long-term plans have not been approved authorities have been classified according to their approved short-term plans). The all-through school with an age range of 11-18 is the most popular, chosen by 62 authorities. Various kinds of middle school system have been chosen by 52 authorities, and two-tier arrangements by 32. Taken together, schemes which involve some sort of a break or transfer at 13 or 14 are more popular than all-through 11-18 schools, but they include a great many variations. Schemes involving transfer at 16 are less popular, at least at present. The schemes involving a break or transfer at 13 or 14 and those with one at 16 figure more prominently in schemes approved in the last two years than previously, and it may be that this marks the beginning of a trend away from the 11-18 school. The shortage of highly qualified teachers and the rapidly expanding numbers of pupils staying on at school after the age of sixteen are impelling authorities to search for ways of concentrating their sixth form resources. Some are looking at the possibility of educating all pupils over the age of 16 at colleges of further education. Others are considering the possibility of linking and co-ordinating the sixth form work of groups of comprehensive schools so that each specialises in particular fields. The pattern is complicated and changing; it may develop a good deal further in unforeseen ways.

92. The figures in the Table are for plans approved but not necessarily implemented. Some schemes cover county and voluntary controlled schools only, and do not settle the role of voluntary aided schools. The speed of implementation often depends on the availability of teachers and of resources for capital expenditure, and for this reason a number of plans set no firm date for completion or the date proposed is far in the future—20 years hence or more. When a school is reorganised it may be some years before it becomes comprehensive. For example, a grammar school being reorganised as a comprehensive school will normally start with an unselected entry in the first form only, the following year the first two forms would be unselected and so on. It would not be fully developed as a comprehensive school until the seventh year after taking its first unselected entry.

Aided Schools

93. The reorganisation of the voluntary aided schools presents special difficulties. In the first place these schools tend to be small in size, so that building is

Table 2

Patterns of Comprehensive Organisation Chosen by Local Education Authorities
(as at December,1969)

	Number of authorities
All-through comprehensive schools (11-18)	62
Schemes including 11-16 schools	
11-16 with sixth form college to follow	18
11-16 schools working in concert with 11-18 "mushroom" schools to which pupils transfer at 16	24
*11-16 schools working in concert with 13-18 schools to which *some* of the pupils in the 11-16 schools transfer at 13 on parental choice	4
*11-16 schools working in concert with 14-18 "mushroom" schools to which pupils transfer at 16	2
Total	48
Two-tier arrangements	
Transfer at 14 (11-14 + 14-18)	22
Transfer at 13 (11-13 + 13-18)	2
*13-18 schools to which *some* pupils transfer on parental choice at 13 from 11-16 schools	4
11-13 schools from which *some* pupils transfer to 13-16 schools and the *others* to 13-18 schools according to parental choice	2
*11-14 + 14-18 "mushroom" schools to which pupils can transfer at 16 from 11-16 schools	2
Total	32
Middle school arrangements	
9-13 + 13-18	29
8-12 + 12-18	11
10-13 + 13-18	5
*8-12 + 12-16 with sixth form college to follow	7
Total	52
Sixth form colleges	
*Following 11-16 schools	18
*Following middle school arrangements (8-12 + 12-16)	7
Total	25

Source: Department of Education and Science.

Notes: 1. When an authority has had both a short-term and a long-term scheme approved, it is the long-term scheme which has been used for the table.

2. Some authorities have more than one type of scheme, either in different parts of their areas or as between county and denominational schools. The schemes of such authorities will therefore appear under more than one heading.

3. The sixth form college schemes include schemes at Exeter and Barnstaple for the provision of all post-16 work in the local college of further education.

4. Schemes marked with an asterisk appear more than once in the table.

usually needed before they can become part of a comprehensive system. The arrangements for the financing of new building in a voluntary aided school demand a contribution from the voluntary body which it may not be willing or able to produce, especially if it has already incurred such expenditure for earlier (and possibly very recent) reorganisation of all-age schools. The distinctive status of the voluntary aided schools makes merging with county schools difficult. Two-tier arrangements often seem to provide a convenient solution but they may not suit the voluntary body or the authority. No voluntary aided school which is unwilling to adopt a comprehensive role can be compelled by law to do so. If the local authority so proposes and the Secretary of State agrees, it may cease to maintain the school. But even if resources for building a new county school were readily available, few authorities would consider taking such action against a local school. In any case the churches which are responsible for most of the voluntary aided schools have declared that they are not in principle opposed to comprehensive reorganisation and are working with many local authorities to introduce comprehensive schemes as soon as possible.

Survey of Comprehensive Schools

94. In 1966 the National Foundation for Educational Research in collaboration with the School of Education of the University of Manchester was commissioned to collect information about comprehensive schools, to chart the growth of comprehensive education and the practical educational problems it posed, and to devise means for measuring how far various forms of comprehensive education attained their declared objectives. A report on the first stage of the enquiry—a factual description of comprehensive education as it existed in 1965-66—was published in 1968.[1] A further report is expected during 1970, giving the result of an intensive survey of some 50 comprehensive schools, providing information about their organisation, staffing, libraries and equipment, their curricular and extra-curricular activities, work and human relationships within the schools, and much else besides.

95. Although we cannot summarise the findings of the 1968 Report, a few points emerge which are particularly relevant to our own discussions. Comprehensive schools have often had to work in difficult and unpromising circumstances. It would, therefore, be inappropriate to make direct comparisons between the performance of children in comprehensive and selective schools. In particular, the comprehensive schools generally have had less than their fair share of pupils of the highest ability. Thus the intake of nearly 60 per cent of the schools included 15 per cent or less of pupils in the top 20 per cent of the ability range. The schools generally had more pupils from unskilled and semi-skilled families and fewer pupils from professional and clerical families than the national average. Most comprehensive schools have been recently founded, and few have yet had time to develop large and flourishing sixth forms.

Variety of Approach

96. The Government did not ask authorities to adopt any particular pattern of comprehensive education. The possibilities were listed and discussed and the authorities were asked to decide what form suited their particular circumstances. This means that reorganisation is being tackled in many different ways. The

---

1 Comprehensive Education in England and Wales by T. G. Monks, N.F.E.R., 1968.

comprehensive system is not by any means a monolithic system. Schools may be single-sex or co-educational, they provide for diverse age ranges, and they are linked with other schools in all sorts of different ways. Within the school, too, there is great variety of organisation and approach. Different policies are followed on streaming, banding, setting and the mixing of abilities, on teaching methods and discipline; even the basic aims and principles of the schools vary.

Conclusion

97. It is now over four years since Circular 10/65 was published. What progress has been made? The number of comprehensive schools was already growing then and this trend has been greatly accelerated since. Figure 9 shows how the number of comprehensive schools has risen in the last two decades. Nevertheless, nearly three-quarters of secondary school children are still in schools not yet reorganised, and many of the remainder are in comprehensive schools which will only gradually offer them the full range of opportunities which comprehensive education is designed to provide.

98. Progress will depend on the resources available, the support of parents, and the determination and skill of central and local authorities, school governors and teachers. The variety of patterns already evolving makes it clear that schools cannot be classified as "comprehensive"—still less evaluated—in isolation from the local system of education in which they work. It is these systems which are becoming comprehensive, and there are many different parts which schools can play within such systems.

Table 3

Comprehensive Schools

	1965	1966	1967	1968	1969
Number of comprehensive schools	262	387	507	745	962
Number of pupils	239,619	312,281	407,475	604,428	772,612
Average of pupils per school	915	808	804	810	803
Percentage of total maintained secondary school population	8·5%	11·1%	14·4%	20·9%	26·1%
Number of authorities operating some comprehensive schools	48	57	72	81	94

Source: Statistics of Education.

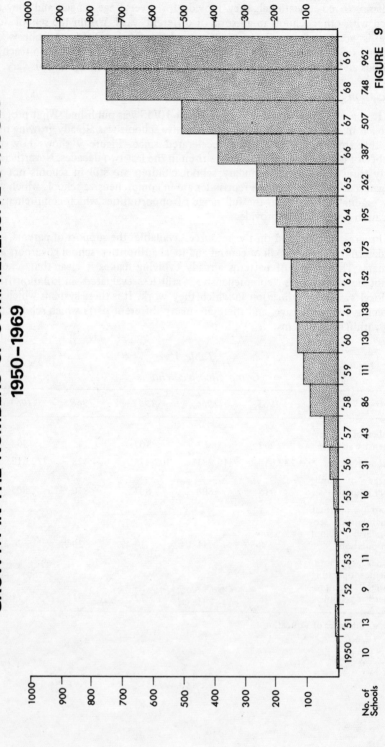

GROWTH IN THE NUMBERS OF COMPREHENSIVE SCHOOLS
1950–1969

FIGURE 9

No. of Schools	1950	'51	'52	'53	'54	'55	'56	'57	'58	'59	'60	'61	'62	'63	'64	'65	'66	'67	'68	'69
	10	13	9	11	13	16	31	43	86	111	130	138	152	175	195	262	387	507	748	962

Source: Statistics of Education.

CHAPTER 4

Direct Grant Grammar Schools

99. "Direct grant" is a term used to describe schools which receive money from the Exchequer: it tells nothing about the kind of education which the schools provide.[1] In this Chapter we briefly describe the schools, their history, organisation and character, and their response to the reorganisation discussed in the previous chapter.

History of the Direct Grant System

100. The present position of the direct grant schools is the outcome of a long history. There is a fuller account of this story in a thesis by Mr. J. A. Partington,[2] to whom we are indebted. At the beginning of this century there were no "direct grant schools", just as there were no "maintained secondary schools". Most secondary schools were financed and administered by voluntary bodies (for example, churches or charitable foundations) and a few had been set up by local authorities acting on their own initiative. The Act of 1902 regularised the situation and the principle was established that, if a school observed certain standards and undertook a definite responsibility in the public educational field, it could secure grants from the central government. If the local education authority conducted the school, they received an appropriate grant from the central government. If a voluntary body controlled the school it could receive grants from the central government, or from the local authority, or from both. In 1926, this situation was simplified and a secondary school conducted by a voluntary body had henceforth to draw its grant from either central or local government but not from both. This ruling, in Circular 1381, effectively established the direct grant list but had neither the intention nor the effect of creating a new category of school. Direct grant schools, schools run by voluntary bodies and grant aided by local education authorities, and secondary schools which the local authorities maintained with the help of percentage grants from the Board of Education, all shared the same objectives and assumptions. Taken together, they provided secondary education only for a minority. In 1926 most children never went to a secondary school.

101. Under the 1944 Act, secondary education eventually became available for all children within the same system of administration and finance as the other sectors of public education. Fees were abolished in the secondary schools

---

[1] In addition to making capitation and other grants to the 178 direct grant grammar schools, the Department of Education and Science also makes smaller grants under the Direct Grant School Regulations on a different basis to four other secondary schools and to 15 nursery schools. These are not within the Commission's terms of reference, and references to direct grant and to the direct grant schools in this Report relate only to the direct grant grammar schools.

[2] "The History of the System of Direct Grants to Secondary Schools" by Mr. J. A. Partington, September, 1967. Available at the University of Durham.

maintained by the local authorities; those schools run by voluntary bodies which had been receiving grants from the local authorities became for the most part voluntary aided or voluntary controlled schools within this newly defined maintained sector. The 231 schools which were receiving direct grant had the choice of applying to become direct grant schools on new terms, or becoming voluntary aided or controlled schools, or becoming independent schools. No-one seriously questioned their educational role as grammar schools at this stage.

102. Before the Act was passed the new terms to be offered to the direct grant schools had been considered by the Fleming Committee. Their final Report, published in July 1944[1], made proposals under "Scheme A" which were designed to attract direct grant and independent day schools into a new association with the State. According to this Scheme, the local education authorities would have the right to reserve places in these schools to a number to be agreed between governors and the authorities, with reference to the Board of Education if necessary, and the remaining places would be free or assisted according to income. The Board was to pay the school the difference between the approved fee and the amount received from parents (if any). Capitation grants would no longer be paid to the schools.

103. The Government modified the Committee's scheme. Regulations made under the Act stipulated that at least 25 per cent of the schools' places should be free, and filled by pupils who had been educated for at least two years at a maintained or grant-aided primary school. Over and above this, a local education authority could reserve up to a further 25 per cent of places, or still higher proportions if the governors agreed. The Fleming recommendation that for the remaining places fees should be remitted according to an income scale was accepted for day pupils.[2] But payment of capitation grants continued.

104. In March 1945, the newly established Ministry of Education invited applications for a modified form of direct grant status. Only schools which had previously been grant-aided, either direct or through the local education authorities, were considered. Of the 231 schools on the direct grant list, 35 decided to become independent, 160 applied for direct grant and were accepted, and 36 applied and were rejected. Among schools grant aided by local authorities, 4 applied and were accepted, and 27 applied and were rejected.

105. In 1957 the list was reopened to permit the addition of a few schools which satisfied the conditions applied to those already on the list. Schools eligible for consideration were those which were then independent and those still being assisted transitionally under Section 32 of the 1944 Act pending determination of their status as voluntary schools. Circular 319, announcing the reopening, stated that the Minister would give particular attention to educational standards (staff, size of the sixth form, normal leaving age and proportion of pupils proceeding to higher education would be relevant), the size of the school (small schools would normally be ineligible), ability to comply with free place requirements, and financial standing. There were 46 applications, all but three from independent schools, and 15 schools were eventually added to the list, making a total of 179 direct grant grammar schools. This total remained

---

[1] "The Public Schools and the General Educational System", H.M.S.O., 1944.

[2] The Committee envisaged two possibilities, either that schools should remit fees for residuary places or that all places should be free. In the event the Ministry adopted the former alternative only.

unchanged until the Trinity School of John Whitgift, Croydon, relinquished direct grant from 1st August, 1968.

The Direct Grant System Today

106. The current direct grant regulations are set out in Appendix 9. Direct grant grammar schools are required to see that at least 25 per cent of the places in their upper (i.e. secondary) school are "free places", available without charge to pupils who have been educated for two years in a maintained primary school. These places are usually paid for by the local education authority but authorities are under no obligation to take up places: the Governors may pay for some (or all) of them out of foundation income or (subject to the approval of the Department) by increasing fees. Over and above these free places, the local education authorities may, if they wish, pay for further "reserved places", also without charge to parents, to bring the total of free and reserved places up to 50 per cent. If the governors agree, the authorities may reserve further places beyond their 50 per cent entitlement; the authorities take more than 50 per cent of places in 93 of the 178 schools. Reserved place holders need not have attended maintained schools. Pupils taking the remaining places ("residuary places") pay fees. Day pupils' fees are remitted according to an income scale approved by the Department of Education and Science. The tuition fees of boarding pupils taking residuary places are not remitted. The standard scale is set out in Appendix 9. The difference between the amount paid by the parents and the full fee is paid by the Department. The Department also pays a capitation grant in respect of all pupils in the upper school (£32 per annum as from the 1st £52 ? August, 1968) and an additional *per capita* grant for pupils in the sixth form (£84 per annum since 1963).

107. The most important conditions attached to these grants are:

   (i) One third of the Governors must be appointed by local education authorities, or there must be a majority of "representative" Governors (defined in the regulations).
  (ii) The approval of the Secretary of State is required for any new premises or alterations.
 (iii) Fees and other charges require the approval of the Secretary of State.
 (iv) Pupils must be excused religious worship or instruction if their parents wish.
  (v) Adequate provision must be made for the medical inspection of all pupils and the medical care of boarders: mid-day meals must be available for day pupils.
 (vi) Other conditions relating to standards of the premises and efficient conduct of the school.

The Schools

108. The direct grant schools as a group are unusual in that only two out of 178 offer co-education: 81 are boys' schools and 95 are girls' schools. They teach about 3 per cent of the secondary school population, but that includes 10 per cent of all sixth formers. All but one are selective schools but otherwise they differ enormously in character. They range in size from about 200 to 1,400 pupils with an average of 616 for boys' schools and 518 for girls' (see Table 6). Only three have more than 1,000 secondary places and 17 more than 800. The

5

sizes of sixth forms also range widely, from 30 to 535 (see Table 7), averaging 164 for boys' schools and 112 for girls'.

109. Most of the schools stand in towns, and they are heavily concentrated in the North and a few cities elsewhere: 46 are in the county and county boroughs of Lancashire—over a quarter of the schools, including half the Roman Catholic schools. Another 19 are in Yorkshire, 20 in Greater London, 7 in Bristol and 6 in Newcastle. There are only 4 schools in Wales. The map at the end of this Chapter shows the distribution of the schools.

110. The areas of school sites vary enormously, from one acre for one girls' school to 58 acres for a boys' day school and 400 acres for a boys' boarding school. Boarding schools have larger sites than day schools: the average size for boys' schools with over 50 per cent of their pupils boarding is 78 acres compared with an average of 22 acres for boys' schools without any boarders at all. The girls' schools generally have smaller sites—those without boarders average 9 acres. The boys' day schools have more land, on average, than is required by the regulations for new maintained schools,[1] but the average site of the girls' day schools is smaller than those requirements. Further information about sites and premises can be found in Appendix 6, Section 2.

Teachers

111. The teacher/pupil ratios in the direct grant schools are very similar to those in maintained grammar schools; the averages are 1:16·7 and 1:16·6 respectively. This is not surprising since the Department of Education and Science approves the fees charged and has regard to ratios in maintained grammar schools when appraising the schools' expenditure on teachers' salaries. Perhaps more unexpected is the finding that the proportion of teachers who are graduates and the proportion with first and second class honours degrees are slightly lower in the direct grant schools than in the maintained grammar schools. (See Table 21). So far as teachers are concerned, there is no evidence that direct grant schools generally are in a specially favoured position compared with maintained grammar schools.

Religious Worship and Instruction

112. Nearly a third of the schools are Roman Catholic (56 schools: 19 for boys and 37 for girls). Of the remainder, 39 are Church of England, 69 are non-denominational and six are interdenominational. There are seven Methodist boarding schools and one Congregationalist. Under the direct grant regulations, parents may withdraw their sons or daughters from religious worship or instruction. In practice this provision is not used greatly—only about 1½ per cent of pupils being withdrawn, most of whom are Roman Catholic children in non-Catholic schools, non-Catholic children in Catholic schools and Jewish children. Small numbers of Hindus, Moslems, Christian Scientists, Jehovah's Witnesses and of Humanists are also withdrawn.

Local Education Authority Places

113. In January 1968, there were 101,236 pupils (51,263 boys and 49,973 girls) in the upper schools. Local education authorities paid the fees for 60 per cent of these (60,550 pupils), the governors paid for 1½ per cent (1,502), parents

---

[1] "Standards for School Premises Regulations", H.M.S.O., 1959.

paid fees in full for 28 per cent (28,758) partially remitted fees were paid for 9 per cent (9,284) and fees were completely remitted for 1 per cent (1,142). The proportions of places taken up by education authorities vary widely, as can be seen in Table 9. The proportions taken up at the Roman Catholic schools are much higher than in the other schools, averaging 86 per cent. At half of the Roman Catholic schools the proportion of education authority places exceeds 90 per cent: only two non-Catholic schools reach this figure. Fewer places are taken up by the authorities in boarding schools: only 18 per cent of the boys' boarding places and 27 per cent of the girls', compared with 64 per cent of the day places in boarding schools. The direct grant schools each tend to serve a wide area: 46 per cent of the schools recruit day pupils from the areas of four or more local education authorities, and 71 per cent take them from three or more authorities. Boarding pupils naturally come from an even wider area.

Recruitment of Pupils

114. Written examinations usually form an important part of selection procedures. Replies to our questionnaires showed that examinations were used in filling education authority places in four out of five of the schools. In about two out of three of these schools the authority set and marked the papers. For residuary places the schools normally used a written examination which they set and marked themselves. Other factors taken into account in the selection of pupils were the impressions of interviewers, reports from primary schools, and denominational preferences. Also taken into account, though of less importance, were the claims of those having a brother or sister in the school, the distance between home and school, and the claims of parents who were former pupils of the school. Pupils paid for by education authorities come mainly from maintained primary schools—nearly 80 per cent of those who entered in Autumn 1968 did so. In contrast, only 38 per cent of residuary place holders in that year came from maintained primary schools: 34 per cent of residuary place holders came from the lower schools, and most of the remaining 28 per cent came from independent preparatory schools. The great majority of day pupils enter at the age of eleven or thereabouts; about 4 per cent enter at 16, and 3 per cent—mostly residuary place holders—enter at 13. Amongst boarding pupils, the girls still enter mainly at eleven, as do the boys holding education authority places; but nearly a third of the boys taking boarding residuary places enter at 13 or 14.

Social Background

115. The direct grant schools are predominantly middle class institutions. Our evidence about parental occupations must be treated with caution, as we explain in Appendix 6, Section 3. But the general pattern is clear. Three out of four pupils come from the homes of white-collar workers: three out of five have fathers in professional or managerial occupations. Only one out of thirteen comes from a semi-skilled or unskilled worker's family. The social composition of pupils differs according to the type of place: 85 per cent of boarding pupils are from professional and managerial homes compared with 57 per cent of day pupils; 72 per cent of residuary place holders are from professional and managerial homes compared with 50 per cent of local education authority place holders. There are also differences between different types of school: at schools with large sixth forms and at boarding schools about 67 per cent of the pupils

come from professional and managerial homes and only 3 or 4 per cent from the homes of semi-skilled or unskilled workers. The equivalent figures for Roman Catholic schools are 37 per cent and 16 per cent respectively.

Ability of Pupils

116. The predominantly middle class background of the pupils in the direct grant schools is in part due to their academic selectivity. The children who do best in the selection tests come more often from the homes of professional and managerial workers than from those of semi-skilled or unskilled workers. If direct grant schools and local education authorities select the academically able they will tend also to select middle class children. And, although a number of the schools take some pupils who would not get into a maintained grammar school, in general the schools do take the academically able. That is what they have been expected to do under the present arrangements. In all the direct grant schools taken together, more than a quarter of the pupils for whom details were available are in the top $2\frac{1}{2}$ per cent of the ability range having Verbal Reasoning Quotients (V.R.Q.s) of 130 or more, and 60 per cent are in the top 9 per cent of the ability range, with V.R.Q.s of 120 or more. The schools vary—those with large sixth forms have a third of their pupils in the top $2\frac{1}{2}$ per cent band (some have more than two-thirds) whereas Roman Catholic schools have 18 per cent and boarding schools 21 per cent. Most schools are less selective in filling their residuary places and boarding places: about a fifth of the residuary pupils and nearly a quarter of the boarding pupils are below the top quarter of the ability range, compared with 8 per cent of those holding local education authority places. All these figures are based on an analysis of the V.R.Q. scores of entrants to the direct grant schools in 1967-68. Such scores should be treated with caution in individual cases, but the general pattern emerging from this analysis of large numbers is clear.

Academic Character of the Schools

117. The academic achievements of the direct grant schools are impressive: 60 per cent of their pupils stay at school until they are eighteen, 62 per cent of boys and 50 per cent of girls get two or more 'A' levels, 75 per cent go on to some form of full-time further education, 38 per cent to a university. There are differences between schools, and pupils in the four main categories of school noted in paragraph 132 do not all fare the same. Nevertheless, as a group, the direct grant schools do better in all these respects than do maintained grammar schools or independent schools which are recognised as efficient (see Tables 11 to 13 and Appendix 6, Section 3). This is to be expected for, although there are individual exceptions and variations, the intake to the direct grant schools is on the whole more highly selective than the intake of either of the other two groups of schools. Moreover the social backgrounds of their pupils tend in general to be more favourable than those of pupils in maintained schools and this must have a considerable effect on their achievements (although as we have shown, the number and qualifications of the staff of direct grant schools are not superior to those in maintained grammar schools). Whether or not the same pupils would do better or worse in other kinds of schools, we cannot say. Even if we could, that would not settle the problems we have to consider, for we must do the best we can for all children, in schools of all kinds. The evidence summarised in Appendix 5 shows that such questions cannot be simply answered. While some

pupils may do better in these schools than they would do elsewhere, others probably do worse. We are unable to demonstrate that either success or failure can be attributed with certainty to the special administrative and financial status conferred by direct grants and the degree of independence resulting from it.

Boarding Schools

118. About two out of three direct grant schools have no boarders—115 schools in all. The proportion of boarders at the other 63 schools ranges from 4 per cent to over 90 per cent. There are 30 schools in which 25 per cent or more of the pupils board. These schools had, in January 1968, 6,427 boarding pupils: 5,373 boys and 1,054 girls. The other 2,260 boarders were at the 33 schools which had fewer than 25 per cent of their pupils boarding. The direct grant schools already play an important part in meeting the boarding needs described in the Commission's First Report. The enquiries for the First Report showed that in 1966 some 4,300 boarding pupils at direct grant schools—46 per cent of all boarders—were assisted from public funds. Of those, 37 per cent were assisted by local authorities and 63 per cent by the central government and other public authorities in their capacity as employer of the boarders' parents.

119. The boarding schools are generally smaller than the other direct grant schools: only eight have more than 500 pupils, and the average size for boys' boarding schools is 454 and for girls' schools 409. The percentage of places (day and boarding taken together) taken up by local authorities ranges from 3 per cent to 75 per cent. In five schools over half the places are taken by local authorities, in ten others over a third, in three between a third and a quarter, and in the remaining 12 less than a quarter (see Table 9).

120. All the boys' boarding schools are members of the Association of Governing Bodies of Public Schools and all the girls' schools are members of the Association of Governing Bodies of Girls' Public Schools. The heads of all but four of the boys' boarding schools belong to the Headmasters' Conference. Seven of the schools are non-denominational, fifteen are Church of England, seven are Methodist, one is Congregational, none is Roman Catholic.

Lower Schools

121. Theré are primary or preparatory departments attached to 119 schools (51 for boys, 67 for girls and one mixed). These are known as lower schools and receive no grants from the Department of Education and Science. Their income is derived from fees and foundation funds. They are small—over half have less than 150 pupils. In January 1968, there were 16,552 pupils (6,449 boys, 10,103 girls) in lower schools. The boys' schools tend to recruit mainly at the age of 8 or thereabouts, whereas the girls' schools mostly take pupils at the age of five. The vast majority of these children—about 93 per cent of those who apply and over 85 per cent of all leavers—enter the upper schools. Of those who do, 28 per cent get free or reserved places and pay no fees in the upper school. The other 72 per cent continue as fee-paying pupils when they move into the upper school.

Finance

122. Tuition fees at the direct grant upper schools in Autumn 1968 ranged from under £100 a year to over £180 a year. The average for boys' schools was £139 and for girls' schools £131. Boarding pupils paid a combined fee, ranging from

under £300 a year to over £400, with averages of £379 for boys and £344 for girls. Tuition fees are lower than they would have been if the schools were independent because they are reduced by capitation grants from the Department of Education and Science. As from the 1st August, 1968 those grants have been £116 for sixth formers and £32 for other pupils, an average of £52 per pupil.

123. The expenditure of the schools is met by fees paid by local authorities and parents, by the capitation grants and the schools' own foundation funds. In 1967-68 nearly 42 per cent of the schools' income came from Department of Education and Science grants, 34 per cent from local education authorities, nearly 22 per cent from parental fees, and nearly 3 per cent from other sources—mainly foundation income. These figures exclude charges for school meals. Though they relate to the latest complete returns from the schools, they precede the cut in the capitation grant that occurred in 1968 as part of the general reductions in public expenditure following devaluation. The proportion of income derived from the Department of Education and Science in the year 1969-70 will probably prove to have been about 30 per cent. These average figures conceal wide variations between schools, depending on the number of places taken by local authorities and various other factors (see Appendix 7).

124. In approving the fees that schools may charge, it is the aim of the Department to ensure generally that expenditure is no higher than in comparable maintained schools. In practice, however, comparison of expenditure at direct grant schools with that of maintained grammar schools is difficult because separate accounts are not generally kept by local education authorities for grammar, comprehensive and secondary modern schools. By using data about numbers and salaries of teachers and pupil/teacher ratios in these different kinds of schools, we arrived at estimates of expenditure per pupil according to the age of pupils and type of school. Our conclusions are set out in Table 18. These estimates suggest that current expenditure per pupil of the same age is about the same on average in direct grant and maintained grammar schools, though differences occur between types of school (see Appendix 7).

125. Capital costs are different, however. Loan charges are a much less important element in direct grant school expenditure than in local authority costs. This is mainly because the direct grant schools finance much of their capital expenditure by means other than borrowing. Between 1950 and 1968 the schools spent nearly £27 million, mainly on improvements, and most of this was financed from private sources (see Appendix 7). The Department of Education and Science sometimes permits schools to borrow up to 80 per cent of the cost of new building and pay the loan charges out of fees. This constitutes some burden on public funds. Perhaps 15-20 per cent of new building has been financed indirectly from public funds in this way.

126. Some of our witnesses argued that local authorities gain financially by sending children to direct grant schools because central government meets a greater share of the cost through capitation grants. Our own investigation of this complex problem is summarised in Appendix 7. Although local situations vary, the local authorities do not, on average, gain or lose by sending children to direct grant schools rather than to maintained schools.

Comprehensive Reorganisation

127. We have been asked to consider how the direct grant schools can best take

part in the movement towards comprehensive reorganisation. When in Circular 10/65 the Secretary of State invited authorities to submit plans for the reorganisation of maintained schools, they were asked to examine this same question. As a result, most of the direct grant schools had discussions of some kind with at least one local authority. Sometimes these broke down after one or two meetings at which the two parties found no common ground. Sometimes both parties agreed that it would be best to continue with existing arrangements for the time being. Nevertheless a number of new agreements have been made. Most of them fall short of the patterns recommended in Circular 10/65 for maintained schools, but in many cases one or both parties regard them as a first instalment of changes which may go further. We describe some of them below.

128. Some take the form of widening the ability range. Loughborough, Bedford and Wakefield are three smallish towns each with two direct grant grammar schools. At Loughborough, the Leicestershire Education Authority has agreed to double the number of places which it takes at the schools from 25 to 50 per cent of the intake. In return the schools will admit pupils from a broader range of ability, taking them in representative proportions from the various bands of ability down to I.Q. 100. This arrangement is subject to review by either party after a period. At Bedford, the Harpur Trust runs two direct grant and two independent schools. They have offered to admit local authority pupils to the direct grant schools from 60 per cent of the ability range at 13+ in order to co-operate with the local authority's scheme. At Wakefield, some children (considerably less than half the age group and mainly, though by no means entirely, in the top half of the ability range) transfer by "guided parental choice" at the age of 13 from maintained comprehensive schools to one of the two direct grant schools, or to the one maintained school which also admits pupils at this age. Places at the direct grant schools are offered in the first instance by parental choice, unless previously fixed quotas at the various maintained feeder schools are exceeded. In these cases pupils are offered to the direct grant schools by random selection. The schools do however reserve the right (sparingly used) not to admit a child sponsored by the local education authority if they believe he or she is unable to profit by the courses they provide. The number of pupils admitted each year under these arrangements is 25 to each of the direct grant schools, and about 200 to the maintained school. All the direct grant schools remain free to make their own arrangements for the admission of fee-payers. Some of them also admit free place holders from authorities other than their home authority and the arrangements described above for the different areas may not apply to these children.

129. A few schools have made arrangements to take local authority pupils at sixth form level. Among them are Dauntsey's School in Wiltshire and Leeds Grammar School. Dauntsey's School will admit any pupils from the local maintained secondary school who wish to follow a sixth form course, and there is already some joint use of staff and facilities in the teaching of younger pupils. Leeds Grammar School will admit up to 30 pupils a year from local authority schools who wish to attend Leeds Grammar School and follow a course which cannot be provided in their own school.

130. For the Roman Catholic direct grant schools the movement towards reorganisation has meant trying to forge links with the voluntary aided Roman Catholic schools in their areas. One school, St. Anne's Convent Grammar School, Southampton, already has a fully comprehensive intake. Another, St. Anthony's

Secondary School, Sunderland, will very shortly receive one. Several other schools have plans to admit sixth formers from maintained Roman Catholic schools so as to form the top tier of a comprehensive system. In general, however, the reorganisation of Roman Catholic maintained schools has proceeded more slowly than that of county schools because of the special difficulties faced by the Catholic schools owing to their limited capital resources, the small size of many of them, and the scattered populations they often serve.

131. In spite of the agreements reached so far, the fact remains that the overall picture is one of little change. In September, 1969 there were about 170 schools out of the total of 178 who will be receiving pupils from at least one authority on the same basis as before Circular 10/65. Agreement has been reached by 31 schools with at least one local education authority for receiving pupils on a different basis but in some cases the differences are slight. Further details are included in Appendix 6 (Section 2, Question 14.) There are several reasons why change has been slow. The reluctance of a number of the schools to admit a non-selective intake is one of them. Another is that some local education authorities have been unwilling to make long-term arrangements when the future status of the school was uncertain. Some authorities and some governing bodies oppose comprehensive reorganisation altogether. A further difficulty is that of financing any expansion or adaptations which may be necessary to fulfil a comprehensive role. A few schools have considered becoming voluntary aided to overcome this, but concluded they would be unable to meet their debts without fee income. The conclusion must be that uncertainty has to be ended and a new situation created in which both sides can negotiate with real purpose and clearly defined objectives.

Conclusion

132. No two schools are alike, and it is particularly dangerous to generalise about a group as varied as the direct grant schools. Nevertheless we think it is possible to identify four recognisable types, to one or other of which most of the 178 schools show a resemblance. First there is the "regional school". It is large, famous and draws from a wide area; it is highly selective, proud of its academic achievements and geared to the needs of the most able; it is more often a boys' school than a girls' school. This is the sort of school which often springs to mind when the term "direct grant" is used, but no more than a quarter of the schools really fit the description. Second is the boarding school. It is smaller and less selective; a higher proportion of pupils pay fees, more of them come from middle-class homes and it is more often a boys' than a girls' school. It is more akin than the other types to the public schools described in the Commission's First Report. Third are the Roman Catholic schools which form a group of their own. Their denominational character means they draw from a wide area, but academically they are much less selective than the regional schools, and socially they are much less selective than the boarding schools. Their higher proportion of local authority places means that they are doing the same job as the voluntary aided Catholic grammar schools. Their lack of endowments, and their low proportions of fee-payers mean that they carry heavier debts than most schools, and depend more heavily on fees to repay these debts. Finally there are the non-denominational local grammar schools. Most of them contain a higher proportion of the most able children than the average maintained grammar school, yet their ability range often extends below the limits usually adopted by

maintained grammar schools. Nevertheless their functions are broadly similar to those of the maintained grammar schools.

133. The principles underlying the system of direct grant finance originated at a time when schools of this sort provided nearly all the secondary education available to children from the elementary schools. The maintained grammar schools which grew up over the next forty years took them as their model, and for a long while there was little but their longer tradition of academic excellence to distinguish the direct grant schools from their maintained neighbours. But the growth and evolution of the maintained system gradually placed the direct grant schools in an increasingly distinctive, isolated—and some would say anomalous—position. They retained their central source of finance when other secondary schools came to depend for public support wholly on the general funds of the local authorities. They retained their largely independent status and their fee-payers when others became maintained and abandoned fees. More recently their commitment to academic selection has distinguished them increasingly sharply from a system which is being reorganised on comprehensive lines. The leaders of a movement are in danger of becoming the odd men out.

134. The direct grant schools have been asked to participate in reorganisation, but the difficulties in their path arise from factors more complex than academic tradition. If more children wish to enter them than they can accommodate, they must select by some means or other, and academic tests have hitherto offered an acceptable means of doing this. Most of the schools are much too small to become 11-18 comprehensive schools without enlargement, and many have cramped, central sites on which expansion would be impossible. Part of the costs of past building projects may have been met from private appeals but many schools have debts on this account which are being paid off from the income from fees (which they have been allowed to increase for this purpose) or from the contributions made by religious orders from the salaries of their members. For many, denominational commitments restrict the range of schools to which they can turn for mergers or the sharing of resources.

135. Underlying these difficulties is the more fundamental question of the nature of the relationship between local authorities, central government, and schools which value both their independence of action and their links with the State. This question must be looked at afresh in the light of the new situation now facing all concerned.

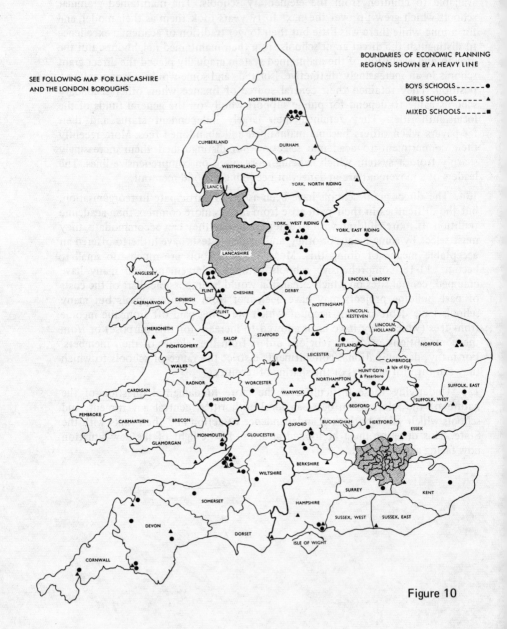

DIRECT GRANT GRAMMAR SCHOOLS
ENGLAND AND WALES

BOUNDARIES OF ECONOMIC PLANNING
REGIONS SHOWN BY A HEAVY LINE

SEE FOLLOWING MAP FOR LANCASHIRE
AND THE LONDON BOROUGHS

BOYS SCHOOLS ------●
GIRLS SCHOOLS ----▲
MIXED SCHOOLS ----■

Figure 10

DIRECT GRANT GRAMMAR SCHOOLS
LANCASHIRE AND THE LONDON BOROUGHS

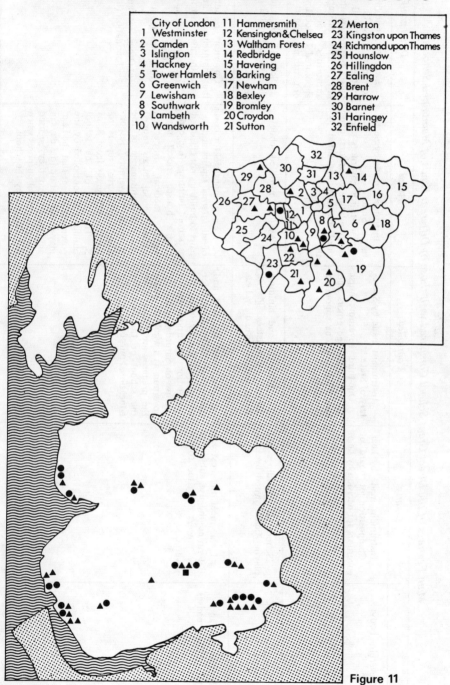

City of London
1 Westminster
2 Camden
3 Islington
4 Hackney
5 Tower Hamlets
6 Greenwich
7 Lewisham
8 Southwark
9 Lambeth
10 Wandsworth
11 Hammersmith
12 Kensington & Chelsea
13 Waltham Forest
14 Redbridge
15 Havering
16 Barking
17 Newham
18 Bexley
19 Bromley
20 Croydon
21 Sutton
22 Merton
23 Kingston upon Thames
24 Richmond upon Thames
25 Hounslow
26 Hillingdon
27 Ealing
28 Brent
29 Harrow
30 Barnet
31 Haringey
32 Enfield

Figure 11

Table 4

Main Features of the Direct Grant School Compared with those of Different Kinds of Maintained Schools

	County	Controlled	Aided	Direct grant
Governing body.	Instrument made by l.e.a. Composition of board of governors for decision by l.e.a.	Instrument made by Secretary of State. One-third governors must be foundation governors and two-thirds must be appointed by the l.e.a.	Instrument made by Secretary of State. Two-thirds governors must be foundation governors: one-third must be appointed by the l.e.a.	*Either* one-third of governors must be appointed by the l.e.a.(s) *or* the majority must be representative e.g. M.P., certain officers of local authorities or governors appointed by local authorities or parish meeting.
Ownership of premises.	School site, buildings and playing fields owned by l.e.a.	School site and buildings owned by trustees. Playing fields usually owned by l.e.a.	As for controlled schools.	School site and playing fields owned by trustees.
Maintenance and use of the premises.	L.e.a. meet the cost and determine the use subject to any powers delegated to the governors.	L.e.a. meet the cost and determines the use except for the use on Sunday when the foundation governors do or the use on Saturday when the governors as a whole do unless the premises are required by the school or the l.e.a. for educational purposes.	L.e.a. responsible for cost of all *internal* repairs and repairs to buildings not classified as school buildings (e.g. caretaker's house, cricket pavilions, medical inspection rooms, school meals rooms) and for maintenance of the grounds. Governors responsible for external repairs receiving 80% grant from S. of S. The use of the school buildings is controlled by the governors except that the l.e.a. may direct (for up to 3 days in any week) that they be used for educational purposes when not required by the school.	Governors responsible for the maintenance and determine the use. Cost met from: (a) Fees paid by parent or l.e.a.s (b) Grants from the S. of S. (c) Other income of the foundation (if any).

Table 4 (cont.)

	County	Controlled	Aided	Direct grant
Tuition fees.	None.	None.	None.	Fixed by governors subject to approval by S. of S. Paid by l.e.a. for l.e.a. free or reserved places. Paid by parents for residuary places but remitted according to income scale approved by S. of S.
Religious worship and instruction.	Day must begin with non-denominational worship. Instruction according to "agreed syllabus" (non-denominational). Parents may withdraw pupil from both or either.	Day must begin with worship. Denomination according to trust deed (or, if this does not specify, as decided by the governors). Agreed syllabus religious instruction. Parents may choose to have religious instruction according to the trust deed (or, if this does not specify, according to the previous practice of the school) up to a maximum of 2 periods per week. Parents may withdraw pupils from worship and/or instruction.	Day must begin with worship. Denomination according to trust deed (or, if this does not specify, as decided by the governors). Religious instruction according to trust deed (or, if this does not specify according to the previous practice of the school). Parents may withdraw pupils from worship and/or instruction.	Worship every day (not necessarily at beginning). Otherwise as for aided schools.
Capital expenditure.	Met and controlled by l.e.a.	As for county school.	Expenditure on school buildings met by governors with 80% grant from S. of S. Public loans available for the other 20%.	Met by governors. Approval of S. of S. required. No grants from S. of S. for capital expenditure.

Subject to control of major building programmes and approval by S. of S.

Table 4 (cont.)

	County	Controlled	Aided	Direct grant
Admission of pupils.	L.e.a. responsible.	According to articles of government for school. These normally say "governors shall be responsible but must act within arrangements agreed with the l.e.a."	As for controlled schools, except that the arrangements should specify in what circumstances extra-district pupils may be admitted.	25% of places must be "free places" offered either by l.e.a.s or governors to pupils who have spent 2 years at maintained primary schools. Further "reserved places" must be offered to l.e.a.s (which need not be taken up). The total of "free" and "reserved" places may not exceed 50% without the agreement of the governors. L.e.a.s are responsible for the selection of pupils for "free" or "reserved" places which they take up (subject to the pupils being suitably qualified). Governors' free places and residuary places are the responsibility of the governors.
Secular instruction.	Under control of l.e.a. except in so far as delegated to the governors and/or head.	Under control of l.e.a. except where otherwise provided in the articles of government. These usually provide that the l.e.a. determine the general educational character of the school and its place in the local educational system while the governors have the direction of the conduct and curriculum of the school, except in so far as delegated to the head.	Under control of governors (except where otherwise provided in the articles of government). Subject to the provisions of the Development Plan approved for the area by the S. of S. as to the educational character of the school, the governors, in consultation with the head, have direction over the conduct and curriculum of the school.	Under control of governors except in so far as delegated to head.

Table 4 (cont.)

	County	Controlled	Aided	Direct grant
Appointment of teachers.	Under control of l.e.a. unless delegated to governors.	Apart from "reserved teachers" under control of l.e.a. unless delegated. L.e.a. must get approval of foundation governors to appointment of a "reserved teacher" as to his fitness to give religious instruction. L.e.a. must inform governors of proposed appointment of head teacher and consider any representation made.	Teachers to be appointed by the governors. Articles may enable l.e.a. to give directions on the educational qualifications of teachers. L.e.a. will determine the total numbers.	Under control of governors but S. of S.'s power to approve fees, enables him to influence total numbers.

Abbreviations: l.e.a.–local education authority.   S. of S.– Secretary of State for Education and Science.

Table 5

Size of Direct Grant Schools at January, 1968 (including both upper and lower schools)

Size	Numbers of schools									
	Under 200 pupils	201 to 300	301 to 400	401 to 500	501 to 600	601 to 700	701 to 800	801 to 900	901 to 1000	1001 and over
Boys	–	1	6	12	10	17	13	9	2	12
Girls	–	2	5	8	32	15	19	9	4	1
Mixed	–	–	–	–	–	1	–	–	1	–
Total	–	3	11	20	42	33	32	18	7	13

Source: Department of Education and Science returns for January, 1968.
Average size: Boys 685   Girls 633.

Table 6

Size of Direct Grant Schools at January, 1968 (upper schools only)

Size	Numbers of schools									
	Under 200 pupils	201 to 300	301 to 400	401 to 500	501 to 600	601 to 700	701 to 800	801 to 900	901 to 1000	1001 and over
Boys	–	1	10	18	10	18	11	7	4	3
Girls	1	2	17	29	17	17	10	–	2	–
Mixed	–	–	–	–	–	1	–	1	–	–
Total	1	3	27	47	27	36	21	8	6	3
Boarding upper schools (included in figures above)										
Boarding upper schools	–	3	9	10	6	1	–	1	–	–

Source: Department of Education and Science returns for January, 1968.
Average size for all schools: Boys 616   Girls 518.
Average size for boarding schools: Boys 454   Girls 409.

Table 7

Size of Sixth Forms at Direct Grant Schools at January, 1968

Number of pupils in sixth forms	Numbers of schools			
	Boys	Girls	Mixed	All
30-59	2	4	–	6
60-89	5	22	–	27
90-119	16	38	–	54
120-179	35	24	–	59
180-239	12	6	2	20
240 or over	12	1	–	13
	Number of pupils			
Average size of VIth form in direct grant schools	164	112	201	137
Average size of VIth forms in maintained grammar schools	127	102	112	113

Source: Department of Education and Science returns for January, 1968.

Table 8

Proportion of Boarding Pupils in Upper Schools at January, 1968

Percentage of boarders	Boys	Girls	Mixed	Total
Over 50% boarders				
No. of schools	14	1	–	15
No. of boarding pupils	3,765	230	–	3,995
25%-50% boarders				
No. of schools	9	6	–	15
No. of boarding pupils	1,608	824	–	2,432
Under 25% boarders				
No. of schools	18	14	1	33
No. of boarding pupils	1,259	879	65 B 57 G	2,260
No boarders				
No. of schools	41	74	1	116
Total No. of schools	82[1]	95	2	179
Total No. of boarding pupils	6,632	1,933	122	8,687

Source: Department of Education and Science returns for January, 1968.

Note: [1] There were 81 boys' schools from August 1968 when Trinity School of John Whitgift became independent. It had no boarders.

Table 9

Local Education Authority Places in Direct Grant Schools at January, 1968

Percentages taken by l.e.a.s	Day schools		Boarding schools[1]	Total number of schools
	Roman Catholic	Other		
Under 20%	–	1	7	8
20%-24%	–	2	5	7
25%-29%	1	11	1	13
30%-39%	1	24	5	30
40%-49%	–	20	7	27
50%-59%	2	14	1	17
60%-69%	6	10	2	18
70%-79%	6	6	2	14
80%-89%	12	3	–	15
Over 90%	28	2	–	30
Total	56	93	30	179[2]

Source: Department of Education and Science returns for January, 1968.

Notes: [1] Schools with 25% or more boarding pupils.

[2] These figures include Trinity School of John Whitgift which fell in the 50-59% category.

Table 10

Pupils Admitted in Autumn Term 1968 to Upper Schools of Direct Grant Grammar Schools

Schools attended in 1967-68	Free place pupils		Reserved place pupils		Residuary place pupils		All pupils	
	Nos.	Percentages of col. total	Nos.	Percentages of col. total	Nos.	Percentages of col. total	Nos.	Percentages of col. total
Maintained or grant-aided primary schools	5,815	85	1,973	64	2,898	38	10,686	61
Lower school	478*	7*	542	18	2,627	34	3,647	21
Other schools or no previous school	514*	8*	549	18	2,150	28	3,213	18
Total	6,807	100	3,064	100	7,675	100	17,546	100

Source: Department of Education and Science returns for September, 1968.

Note: *Free place pupils must have attended a maintained or grant-aided primary school for two years or more. Where they attended a lower school or other non-maintained school immediately prior to admission they will have attended a maintained primary school at an earlier age.

Table 11

School Leavers: Age of Leaving, 1967-68

Percentages

	Direct grant*			Maintained grammar			All maintained (including grammar)			Independent recognised efficient		
	Boys	Girls	Total	Boys	Girls	Total	Boys	Girls	Total	Boys	Girls	Total
15	1·9	2·7	2·3	5·6	7·0	6·3	53·8	54·4	54·1	4·0	7·9	5·8
16	13·1	18·9	16·0	24·6	31·7	28·1	25·2	26·4	25·8	14·6	32·6	22·8
17	23·9	18·4	21·2	18·7	17·2	18·0	7·5	7·4	7·4	28·7	29·9	29·3
18	50·0	56·5	53·2	41·6	41·5	41·6	11·1	11·1	11·1	45·7	26·4	36·9
19 and over	11·1	3·5	7·4	9·6	2·5	6·1	2·4	0·8	1·6	6·9	3·1	5·1
Total	100·0	100·0	100·0	100·0	100·0	100·0	100·0	100·0	100·0	100·0	100·0	100·0
Number of leavers	7,369	7,177	14,546	52,920	52,240	105,160	288,980	271,910	560,890	15,080	12,760	27,840

Sources: Statistics of Education, 1968 (based on a 10 per cent sample) for maintained and independent recognised efficient schools.
Direct grant schools—P.S.C. questionnaire.

* Excluding seven pupils (five boys and two girls) for whom the age of leaving was not given.

Table 12

Destination of School Leavers, 1967-68

Percentages

	Direct grant*			Maintained grammar			All maintained (including grammar)			Independent recognised efficient		
	Boys	Girls	Total	Boys	Girls	Total	Boys	Girls	Total	Boys	Girls	Total
Universities	47·9	29·1	38·5	25·6	13·2	19·5	6·1	3·1	4·6	30·3	11·4	21·6
Colleges of Education	3·9	21·5	12·7	4·8	18·5	11·6	1·4	5·1	3·2	1·4	7·8	4·3
Other full-time further education	23·1	23·4	23·2	13·2	19·4	16·3	7·8	10·6	9·2	25·1	40·4	32·1
Temporary employment pending further education	—	—	—	1·7	1·2	1·4	0·5	0·4	0·5	6·1	3·4	4·8
Employment or destination not known	24·9	25·8	25·5	54·6	47·7	51·2	84·2	80·7	82·5	37·1	37·1	37·1
Total	100·0	100·0	100·0	100·0	100·0	100·0	100·0	100·0	100·0	100·0	100·0	100·0
Number of leavers	7,374	7,179	14,553	52,920	52,240	105,160	288,980	271,910	560,890	15,080	12,760	27,840

Sources: Statistics of Education 1968, (based on a 10 per cent sample) for maintained and independent recognised efficient schools.
Direct grant schools—P.S.C. questionnaire.

* Pupils in direct grant schools entering temporary employment pending further education have been included in the appropriate category of further education.

Table 13

G.C.E. Advanced Level Achievements of School Leavers, 1967-68

Percentages

	Direct grant			Maintained grammar			Independent recognised efficient		
	Boys	Girls	Total	Boys	Girls	Total	Boys	Girls	Total
No subjects attempted	25·3	33·6	29·4	42·9	51·6	47·3	32·7	61·1	45·7
All subjects failed	4·7	5·7	5·2	5·0	4·9	4·9	5·8	4·4	5·1
1 pass	7·5	10·4	8·9	8·1	9·3	8·7	8·7	7·8	8·3
2 passes	14·1	15·9	15·0	13·2	14·5	13·9	16·3	12·2	14·4
3 passes	35·4	27·5	31·5	24·2	17·2	20·7	28·8	12·7	21·4
4 or more passes	13·0	7·0	10·0	6·6	2·4	4·5	7·6	1·7	4·9
Total	100·0	100·0	100·0	100·0	100·0	100·0	100·0	100·0	100·0
Number of leavers	7,374	7,179	14,553	52,920	52,240	105,160	15,080	12,760	27,840

Sources: Statistics of Education 1968, (based on a 10 per cent sample) for maintained grammar and independent recognised efficient schools.
Direct grant schools—P.S.C. questionnaire.

Table 14

Oxford and Cambridge Applications, Admissions and Open Awards by Type of School (men only)

Type of School	Percentages					
	Cambridge			Oxford		
	Appli-cations	Admissions	Awards	Appli-cations	Admissions	Awards
Independent	35	38	44	41	41	43
Direct grant	17	20	23	15	16	18
Maintained	42	39	32	42	41	38
Other	6	3	1	2	2	1
Total	100	100	100	100	100	100
Number of men	5,253	2,404	564	3,776	1,866	650

Source: The Universities of Oxford and Cambridge.

Notes: The Times Educational Supplement survey of the 3rd October, 1969 showed that of the 27 schools with 10 or more awards:

    20 were H.M.C. independent schools
    7 were direct grant schools

We record these facts because the Oxford and Cambridge scholarship results are often quoted in connection with direct grant and independent schools. It should not be thought that the Commission regards these results as the only measure of academic success or as the only mark of a "good" school. A school's results in the examinations depend on a great many factors including the ability of the pupils going to the school, the number of pupils who want to go to these universities and therefore apply, the aims of the school, and so on.

Table 15

Financial Responsibility for Tuition Fees in Different Groups of Direct Grant Schools at January, 1968

Column percentages

Fees paid by: (1)	All schools (2)	Boys'[1] schools (3)	Girls'[1] schools (4)	(5) All R.C. schools			H.M.C. schools (6)	Mainly boarding schools (7)	Schools with over 25% boarding (8)	GPDST schools (9)	Schools with large VIth forms (10)
				R.C. boys	R.C. girls	R.C. total					
1. L.e.a.	60	55	64	89	84	86	44	29	38	42	50
2. Governors	1	2	1	*	*	*	2	5	5	*	1
3. Parents or Guardians:											
(a) remitted in full	1	2	1	1	1	1	2	2	2	*	2
(b) partly remitted	9	10	8	5	8	7	12	6	8	8	11
(c) wholly paid by parents[2]	28	31	26	5	7	6	40	58	47	49	37
Numbers of pupils	101,236	50,550	49,215	13,076	21,812	34,888	35,413	5,961	13,312	9,697	29,069

Source: Department of Education and Science returns for January, 1968.
Notes: [1] Excluding mixed schools.
          [2] Including places paid for by other bodies or from scholarship funds.
    * Negligible percentage.
Abbreviations: L.e.a.—Local education authority; R.C.—Roman Catholic; H.M.C.—Headmasters' Conference; G.P.D.S.T.—Girls' Public Day School Trust.

Table 16

Tuition Fees for Direct Grant Upper Schools at September, 1968

Fees	All schools (incl. two mixed)	Boys' schools	Girls' schools	Number of schools R.C. schools Boys	R.C. schools Girls	H.M.C. schools	25% or more boarding	GPDST schools	Schools with large VIth forms
Below £90	–	–	–	–	–	–	–	–	–
£90-£100	1	–	1	–	1	–	–	–	–
£101-£110	6	1	5	1	5	–	–	–	–
£111-£120	25	7	18	2	11	5	3	–	5
£121-£130	32	14	18	10	13	4	1	–	6
£131-£140	30	16	13	5	5	9	4	–	6
£141-£150	56	20	35	1	2	19	11	22	13
£151-£160	22	18	4	–	–	16	9	–	8
£161-£170	4	4	–	–	–	4	–	–	2
£171-£180	1	1	–	–	–	1	1	–	–
above £180	1	–	1	–	–	–	1	–	–
Number of schools	178	81	95	19	37	58	30	22	40
Average fee	135	139	131	126	120	144	147	147	140

Source: Department of Education and Science returns for September, 1968.

Note: Average fee calculated by multiplying the numbers of pupils at each school by the annual fee charged at September, 1968 and then dividing the aggregated total for all schools by the total number of pupils.

Abbreviations: R.C.–Roman Catholic; H.M.C.–Headmasters' Conference; G.P.D.S.T.–Girls' Public Day School Trust.

Table 17

Combined Tuition and Boarding Fees for Direct Grant Upper Schools for September, 1968

Fees	All schools (incl. one mixed)	Boys' schools	Girls' schools	R.C. schools		H.M.C. schools	25% or more boarding	Less than 25% boarding	GPDST schools	Schools with large VIth forms
				Boys	Girls					
Below £300	9	3	6	2	4	–	2	7	–	–
£300–£320	5	3	2	1	1	2	1	4	–	2
£321–£340	8	3	4	1	–	1	4	4	2	1
£341–£360	9	6	3	–	–	6	3	6	1	2
£361–£380	11	8	3	–	1	8	6	5	–	3
£381–£400	13	10	3	–	–	9	8	5	–	1
£401–£420	2	2	–	–	–	2	2	–	–	1
£421–£440	3	3	–	–	–	3	2	1	–	–
Over £440	3	3	–	–	–	3	2	1	–	1
Number of schools	63	41	21	4	6	34	30	33	3	11
Average fee	371	379	344	307	294	386	379	347	336	399

Source: Department of Education and Science returns for September, 1968.

Note:　Average fee calculated by multiplying the numbers of boarders at each school by the annual fee charged at September, 1968, and then dividing the aggregated total for all schools by the total number of boarders.

Abbreviations: R.C.–Roman Catholic; H.M.C.–Headmasters' Conference; G.P.D.S.T.–Girls' Public Day School Trust.

Table 18

Comparison of Costs Between Direct Grant and Maintained Grammar Schools

1. Estimated average costs per pupil (exclusive of capital charges and school meals) for maintained grammar, secondary modern, comprehensive and other secondary schools were calculated using information about the numbers and salaries of teachers and pupil/teacher ratios at different ages in the different kinds of school. Costs other than teachers' salaries were distributed between the three categories of pupil on the assumption that in each case they form the same ratio to the cost of teachers' salaries. The estimates for grammar school pupils in 1967-68 were:

	Pupil/teacher ratios (full-time equivalent)	Teachers' salaries per pupil £	Total cost per pupil £
Pupils wholly or mainly under 15 years of age	20:5	92	132
Pupils aged wholly or mainly 15 years and over, but not in sixth forms	16:2	115	165
Sixth form pupils	10:8	174	250
All pupils	16:8	112	161

2. To obtain the notional average cost per pupil if the children now at direct grant schools were in maintained grammar schools, the number of children of various ages in the direct grant schools were multiplied by the average costs given above.

	1 Average cost at maintained grammar school	2 Numbers in direct grant schools	3 (1) x (2) £
Pupils under 15 years	132	57,281	7,561,092
Pupils of 15 years* and over, not in sixth forms	165	19,456	3,210,240
Sixth form pupils	250	24,499	6,124,750
Total		101,236	16,896,082

Average cost for all pupils = $\dfrac{£16,896,082}{101,236}$ = £167

Source: Department of Education and Science.

* This classification has to be slightly different from that adopted for maintained grammar schools, but the difference is small.

3. In 1967-68, the actual average cost per pupil in direct grant grammar schools, excluding school meals expenses, loan charges and transfers to other funds, was £169. This includes an element of administrative costs borne by a local authority in the case of maintained schools. Taking this into account there is very little difference between the overall average expenditure per pupil on current resources in the two types of school.

Table 19

Distribution of I.Q. or V.R.Q. of Pupils Admitted to Upper School in the Academic Year 1967-68 by Categories of Schools

	Percentages of entrants for whom I.Q. or V.R.Q. is known								Number of entrants for whom V.R.Q. is known	Number of entrants
	Less than 90	90-99	100-109	110-119	120-129	130-139	140+			
Schools with large sixth forms	—	1	6	22	34	26	10		2,432	4,948
Roman Catholic schools	1	2	9	31	38	15	3		2,568	6,460
Boarding schools	1	3	15	33	27	15	6		936	2,504
Other schools	2	1	9	28	33	22	5		2,306	4,712
All schools	1	2	9	27	34	20	7		8,030	18,144

Source: P.S.C. questionnaire.

Notes: 1. Figures for some schools have been included more than once since some boarding schools fall within the large sixth form category also.
2. For further tables on I.Q./V.R.Q. distribution and notes on categories of school see Appendix 6, Volume II.

Table 20

Social Class of Fathers of School Leavers (by categories of schools)

	Percentages				
	Schools with large VIth forms		Roman Catholic schools	Boarding schools	All direct grant schools
	Boys	Girls			
I and II Professional and Managerial	64·4	71·3	37·5	72·8	59·6
IIIa Other non-manual	13·5	11·2	13·7	11·9	12·8
IIIb Skilled manual	19·0	12·9	32·8	12·0	20·1
IV and V Semi and unskilled	3·1	4·6	16·0	3·3	7·5
Number where father's occupation stated excluding those not classifiable	2,178	1,657	4,084	1,638	12,716
Total number of leavers	2,384	1,796	5,024	1,934	14,553

Source: P.S.C. questionnaire.
Note: For further tables on social class and notes on categories of school see Appendix 6 Volume II.

Table 21

Proportions of Graduate Teachers in Maintained and Direct Grant Schools at March, 1967

	Men and women		Men only		Women only	
	Maintained grammar schools	*Direct grant schools*	*Maintained grammar schools*	*Direct grant schools*	*Maintained grammar schools*	*Direct grant schools*
(a) Number of graduates with 1st class honours	2,146	352	1,415	220	731	132
(b) All teachers	38,595	6,530	23,444	3,374	15,151	3,156
(c) (a) as a percentage of (b)	5·6	5·4	6·0	6·5	4·8	4·2
(d) Number of graduates with 1st or 2nd class honours	18,764	2,555	11,766	1,524	6,998	1,031
(e) (d) as a percentage of (b)	48·6	39·1	50·2	45·2	46·2	32·7
(f) All graduates as a percentage of all teachers	73·9	61·3	77·2	72·2	68·7	49·7

Source: Statistics of Education 1967, Volume 4.
Note: This table applies to full-time teachers only.

CHAPTER 5

The Independent Day Schools

136. The Commission's First Report dealt with independent boarding schools: now we turn to the day schools, which for our present purposes we define as those in which fewer than 25 per cent of the pupils board. By this definition, there were 2,571 independent day schools in January, 1968, out of a total of 3,066 independent schools. Of these, 117 were nursery schools[1], 1,857 were primary or preparatory schools, and 597 were secondary schools.[2]

Registration and Recognition

137. Part III of the Education Act, 1944, which came into operation on 30th September, 1957, requires the Secretary of State to appoint a Registrar of Independent Schools whose duty it is to keep a register of all independent schools. Subject to appeal to an Independent Schools Tribunal, schools found to be unsatisfactory may be struck off the register. It is illegal to run an independent school not on the register. The general standards hitherto adopted by the Department for the purposes of registration under Part III of the Act are lower than those looked for before an independent day school is recognised as efficient under the Department's Rules 16. Of the 597 independent secondary[2] day schools, 265 are recognised as efficient, and 65 of these are public schools as defined in our terms of reference (18 boys' and 47 girls' schools). These figures are set out in detail in Tables 23 to 28 at the end of the Chapter.

138. Our terms of reference were particularly directed towards the public schools although we were also asked whether "any action is needed in respect of other independent schools whether secondary or primary". In the first Report it was concluded that there was no hard and fast line which could be drawn between the public schools as defined in our terms of reference and other independent schools recognised as efficient. The Secretary of State has already initiated action to bring all independent boarding schools up to the standards required for recognition as efficient. He has also made it plain that when this has been achieved for boarding schools the standards in the non-recognised independent day schools will be raised in the same way. We shall therefore concentrate our attention on schools which have been recognised as efficient. We have also decided to confine our proposals for the future to independent secondary schools rather than primary schools. This Chapter therefore deals mainly with independent day schools which are recognised as efficient and take pupils who stay beyond the age of 15.

---

[1] Nursery schools do not have to be registered as independent schools unless they have at least five pupils of compulsory school age. The 117 schools mentioned above thus represent a small proportion of all nursery schools or groups.

[2] Including schools with a secondary department which cater also for primary pupils.

The Schools

139. The independent day schools vary even more widely in size and character than the independent boarding schools; the range is from the very small school only locally known to large and famous grammar schools such as Dulwich and St. Paul's. The 265 recognised efficient secondary schools range in size from under 50 to over 1,000 pupils: 29 per cent have 400 or more pupils, 71 per cent have less than 400 pupils, and 26 per cent have less than 200. Only 11 schools have more than 800 pupils.

140. Most of these schools cater for boys or for girls only. Only 50 out of the 265 are co-educational schools, although some of the others have small numbers of the opposite sex, usually in their junior departments. The majority of the 265 schools we shall consider are girls' schools (162, compared with 53 boys' schools) and although girls' schools tend to be smaller, more girls than boys attend independent secondary day schools. The total number of boys of secondary age in independent schools (including boarding and day pupils) is not very different from the total number of girls, but parents are more likely to send their sons than their daughters to boarding school.

141. There are more independent schools in the South than in the North and the larger and more famous day schools tend naturally to be situated in the big conurbations. The distribution of day pupils at independent recognised schools is shown in the map (Figure 12) and in Tables 25 and 26 at the end of this Chapter. The location of the public schools with day pupils is shown in Figure 13.

142. Records of the numbers of unrecognised schools are available from 1958. Since then the total number of independent schools on the register (other than nursery schools) has fallen by 1,286—from 4,235 in 1958 to 2,949 in 1968. It is mainly the unrecognised schools which have been closing: the number of those on the register has dropped by 1,315 from 2,799 in 1958 to 1,484 in 1968. Recognised schools which have closed or changed their status have been more than replaced by unrecognised schools gaining recognition, and the total number of recognised schools which was 1,436 in 1958 shows a net gain of 29 to 1,465 in 1968.

143. This trend in the numbers of schools which is illustrated in Figure 14 is matched by a similar trend in the numbers of pupils. The number of pupils (both day and boarding) in all independent schools, other than nursery schools, has fallen from an estimated 498,000 in 1947 (500,000 in 1958) to 426,000 in 1968—299,000 of the latter were day pupils. Over the 21 years, the school population as a whole has risen and the percentage of pupils in independent schools has dropped from 8·8 per cent in 1947 to 6·7 per cent in 1958 and 5·3 per cent in 1968. When the pupils in recognised efficient schools are counted separately a different picture emerges. As more independent schools have gained recognition the number of pupils in recognised schools has increased from 165,000 in 1947 to 281,000 in 1958 and 301,000 in 1968. Seven out of ten pupils receiving independent education are now in recognised efficient schools compared with just over three out of ten in 1947. The percentages of fourteen-year-old boys and girls in independent schools are shown in Figure 15.

144. The fall in numbers over the independent sector as a whole should not be exaggerated. The independent sector is not "withering away". The number of pupils in all independent schools has fallen by 14 per cent in 21 years. If it falls

by the same proportion over the next 21 years (and that by no means follows) it would still represent 366,000 pupils—more than the present number in independent recognised efficient schools and 3 per cent of the total school population. The independent schools with the most influence and prestige have not been affected by this fall in demand. Generally speaking, it is the smaller and the less efficient schools which are closing. The comparison of the 1958 figures with those for 1968 in Table 28 shows that day pupils, girls and primary pupils in independent schools as a whole have all decreased in numbers whereas the numbers of boy boarders at secondary schools have increased. Numbers of pupils in recognised efficient schools have in most categories increased as more independent schools seek and obtain recognition.

Places taken by Local Education Authorities

145. There are 79,500 senior[1] day pupils in independent schools recognised as efficient. They represent 2·6 per cent of all senior day pupils. Of these 79,500 pupils, about 18,000[2]—23 per cent—have their fees paid in full by local education authorities. About 1,800 pupils more get partial assistance. Thus one in four senior day pupils at independent recognised efficient schools have their fees paid either in full or in part by local education authorities. The pupils paid for by local education authorities are not evenly spread over the schools, since in 152 schools (57 per cent) there are no places paid for by local education authorities and in seven schools (3 per cent) over 75 per cent of the places are paid for by local education authorities. Table 29 gives more details.

146. The authorities provide free or assisted day places at independent schools in three main types of situation: first, where the independent school provides a denominational education (usually selective) which is not available at maintained schools in the area (about 60 per cent of all the places taken up by the authorities are at Roman Catholic schools); second, where the independent school has traditionally served as the grammar school for its district, and third, where the independent school has high academic prestige and draws from a wider area on a highly selective basis in competition with grammar schools. In each case, the independent school is playing a part much like one or other of the main types of direct grant day school we distinguished in paragraph 132.

147. The Department of Education and Science in its Manual of Guidance (Schools Number 1 re-issued in 1960) advised that free places should not be taken up at independent schools if maintained or direct grant schools could provide what was needed. As authorities reorganise along comprehensive lines and provide more places in new maintained schools, they will probably take up fewer free day places at selective independent schools.

Staffing and Fees

148. The Commission's First Report (Volume I Table 13) showed that independent schools are on average more generously staffed than maintained schools,

---

[1] This excludes pupils of secondary age in independent preparatory schools. It represents day pupils in secondary independent schools which are recognised as efficient, and pupils aged 12 and over together with two thirds of those aged 11 years in recognised efficient schools with both primary and secondary departments.

[2] There were 18,597 pupils assisted by local education authorities—almost all at independent secondary schools but a few may be under the age of 11.

7

and their classes tend generally to be somewhat smaller. The qualifications of teachers in independent schools vary. In the public schools a high proportion of teachers are graduates and only about 5 per cent of them would not be regarded as qualified in maintained schools. In other recognised efficient independent schools about 75 per cent of teachers would be classed as qualified teachers. In unrecognised schools the proportion is substantially lower.

149. Teachers' salaries are not tied to national scales. Many of the girls' public schools pay according to Burnham scales. A number of the boys' public schools pay salaries above these scales. Salaries at other independent schools vary considerably.

150. Fees depend on many factors such as the staffing ratio, the size of the sixth form, the salary scales of teachers, the rate of expenditure on materials, equipment and new building, past debts and endowment income. For day pupils they range from under £100 to over £300 in recognised efficient secondary day schools. The average fee at boys' schools is £180, at girls' schools £164. Table 27 provides more information about this.

Social Composition and Parental Expectations

151. The independent secondary day schools are less isolated from the rest of the community than the public boarding schools: more of their pupils have previously attended maintained primary schools.[1] In recognised independent schools other than the public schools, about 46 per cent of the day pupils enter direct from maintained schools and 49 per cent from independent schools, the remaining 5 per cent coming from direct grant schools, schools abroad, and other forms of education. The day schools make this easy by admitting pupils at age eleven; more day pupils enter at that age than at thirteen, particularly at schools other than the boys' public schools.[2]

152. Analysis of the backgrounds of pupils at independent schools according to the Registrar General's social categories can only be a rough guide to social backgrounds, and comparison between boarding and day pupils is complicated by the 11-12 per cent of boarding pupils whose fathers are in the Armed Forces. If parents in the services are discounted, the proportions of children from the different home backgrounds found in the survey carried out for the First Report[3] were as set out in Table 22. Among parents of direct grant school day pupils, 58 per cent fall into the professional and managerial category. (Registrar General's categories I and II). In the economically active adult male population as a whole, 20 per cent are in this category.

153. Information about I.Q. or V.R.Q. scores of pupils at independent schools is limited and difficult to interpret. All one can say with confidence is that a few independent day schools are highly selective and take pupils academically similar to those of the more highly selective direct grant schools, whereas others take pupils with abilities well below that of entrants to maintained grammar schools.

154. Why do parents pay £250 a year or more to send their children to independent day schools when they could be educated free of charge in a maintained school? The Incorporated Association of Preparatory Schools, the

---

1 First Report Volume II Table 7 page 102.
2 First Report Volume II Table 3 page 46.
3 First Report Volume II Table 5 page 101.

Table 22

Social Class of Parents of Pupils at Independent Schools

Social Class of Parent: Registrar General's Categories	Boarding pupils		Day pupils	
	Public schools	Other recognised efficient schools (sample)	Public schools	Other recognised efficient schools (sample)
	%	%	%	%
I and II—Professional and Managerial	94	93	88	87
III(a)—Other Non-Manual	5	6	8	7
III(b), IV and V—Manual	1	1	4	6
Total	100	100	100	100

Bow Group and the Advisory Centre for Education all made surveys dealing with this question and sent the results to us. We talked to teachers and pupils on our visits to schools. In many cases family tradition and social background have meant that education at a maintained school has not been seriously considered. Many parents have loyalties to particular schools. Many believe that their children will receive a better education at an independent school. Their reasons for such a choice are varied. Styles of teaching and discipline may be valued. Or it may be thought that the school has better laboratories, or better equipped classrooms, or larger playing fields. Parents may be attracted by the reputation which the school enjoys for assisting pupils on their way to universities or good careers. Most important of all, many parents believe that in an independent school their children will be taught in smaller classes and attach great value to this apparent advantage.[1]

155. When choosing a school, many parents lay weight on its formal academic achievements. Our impression is that ability and home background account for most of the differences between the attainments of pupils in these and other schools. There is not much evidence about academic achievements of schools which takes account of both the ability and the home background of their pupils. Dr. Douglas,[2] comparing attainments of middle class pupils at independent and at maintained schools, concluded that boys of the highest ability gained more good certificates at independent schools than their counterparts in maintained schools, but that there was little difference at other levels of ability.

[1] We are here summarising and not evaluating the reasons for which parents are prepared to pay fees. Nevertheless, attention should be directed to the most recent and significant research on the effects of class size on achievement (see e.g. paragraphs 780 to 788 of "Children and their Primary Schools" Volume I). Most of this research applies particularly to primary education, which differs significantly in method and organisation from secondary education, but it does point to the conclusion that class size by itself, within the limits normally found in schools, has little effect upon the attainment of pupils. However, parents still plainly believe that smaller classes produce "a better education" for their children, and for this reason are often prepared to make considerable financial sacrifices.

[2] "All our Future" by J. W. B. Douglas, J. M. Ross and H. R. Simpson; Peter Davies, London, 1968.

Girls, on the other hand, tended to do better at all levels of ability at the maintained school. But the research which Dr. Douglas has so far published has dealt with attainment only up to 'O' level; and his social class categories are sufficiently broad to make it uncertain whether further social differences within his categories may influence these results.

156. Some parents lay more stress on social considerations: they feel that independent schools will more effectively develop the sort of character, disposition or manners they want their child to have. For some, religious considerations are most important. If there were a maintained school of their religious denomination in the neighbourhood many of them would be happy to send their children there. Some parents living in areas where there is still a selective system may choose an independent school because they fear their child is unlikely to get to a grammar school. Others in areas where comprehensive schools have been recently introduced may prefer an established independent grammar school. A small, homely independent school may be chosen in preference to a large maintained school, progressive (or conventional) independent schools may be chosen in preference to more conventional (or progressive) maintained schools, and single-sex schools may be chosen in preference to co-education.

157. There is no single reason why parents pay fees to have their children educated at independent schools. What is certain is that independent schools survive because they are believed to offer something which is *different* from what is available in maintained schools. In so far as they depend on being different, the question we shall have to consider is whether these differences are of a kind that justify public expenditure on the services they offer.

Table 23

Numbers of Independent Secondary Schools Mainly for Day Pupils at January,
1968

		Number of schools		
		1 *Day only*	*2* *With less than 25% boarding places*	*3* *With less than 50% boarding places*
Public schools	Boys	9	18	30
	Girls	29	47	65
	Total	38	65	95
All independent recognised efficient schools (including public schools)	Boys	33	53	73
	Girls	95	162	216
	Mixed	36	50	60
	Total	164	265	349
Non-recognised independent schools	Boys	35	51	65
	Girls	54	77	92
	Mixed	161	204	204
	Total	250	332	361

Source: Department of Education and Science returns for January, 1968.

Notes: 1. Schools have been classified as secondary if they make provision for pupils aged 15 or over even though they may have some pupils of primary school age.

2. The figures given in Column 2 include the figures in Column 1 and the figures in Column 3 include the figures in Columns 1 and 2.

3. Public schools have been defined as independent schools in membership of the H.M.C., G.B.A., or G.B.G.S.A.

4. Schools which contain both boys and girls but which have less than 10 per cent of pupils of the opposite sex have been classified according to the sex of the majority of their pupils.

PART TWO. THE BACKGROUND

Table 24

*Sizes of Independent Secondary Schools
with under 25 per cent of Pupils Boarding at January, 1968*

| No. of pupils in school | Number of schools | | | | | |
| | Recognised as efficient | | | Other independent | | |
	Boys schools	*Girls schools*	*Mixed schools*	*Boys schools*	*Girls schools*	*Mixed schools*
Under 200	12	38	20	44	65	172
201-300	9	46	13	6	9	26
301-400	6	34	10	–	2	3
401-600	7	34	5	1	1	–
601-800	10	9	1	–	–	3
801-1000	7	–	–	–	–	–
1001 and over	2	1	1	–	–	–
Total	53	162	50	51	77	204

Source: Department of Education and Science returns for January, 1968.

Notes: 1. Schools have been classified as secondary if they make provision for pupils aged 15 or over even though they may have some pupils of primary school age.

2. Schools which contain both boys and girls but which have less than 10 per cent of pupils of the opposite sex have been classified according to the sex of the majority.

Table 25

Number of Secondary Day Schools in Each Region at January, 1968
(Independent recognised efficient, direct grant grammar and maintained)

	Independent secondary day schools recognised as efficient		Direct grant day grammar schools		Maintained secondary day schools		Total
	Number of schools	% Col. 7	Number of schools	% Col. 7	Number of schools	% Col. 7	Total of Cols. 1, 3 and 5
	1	2	3	4	5	6	7
Northern	17	3·5	10	2·1	458	94·4	485
Yorkshire and Humberside	10	1·7	15	2·6	556	95·7	581
North West	26	3·0	55	6·3	797	90·8	878
East Midlands	11	2·5	6	1·4	427	96·2	444
West Midlands	17	2·6	8	1·2	632	96·2	657
East Anglia	10	4·5	6	2·7	204	92·7	220
Wales	13	3·5	–	–	354	96·5	367
South East	133	7·2	35	1·9	1,674	90·9	1,842
South West	28	5·8	13	2·7	639	91·5	480
Total	265	4·5	148	2·5	5,541	93·1	5,954

Notes: 1. Schools have been counted as day schools if they have less than 25% per cent of the pupils boarding.
2. Independent schools have been classified as secondary if they make provision for pupils of 15 or over even if they have some pupils of primary age.

Source: Department of Education and Science returns for January, 1968.

Table 26

Number of Day Pupils in Recognised Efficient Independent Secondary Schools, Direct Grant Grammar Schools and
Maintained Secondary Schools in Each Region at January, 1968

	Independent secondary schools recognised as efficient		Direct grant grammar upper schools		Maintained secondary schools		Total
	Pupils[1]	% of Col. 7	Pupils	% of Col. 7	Pupils	% of Col. 7	Total of Columns 3 and 5
	1	2	3	4	5	6	7
Northern	4,678	2·1	5,917	2·7	212,665	95·3	223,260
Yorkshire and Humberside	2,096	0·7	10,173	3·2	302,484	96·1	314,753
North West	8,585	2·0	34,757	7·9	395,596	90·1	438,938
East Midlands	3,082	1·4	3,790	1·8	206,620	96·8	213,492
West Midlands	5,826	1·8	5,694	1·7	317,563	96·5	329,083
East Anglia	2,644	2·8	3,142	3·3	88,079	93·8	93,865
Wales	2,563	1·4	957	0·5	181,322	98·1	184,842
South East	41,180	4·0	20,794	2·0	962,567	94·0	1,024,541
South West	8,877	3·8	7,633	3·3	217,458	92·9	233,968
Total	79,531	2·6	92,857	3·0	2,884,354	94·4	3,056,742

Source: Returns to the Department of Education and Science for 1968.
Note: [1] Pupils in independent secondary schools and pupils aged 12 or over together with two thirds of those aged 11 years in schools with both primary and secondary departments.

Table 27

Tuition Fees at Recognised Efficient Independent Secondary Day Schools at January, 1968 (England and Wales)

£	Number of schools		
	Boys	*Girls*	*Mixed*
Under 100	8	42	17
100-149	15	52	19
150-199	14	38	10
200-249	11	24	2
250-299	3	4	2
300 or more	2	2	–
Average fee per pupil (weighted)	180	164	131

Source: Department of Education and Science returns for January, 1968.

Notes: 1. Schools have been classified as secondary if they make provision for pupils aged 15 or over even though they may have some pupils of primary school age.

2. Schools have been counted as day schools if they have less than 25 per cent of the pupils boarding.

3. Schools which contain both boys and girls but which have less than 10 per cent of pupils of the opposite sex have been classified according to the sex of the majority.

4. Average fee calculated by multiplying the numbers of day pupils at each school by the annual fee charged at January 1968 and then dividing the aggregated total for all schools by the total number of day pupils.

Table 28

Comparison of Numbers of Pupils in Independent Schools in 1958 and 1968

(a) *Pupils in all independent schools with a secondary department (recognised and unrecognised)*

	Numbers of pupils		Percentage increase or decrease
	1958	1968	
Boarding	100,359	96,300	− 4
Day	211,635	160,800	− 24
Boys boarding	56,265	56,544	+ 0·5
Boys day	81,255	61,975	− 24
Girls boarding	44,094	39,756	− 10
Girls day	130,380	98,825	− 24

(b) *Pupils in independent primary schools (recognised and unrecognised)*

Boarding	34,949	30,586	− 12
Day	153,203	138,564	− 10
Boys	112,298	105,001	− 6
Girls	75,854	64,149	− 15

(c) *Recognised efficient independent schools with a secondary department*

Boarding	86,079	89,918	+ 4
Day	108,616	118,868	+ 9
Boys boarding	48,392	52,678	+ 9
Boys day	37,177	43,834	+ 18
Girls boarding	37,687	37,240	− 1
Girls day	71,439	75,034	+ 5

(d) *Recognised efficient primary schools*

Boarding	29,803	28,306	− 5
Day	56,560	64,288	+ 14
Boys	59,300	64,015	+ 8
Girls	27,063	28,579	+ 6

Source: Department of Education and Science Statistics for January, 1958 and 1968
Note: All figures exclude pupils in nursery schools.

Table 29

Local Education Authority Places at Independent Day Schools

	More than 75% of places	50-74% of places	25-49% of places	Schools with l.e.a. places but not exceeding 25%	Schools with no l.e.a. places	All schools
Numbers of schools	7	15	34	57	152	265
Percentage of all independent day schools	3	6	13	21	57	100

Source: Commission's questionnaire.

Note: The definition of an independent day school used here is a school with less than 25 per cent boarding pupils. The percentage of day pupils paid for by local education authorities was calculated on the basis of all pupils including boarders. Local education authorities do pay for some day pupils attending boarding schools but these are not included here.

DENSITY OF INDEPENDENT SECONDARY DAY PLACES
BY COUNTY AUTHORITY
EXCLUDING NON-RECOGNISED SCHOOLS

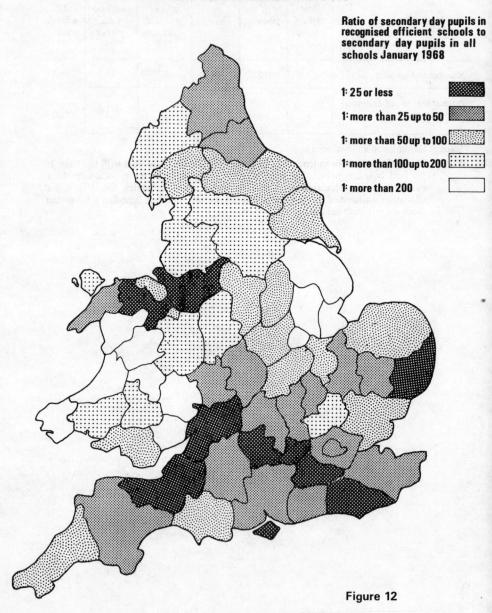

Ratio of secondary day pupils in
recognised efficient schools to
secondary day pupils in all
schools January 1968

1: 25 or less

1: more than 25 up to 50

1: more than 50 up to 100

1: more than 100 up to 200

1: more than 200

Figure 12

PUBLIC SCHOOLS IN ENGLAND AND WALES
WITH DAY PLACES

Schools with 10 day places or less have been omitted

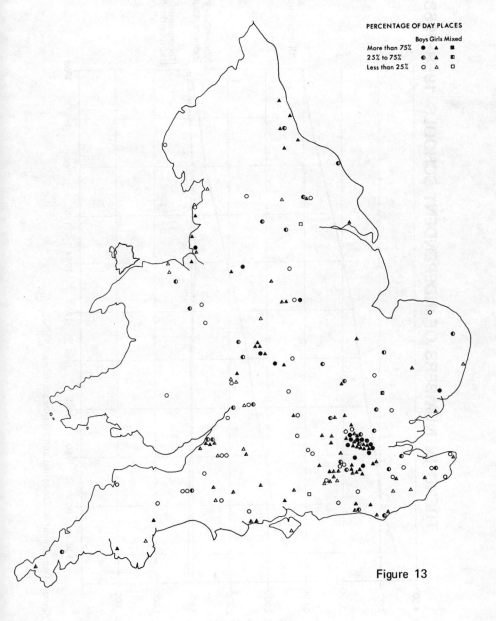

PERCENTAGE OF DAY PLACES

	Boys	Girls	Mixed
More than 75%	●	▲	■
25% to 75%	◑	▲	◪
Less than 25%	○	△	□

Figure 13

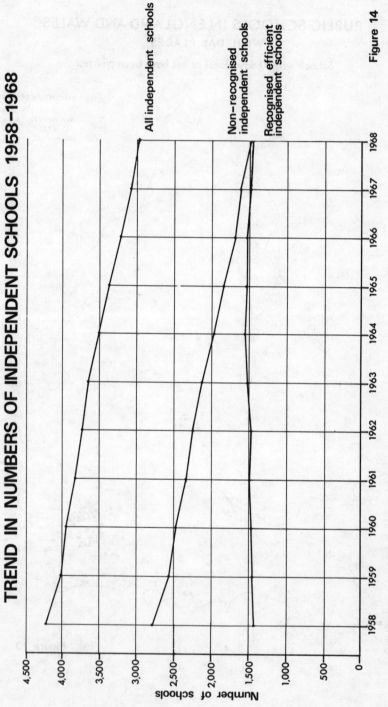

TREND IN NUMBERS OF INDEPENDENT SCHOOLS 1958–1968

Figure 14

All independent schools

Non-recognised independent schools

Recognised efficient independent schools

Number of schools

Source: Department of Education and Science Statistics, 1958-68.

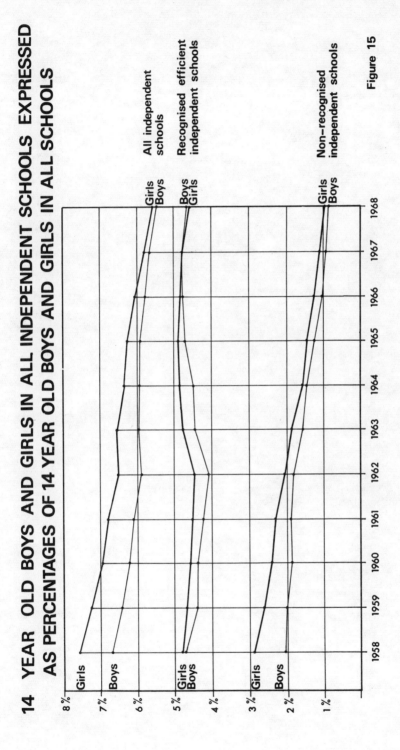

14 YEAR OLD BOYS AND GIRLS IN ALL INDEPENDENT SCHOOLS EXPRESSED AS PERCENTAGES OF 14 YEAR OLD BOYS AND GIRLS IN ALL SCHOOLS

Figure 15

Source: Department of Education and Science Statistics for 1958-68.

Part Three

Argument and Proposals

CHAPTER 6

The Evidence We Considered

158. We read the statements of evidence prepared for us by 62 organisations and individuals, and had helpful discussions with the 17 individuals and representative groups who met the Commission to expand on their views and answer further questions. We also had less formal but equally useful discussions with councillors, administrators, school governors, teachers and pupils in the 20 local authorities and 88 schools and colleges which we were able to visit in the course of our work. We carefully considered everything they told us, and read many other contributions to the debates about education now going on in this country. Before presenting our own proposals we want to outline the main opinions that must be considered by anyone dealing with the problems we have been asked to examine. This will not be a record of our procedures for gathering evidence or a roll-call of the witnesses who presented it—both of which can be found in the Appendices to our Report—but an account of the main points of view on the principal questions we have to answer, illustrated by statements which most clearly express these contrasting opinions. It shows the conflicts and uncertainties now exercising the minds of all who wish to play their part in the development of secondary education in this country; and it shows that those who must decide policies for the future will find no consensus of expert opinion to guide them.

THE DIRECT GRANT SCHOOLS

Selection

159. On the subject of selection very diverse views were presented to us. The Comprehensive Schools Committee took the view that any system whereby children under the statutory school leaving age are selected for one school rather than another on grounds of academic ability is wrong. At the other end of the spectrum, amongst those who wanted to preserve an element of selection, hardly anyone said that selection of the top 20 per cent of the ability range for separate education at the age of 11 is desirable. There was scant support in our evidence for selection of the kind used in the grammar schools of the 1950's.

160. There were three broad strands of opinion among those who wanted to retain selection. Some wished to select pupils of a much broader range of ability than at present; others wished to form super-selective schools recruiting from a narrow band of the highest abilities; and others favoured selection at a later age than 11. This last proposal can be combined with either of the two preceding—a broadly selective or a super-selective school could recruit at age 13 or later.

161. Many heads in their replies to Question 14(iv)[1] of the General Question-naire said they would be willing to broaden the ability range in their schools.

---

[1] "What are your personal views about the part your school could play in the movement towards comprehensive reorganisation?"

Some defined this by giving a proportion of the ability range (50 per cent for example) and others specified a minimum I.Q. (usually 100 or 105). These heads were not advocating a national system of education providing separate schools for children above the levels they specified. They recognised that if such a system were set up the schools for non-selected pupils would face problems still more acute than those which now trouble the secondary modern schools. They were considering what their own schools could do and what effect this might have on other schools. Typically the argument ran,"My school is too small to be a comprehensive and my staff are not equipped for the task. Nevertheless I admit that the maintained comprehensives will face problems if all the ablest children are selected for my school. Therefore I can best help by selecting children from a broader range of ability, thus leaving some of the more able for the comprehensive schools".

162. If a super-selective school is defined as one which accepts the top 5 per cent of the ability range or less, only a small minority of direct grant schools are super-selective at present. This may explain why the super-selective school was rarely pressed on us in evidence. However the High Master of Manchester Grammar School, Mr. P. G. Mason, and his predecessor, Lord James, argued the case for it with conviction. The arguments were partly on administrative, partly on educational grounds. There is a national shortage of academically highly qualified teachers. If you believe that while this shortage lasts these highly qualified teachers should concentrate their efforts on the most able pupils, a super-selective school offers one way of achieving this. The educational argument was that with a group of uniformly very able pupils it is possible to depart from examination syllabuses and go far beyond them; the pupils can quickly absorb information, and all will be clever enough to secure examination results which give them good opportunities for higher education. If the group contains some less able pupils, there is a tendency to concentrate for their sake on what is necessary to get them through the examination. In an article published in "Science Teacher" in October, 1968, Lord Snow (in the context of a discussion of Russian mathematical schools) developed another argument for the super-selective school; "Most people who have studied the problem believe the real secret lies in what physicists call "critical mass". That is, if you assemble enough bright pupils and enough good teachers, you produce a level of excellence which is far higher than if the bright pupils and good teachers were split up and scattered in penny packets". Our own views on the super-selective school are given in Chapter 14.

163. Many heads were prepared to alter the age range of their schools. Again they had various reasons. Some schools were in areas where local authorities had adopted middle school schemes of reorganisation involving transfer to secondary education at 12+ or 13+; the direct grant schools wished to keep in step. Others believed that by shortening their age range they could move towards comprehensive reorganisation without heavy expenditure on extensions to their buildings. One head wrote "It would be possible to co-operate with the comprehensive movement by widening the ability range and changing the entry to 13, making a 5-stream school". Still others felt that if selection at 11 had to be abandoned, there might be some age between 11 and the school leaving age (when pupils select themselves) at which it would be more acceptable. Thus one or two direct grant schools have made arrangements with local authorities whereby they admit, say, from the top half of the ability range (selected by guided parental

choice) at the age of 13 from a maintained comprehensive school. But several of our witnesses opposed postponing the age of selection on the grounds that the later it occurs the more likely tests are to reflect acquired knowledge rather than innate ability; this would handicap socially and educationally deprived children. Another point made was that children should be taught within the framework of the same organisation over a period of years in order to achieve continuity in their studies.

Sixth Form Organisation

164. We received a good deal of advice on the subject of sixth form provision. There was widespread agreement that the modern sixth form must offer a wide range of courses—at least 10 'A' level subjects was suggested by the Inner London Education Authority Report on "Sixth Form Opportunities". There should also be courses suitable for pupils not taking 'A' level examinations. Projections of the supply of graduate teachers up to 1986, made by the Department of Education and Science, show that the country cannot afford very small classes in sixth forms—there are just not enough highly qualified teachers to go round. Larger classes and more subjects can only be provided by larger sixth forms. The Bow Group, observing that many direct grant schools already have large sixth forms and suitable staff, suggested that many of them might become junior colleges for the 15-18 or 16-18 age group. The idea had a mixed reception among the schools. A few supported it, but many were opposed to it, and to the more selective alternative of an academic sixth form college the Direct Grant Joint Committee said "We strongly oppose the idea of the Sixth Form College as a separate two-year school".

165. An alternative to the sixth form college is the "mushroom" school which continues to admit pupils under 16 but also admits pupils from other schools for sixth form courses. Many heads of direct grant schools thought that their schools might adopt this role, either linked with specific maintained 11-16 schools or admitting pupils from a wide area for "minority" courses such as Greek or Music. Other evidence criticised the "mushroom" arrangement because these schools would attract good staff at the expense of the 11-16 schools linked with them, and the pupils under 16 in the "stalk" of the "mushroom" would enjoy advantages over similar pupils in the schools which do not have sixth forms. We were assured by the Chief Officer of an Education Authority which maintained a mushroom school that this criticism was unfounded, but the head of a comprehensive school who had formerly been head of an 11-16 school said it had been a disheartening experience.

Payment of Fees

166. Perhaps the chief difference between the direct grant school and the maintained grammar school is that in direct grant schools some parents pay fees. The schools themselves like this. In reply to Question 16[1] of the General Questionnaire the great majority of heads supported fee-paying. They claimed it promoted parental interest in the school, saved public money and guaranteed the school's independence because it provided a separate source of income. One head said "Here in Yorkshire they only pay for what they value, and after demonstrating their interest not only in words but cash, they watch their

---

[1] "What do you consider to be the effect upon your school of the payment of full or graded fees by the parents of some of your pupils?"

investments carefully". But there was criticism of the details of present arrangements. Many felt that the present scale for remission of fees was far too severe on parents with modest incomes. It was also argued that parents whose children won free places often had higher incomes than those who had to pay. The Direct Grant Joint Committee made a tentative suggestion which would meet both these criticisms; free places should be abolished and all pupils assessed for fees on a more generous scale. They also urged that the Department of Education and Science should allow remission for the tuition fees of boarding pupils.

167. Fee-paying also had many opponents, among them the National Union of Teachers. They were opposed to fee-paying for secondary education in general but found it particularly objectionable in the direct grant schools. They argued that the direct grant schools won reputations, which enabled them to recruit good staff and pupils, largely because the local education authorities paid for the brightest children to go to them. It was unfair that wealthy parents could buy these advantages, even if their children were not particularly bright, while poorer parents with children of equal intelligence had no such opportunity.

Social mix

168. Connected with the issue of fee-paying is the mixing of social classes achieved by direct grant schools. This threw up a good deal of controversy. On the one side, a Member of Parliament, in a widely reported speech, said "The nearest approach to a school which over-rides and obliterates class is probably the direct grant school in a large town or city such as that to which it was my own good fortune to gain admission from a State secondary school: I doubt if many can have covered a wider gamut of all kinds and conditions of home". But others, such as the Comprehensive Schools Committee, while conceding that direct grant schools contained some representatives from each social class, maintained that this did not make them socially representative;" . . . we feel we would not be overstating the case to say that half the pupils in direct grant grammar schools are drawn from professional and managerial homes". The conclusions to be drawn from the statistics we present in Table 22 of Section 3 of Appendix 6 depend on whether the social composition of direct grant schools is compared with that of independent schools or with the national proportions of the different social classes. We discuss this question further in Chapter 8.

169. When the spokesmen for direct grant schools claimed that their schools were socially mixed they meant that their schools included working class children whose parents would not be able to afford to send them to a fee-paying independent school. Their claim was not that they contained a cross section of social classes representative of the community but that they had a higher proportion of working class children than independent schools charging full fees and a higher proportion of middle class children than some neighbourhood comprehensive schools reflecting the social composition of their immediate surroundings. Certainly some direct grant schools have large catchment areas. The Parents and Staff Association of one suburban school sent us the results of a survey they had made, showing that 22 per cent of parents lived within two miles of the school, 56 per cent between two and five miles, 21 per cent between six and ten miles, and the remaining one per cent still further away. Such wide catchment areas have their advantages for the schools but some heads thought they had pupils who spent too much time travelling.

The Freedom of the School

170. In the General Questionnaire[1] we invited heads to give their views on the measure of independence and freedom enjoyed by their schools. The governing bodies were asked similar questions in Enclosure 'A'[2]. While many respondents conceded that some local authorities were giving their maintained schools fair scope for initiative, nearly all agreed that governors and heads of direct grant schools had more freedom. It was their school and their responsibility, within the framework of the Direct Grant Schools Regulations, to take all the most important decisions about it; which staff to engage, which children to admit, what curriculum to follow, what equipment to buy, whether to erect new buildings, and so on. This was a stimulus and a challenge to those who had to exercise responsibility and it helped to ensure a sense of community, a feeling that they were not simply cogs in a vast machine but that their own views would be taken into account and their needs sympathetically considered. For example, many heads mentioned that they had the power of giving leave to staff on compassionate grounds or to attend conferences—a power they thought they would not have in a maintained school. It was conceded by governors and heads that the controls exercised by the Department of Education and Science left them less free than independent schools in matters of finance, but many thought that this was a small price to pay for being able to admit pupils irrespective of parental income.

171. These points pose further questions. First, are the freedoms of direct grant schools inseparable from direct grant status? Are they due to the schools' mixture of fee-payers and free place holders, and the central source of their grants? Do the governors and staff of maintained schools now have all the freedom which they can reasonably expect or could these freedoms be extended? Our impression from the replies to the Questionnaire was that many direct grant school heads believed their freedoms arose from the schools' special status, but also held that maintained schools could be given greater independence. Many have urged that greater responsibilities be given to the governing bodies of maintained schools. The Royal Commission on Local Government received evidence from the Association of Education Committees which argued the need for strong governing bodies with wider powers. The same conclusion was reached in a study undertaken for the Royal Commission by Dr. Baron and Mr. Howell of the University of London Institute of Education Research Unit. We devoted much discussion to the government of schools, and give our own views in Chapter 10.

---

[1] *Question 15:*
"Do you consider that the headmaster or headmistress and teaching staff have greater or less freedom than the staff of a maintained school. If so, in what ways? If you wish to distinguish between county, voluntary controlled and voluntary aided schools, please do so."

Question 15(b):
"Do you consider that the headmaster or headmistress and teaching staff have greater or less freedom than the staff of an independent school? If so, in what ways?"

[2] *Enclosure A Question 2(c):*
"In what ways do direct grant schools have greater or less freedom than voluntary aided schools in fulfilling their purpose as schools?"

Enclosure A Question 2(d):
"In what ways do direct grant schools have greater or less freedom than independent schools in fulfilling their purpose as schools?"

Parental Choice

172. We were urged by supporters of the direct grant schools to preserve variety and the right of parents to choose their child's school. The relationship between these two points is complicated. There is variety between schools, and variety of opportunities within a school. Selection certainly increases the variety of types of school. But we were reminded that selection of a minority on grounds of ability generally ensures that the majority of parents and children fail to get the school they most want. When "parental choice" was used as an argument for the preservation of selection it often meant little more than that selective schools were more popular than comprehensive schools with parents whose children get to selective schools. This thesis derives some support from an article in "New Society", 26th October, 1967, on "Education and Opinion". This article also showed that secondary modern schools are very much less popular than comprehensives—and as long as there are academically selective schools there will have to be schools for those who are not selected.

173. Many, when they spoke of the need to preserve parental choice, had in mind characteristics other than academic selection. Headmistresses of direct grant schools said that many parents preferred small, single-sex schools for their daughters. The Girls' Public Day School Trust put it thus in their evidence to the Commission: "The staff in the single-sex schools have developed skill and enterprise in planning academic work, general studies, careers guidance and sex education for girls and it would be a loss to the nation if this accumulated experience became submerged or diluted. Moreover, a significant proportion of parents prefer single-sex schools, and many girls, especially in adolescence, also prefer this kind of education, though some would not admit it."

174. We put these issues of variety and parental choice to some local authorities and heads of comprehensive schools. The Manchester Education Authority pointed out that their admissions procedure allowed parents to list any three of the city's comprehensive high schools in order of preference. Seventy-eight per cent of parents were getting their first choice and 94 per cent their first or second choice. Comprehensive school heads generally argued that variety was not incompatible with a comprehensive system; each school had different approaches to curriculum, discipline, sport and other matters, and this could give parents an adequate choice. Within a large school parent and child might have a wider choice because of the variety of courses that could be offered.

The Scope of Reorganisation

175. Many witnesses discussed the direct grant schools' capacity for becoming "viable comprehensives". Heads of direct grant schools often insisted that their schools were too small to go comprehensive. The Department of Education and Science statistics show that the direct grant grammar schools are not on average smaller than the maintained grammar schools, many of which have been incorporated in comprehensive schemes. But the direct grant schools pointed out that they do not have public money at their disposal for the capital investment required for reorganisation. Indeed many are already carrying heavy capital debts which would prevent them shouldering new burdens. For those which are willing to go comprehensive, direct grant status thus presents major practical problems.

176. It is a matter for debate how large a "viable" comprehensive school must be. There was general agreement that viability depended upon form-entry rather

than overall numbers. It is therefore possible to fit a viable school into small buildings by shortening the age range. The number of form-entries required was controversial. A commonly expressed view was that six form-entry could produce an acceptable school but some would say that eight form-entry was the minimum. Local authorities and heads advised us that in deprived urban areas eight might be the minimum to achieve a sixth form of economic size. Even allowing for the possibility of shortening the age range in some schools and converting others to junior colleges and sixth form colleges, it is clear that many would have to be considerably expanded to become viable comprehensives. But we were reminded that the minimum size for a comprehensive school depends on the alternatives available and the things which can be done to help a school assume new functions. One witness pointed out that in sparsely populated areas teachers in schools with two or three forms of entry are teaching classes of very mixed ability, and the Department of Education and Science and local education authorities could help by encouraging the re-training of staff already in service for new forms of teaching.

Conclusion

177. Underlying all these differences of view were two different ways of looking at the direct grant schools. Those working for the schools saw them as independent institutions providing a service to the nation under contract to central government. Viewed in this way the social mix they contain is admirable, fee-paying is a natural expression of independence, and selection inevitable in schools which cannot admit all the children who would like to go to them. Their critics saw them as an anomalous sector of the national system, retaining the fee-paying and selection which have gone, or are going, from the rest of the system, and outside the control of local education authorities responsible for the development of the educational system of their areas. Standing between opposing forces the direct grant schools are inevitably exposed to fire.

INDEPENDENT DAY SCHOOLS

178. Much of the evidence given us by organisations and individuals representing independent day schools began with a brief justification of the schools' existence. The most common arguments were that it was essential to preserve the individual parent's freedom to choose the kind of education he wanted for his child and that a State monopoly in education would be disastrous. We did not receive much fresh evidence in favour of the abolition of independent schools, but this may have been because the Commission rejected it in its First Report. Some people think that even without legal constraint the independent day schools will wither away in time, since to a much greater extent than the boarding schools they are in direct competition with an increasingly strong maintained system in which no fees are charged. The outcome will depend on the reasons why parents pay fees. We have discussed this question in Chapter 5. In the survey made by the Bow Group of the parents among their members, which was mentioned in that Chapter, the parents who preferred to send their sons to boarding public schools were asked what their second choice would be if their first proved impossible. It was interesting that 50 per cent said a maintained grammar school and only 32 per cent a public day school. However since only 9 per cent opted for a comprehensive school and comprehensive

schools will soon be the only maintained day schools available in many areas, it would be wrong to draw any definite conclusion from this, save that some parents had a special loyalty to the public boarding schools. Our own views on the future prospects for independent day schools are given in Chapter 11.

179. The two arguments for the existence of independent day schools mentioned above might seem to imply a competitive rather than a co-operative relationship with the maintained system (though the two relationships are not necessarily mutually exclusive). If the schools are to offer parents a choice, they must be different from the maintained schools and these differences must be of a kind that parents are prepared to pay for. If maintained and independent schools grow more alike, the argument that independent schools prevent the maintained schools from having a monopoly may be less convincing, though there is continuing support for the view that the co-existence of independent and maintained schools promotes healthy emulation of the best features of both. Nevertheless some of the independent day schools and their governing bodies suggested ways in which they might draw closer to the maintained system. Almost all wanted to retain their independence and the right to admit some fee-paying pupils. Under these conditions, the favoured way of coming nearer to the maintained system was through offering more places to pupils paid for by the local education authorities. Since the schools all stressed that they were too small to admit pupils of all abilities, some selection procedure would be needed. In a few cases, a specialised contribution was offered. Chetham's Hospital School, Manchester, aims to become a musical academy with two forms of entry to which local authorities would send children of high musical ability from the age of seven. Where a school offers no specialism of this sort, how can its assisted pupils be chosen? The Head of King's College School, Wimbledon, put this question to heads of independent day schools who are members of the Headmasters' Conference and reported ". . . strong emphasis upon parental wish, on the ability of a boy to benefit from the type of education offered, and on the Headmaster's ultimate responsibility for deciding upon a boy's suitability". However, the whole idea of the purchase of places at independent schools was strongly opposed by other witnesses, particularly where this would impede comprehensive reorganisation. It was, they said, only justified where independent schools offered something not available in maintained schools. If it ought to be available, then local authorities should be pressed to provide it as soon as possible.

Conclusion

180. Equally humane and responsible people, equally expert in the field we have studied, are profoundly divided both about the facts to be considered and about the action to be taken. No distillation of present knowledge and opinion can produce a consensus among them. Since any action we propose must be controversial, some witnesses advocated that nothing should be done. The Association of Education Committees, for example, urged us to await the reform of local government and a new Education Act before making any proposals. Others urged that present arrangements should continue undisturbed till comprehensive reorganisation had "proved itself".

181. The conflict of expert opinion in the evidence we have been given, and the speed at which such opinions have changed in recent decades, compel us to approach our task with caution, recognising the fallibility of human judgements

in a field so subject to changes of circumstance and fashion. But having done our best to form our own judgements we shall present them as firmly and clearly as we can.

182. One point on which all our witnesses agreed was the crippling effect of the uncertainties which now afflict the direct grant schools. Some of the heads of the schools we visited could not have been more explicit in their appeals to us: if only they knew what would be expected of them in the years to come, they could devote themselves wholeheartedly to developing the kind of schools that would be needed in future. Anything, they said, would be better than the repeated changes they have experienced as national and local elections succeed each other, bringing new majorities with new policies to power. These anxieties are not of the Commission's making; they were widespread long before our appointment and will not be resolved until the country has worked out and applied the new policies now slowly taking shape. If we can help to resolve these uncertainties by presenting our own diagnoses and proposals we must do so.

183. Though we disagree among ourselves about some aspects of the proposals we shall make, we are all convinced that inaction makes it harder, not easier, to resolve the problems we have studied. We have repeatedly found that where reorganisation of secondary education has been pressed furthest without the participation of non-maintained schools, the formulation of a policy for these schools tends to be hardest to devise and apply. A policy of "wait-and-see" designed to "keep the options open" is sometimes best; but in dealing with our terms of reference it would be disastrous.

CHAPTER 7

Participation in a Comprehensive System

Introduction

184. In Part II of our Report we described this country's changing system of secondary education and the contribution made to it by the schools in our terms of reference. In the last chapter we showed how deeply divided people are about the next steps to be taken by these schools. The rest of our Report presents our own diagnoses and prescriptions. Where we differ among ourselves we have explained our disagreements clearly, believing that a clear statement of our differences will be more helpful to those who must ultimately take decisions than a cautiously worded consensus would be.

185. We start with the points on which we agree because these are far more important than those on which we part company. We have been asked to show how the independent day schools and direct grant grammar schools "can participate in the movement towards comprehensive reorganisation", and "to review the principle of central government grant" to the latter schools. We have tried to begin from the beginning and take nothing for granted. This Chapter deals with comprehensive reorganisation, its aims, character and problems. It presents three main conclusions. The first is that day schools which receive grants from central or local authorities or educate children whose fees are paid by these authorities must participate in the movement towards comprehensive reorganisation in some way that accords with local needs and plans. To this conclusion a minority of the Commission add an important qualification in the final chapter of this Report: they think that until the outcome of reorganisation and the pattern of secondary education become clearer, a few of the most highly selective grammar schools already in existence (to be chosen not only from the direct grant schools) should be enabled to continue as "super-selective" schools taking the ablest one or two per cent of pupils. Our second conclusion is that arrangements for participation in the movement towards comprehensive education must be worked out between the schools and the local education authorities on terms approved by the Secretary of State who should arbitrate between them if agreement cannot be reached. Our third conclusion is that no fees should be charged for places in day schools which depend mainly on central or local government for their finance. The arguments for this conclusion, from which two of our members dissent, are presented more fully in the next chapter. Three of the five members who wish to retain some highly selective schools believe that these schools, too, should have no fee-paying pupils.

The Aims of Comprehensive Reorganisation

186. Comprehensive organisation takes different forms in different places and new forms are constantly evolving. Before we can say whether, let alone how, the schools in our terms of reference should "participate" in this process, we must explain what we mean by "the movement towards comprehensive reorganisation".

187. For the next decade or two, the chief and fundamental aim—not only of secondary reorganisation, but of our whole educational endeavour—must be to get more and more children to take their education to a point that enables them to go on learning and adapting throughout their lives. Ultimately all, except some of the severely subnormal, should continue systematic education (in which paid work, if they do any, plays an educational or clearly subordinate part) until the age of eighteen, with good opportunities for further education thereafter. This must be our aim because more and more children and their parents will want a full secondary education; because gross inequalities of education in an urban, industrial society produce pervasive social inequalities and destructive conflicts; because our economy will need more and more people capable of adapting, training and retraining throughout their lives, and will offer poorer opportunities to those incapable of doing this; and because Britain allows larger proportions of her young people to drop out of school at the ages of fifteen and sixteen than her neighbours and major competitors,[1] and is already severely handicapped by this waste of talent. An educational system which enables a minority of the most fortunate children to take their education a long way while turning the rest out into the labour market as soon as it is socially tolerable for them to start work is as obsolete as the early industrial era from which it originated. There is no time to be lost in creating the new system we need: the pupils going to school for the first time this year will go on working, under present retirement arrangements, until about the year 2030. Long before that date our economy will have scant opportunities to offer the untrained and unskilled worker.

188. This is what the movement towards reorganisation is all about. The forms and patterns of education now evolving must be judged by their capacity to attain these aims. The essential features of the movement can be briefly outlined.

189. First we must postpone irrevocable, and nearly irrevocable, decisions about children's educational opportunities to as late an age as possible. The earlier we select, the more mistakes we make; and those errors cannot be much reduced by better techniques of selection. Early selection by academic criteria tends to be a wasteful, self-fulfilling prophecy. (Self-fulfilling because however well-intentioned our endeavours to give different schools equal treatment and status, experience shows that better teaching resources tend to be concentrated upon the children selected, and their morale and performance tend to improve. Wasteful because the excluded majority are penalised and their opportunities tend to be restricted despite the excellence of many secondary modern schools.) Procedures for late transfer, designed to remedy errors in selection, seldom work well in practice and in any case fail to correct the fundamental handicaps which selection imposes on the excluded.

190. Precisely how far can selection be delayed? This is trickier ground. We believe that selection at 11 is too early, and international comparisons indicate that most countries share this view. But by the age of 18 a good deal of selection is taking place, and will already have taken place. For one thing, because of the scarcity of resources we cannot yet offer higher or further education to all; and even when (or if) we can, some institutions of higher education (those in particular which combine teaching and research) will make academic demands

---

[1] See Chapter 2, Figure 1, and paragraphs 49 to 52.

on their entrants not necessarily made by other institutions. Even if it is true that at present the downward pressure of university entrance on school work is too severe, it is appropriate that boys and girls who aspire to higher education should begin serious preparation for it by the age of 16, and acquire suitable intellectual dispositions before that age. More generally, the interests, abilities and vocational aims of many students are differentiated well before the age of 18, and the diverse aspirations that they foster suggest that there should be some differentiation at an earlier age (between 14 and 16), and many other countries have found this to be so. Differences of curriculum, educational style and pace will be found in comprehensive schools before the age of 16—though they should not be of a kind that unnecessarily creates barriers or limits choices.

191. If more and more children are to continue their education to the age of eighteen, our second aim must be to offer them a greater variety of subjects, learned in a greater variety of ways, than the traditional sixth form provides. Some of the new children staying on at school will not want to pursue a course of studies designed mainly for those entering universities, and should not be expected to do so. But encouragement to excel, in varied ways, must be as keen as ever.

192. Third, if selection is to be postponed and the way to an education continuing beyond school is to be opened to all, then children from a wide range of social classes must be educated together wherever this is possible. Children tend to advance together, adopting the aspirations of their peers, and we must therefore try to place all in an environment where high attainment and intellectual interests are sufficiently common and respected to be "catching". Social segregation of young people in their formative years is also likely to impoverish their education in more fundamental ways: it makes it harder for them to understand their fellow countrymen.

193. Parents, teachers and administrators are moving towards an increasingly general agreement about these fundamental aims of educational planning. Difficulties arise when it comes to applying them. In practice there are many obstacles to be surmounted. Some of the main ones must be briefly listed.

194. Our system of education is geared to public examinations, giving entry to higher education and professional training, which assume early specialisation, early entry to sets and classes studying particular syllabuses, and advanced work which attains standards—in relatively few subjects—that would in some countries be found only in universities. This system is changing; in future, children will not specialise so soon or so severely. But continuing competition for entrance to the universities (which are unlikely to expand fast enough to meet the demand for their places) will make these changes a slow and difficult process.

195. Our grammar schools have long been organised specially for this system. They are small. Most of them have less than 600 pupils and fewer than 4 forms of entry. If they cease to be academically selective from the age of eleven or thereabouts and become comprehensive schools, most of them must either be greatly enlarged or must cover a shorter age range. In that event their adaptation to new tasks is not simply a question of numbers and logistics. The strengths they have developed over the years may initially restrict what they can do for the four-fifths of young people who have hitherto been excluded from them—young people whose aspirations and interests cannot all be met within the more academic culture of a traditional grammar school. We shall argue that

schools can only remain academically selective if they recruit at the age of 16+[1] within a system which makes really good provision for carrying forward the education of all young people. Even as sixth form colleges, they should be larger than most of the present direct grant schools if they are to make the most effective use of their teachers and equipment. Schools taking only sixth formers have to provide a wide range of specialist staff at a high academic level. In sixth forms attached to a lower school, these teachers also teach children in lower forms. If they are to be fully employed in a self-contained sixth form college, there will have to be more than one group in their subject and this calls for a college which is much larger than the usual sixth form.

196. Some of the non-grammar schools are large, well-equipped comprehensive schools recruiting plenty of able children and teachers. Others are only beginning what may be a long haul from secondary modern to full comprehensive status. They may also be handicapped by social deprivations afflicting the neighbourhoods in which they stand. Unless other schools or colleges of further education come to their help, their pupils may be as severely handicapped as those in some of the old secondary modern schools.

197. The schools facing these different problems are scattered unevenly across the country. Some of the strongest grammar schools stand in the middle of big cities, often alongside small secondary modern schools. But the proximity of these contrasting problems seldom offers ready scope for mutually helpful solutions. If the schools serve different religious denominations, collaboration and combination may be difficult or impossible. If the population of a central neighbourhood has been falling for many years there may be a surplus of school places, dictating contraction rather than expansion of the schools there. If expansion is possible there may be no room on their restricted sites for the buildings required.

198. These and many other difficulties mean that the process of bringing hitherto selective schools into a comprehensive system is likely to be a slow one. How fast we can proceed depends on the determination of the central and local authorities concerned, and particularly on the resources they can bring and are willing to bring to the task. Existing buildings may be unsuited, without adaptation, to the new demands to be made on them. More staff may be needed. Teaching methods may have to be revised. All these things take time and money. Reorganisation which fails to give all children better opportunities of taking their education further is reorganisation in name only. Only when local education authorities receive finance on as generous scale as they receive exhortation will thoroughly satisfactory advances be made.

199. From this analysis of the task before us and its difficulties we derive the following general principles for evaluating schemes for reorganisation and proposals for the future of individual schools. Such schemes and proposals should:

(a) ensure so far as possible that children of all abilities are educated in such a way as to develop their talents to the highest possible degree;

(b) avoid the segregation of pupils before statutory school leaving age into schools (or clearly distinguishable sections or "sides" within schools) which are designed, staffed, equipped or organised to provide separately for particular levels of ability;

---

[1] But see paragraph 227.

(c) ensure, wherever possible that all pupils are educated in schools which offer adequate opportunities of progressing to further and higher education—opportunities which are actually taken by an appreciable number of pupils;

(d) avoid unnecessarily depressing the expectations and drive of children and their teachers;

(e) avoid deliberately placing schools in a hierarchy of esteem;

(f) prevent, wherever possible, any school becoming a "one class" establishment;

(g) whenever the normal secondary age range (11-18) has to be divided into different, tiered schools, ensure that transfers occur at a point and in a way that encourages children to continue their education, and avoid frequent movement of pupils which permits only a short stay at any one school;

(h) in such cases also ensure that there is the closest possible collaboration between teachers in the different schools over curriculum, teaching methods, guidance of pupils, etc., including opportunities for teachers to teach in both schools whenever this is appropriate;

(i) ensure that suitable buildings and staff are available before new schemes come into operation;

(j) whenever the foregoing objectives cannot soon be attained, create situations which encourage development in these directions, and avoid situations which frustrate development in these directions.

Schools in a Comprehensive System

200. We have explained what we mean by "the movement towards comprehensive reorganisation". We turn next to the schools in our terms of reference. The direct grant schools and many independent day schools have a major contribution to make to this movement. Any school whose governors and staff wish to play their part in meeting the nation's most challenging educational needs will want to contribute in some way. The direct grant schools would not have made the arrangements with the central government which bring them their grants if they had not been determined to play their part in a national system of education and they have all said that they wish to continue to do so. New needs now call equally urgently for their help. Indeed, in some places it is difficult to see how reorganisation can be successfully achieved without their help. The rest of this Chapter deals with these schools and with independent day schools willing to participate in a comprehensive system. We return in Chapter 11 to consider more specialised contributions that can also be made by independent day schools.

201. Before proposing specific ways in which schools can play their part, we must present some more general conclusions about the context within which they will work. First, it should be clear from our principles for evaluating reorganisation schemes that we are talking about local systems of education and all the children they serve, not about particular kinds of school. The part a particular school can play in such a system depends on local needs and resources, and particularly upon the school's links with others in the local system.

202. The development of this local system must be planned and administered largely by the local education authorities, within policies and resources determined by the central government. Any school which intends to play a part in the system must first reach agreement with one or more local education authorities. It cannot simply pick the role of its choice, if that role does not accord with local needs. We hope that all schools will wish to play a part in reorganisation, but we recognise that some may be unable to find a place in comprehensive systems. They may be too small, for example, and lack space or other resources required for expansion. A few of the maintained grammar schools have run into similar dilemmas and they have had to close (though their buildings have often been used for other educational purposes). If they cannot choose independence, or do not wish to, a few of the direct grant schools may also have to close. We regret this, but it would be unrealistic not to recognise that closure will sometimes be the only possible course of action. If so, the interests of pupils and teachers must be safeguarded. Meanwhile the central government, which is responsible for the economical deployment of resources throughout the country, must ensure that local education authorities make the most effective use of the help of direct grant schools willing to participate in the movement towards reorganisation. Thus it must ensure that local authorities neither invite schools to participate in ways which frustrate the aims of reorganisation, nor decline genuine and valuable offers to participate, nor make demands on schools which are destructive of the contribution they could make to reorganisation. We return in later chapters to consider the rights of governing bodies, heads and staffs of schools, the negotiations which must take place between schools and local education authorities, and the responsibilities of the Secretary of State who should arbitrate in cases of disagreement.

203. It follows from our principles for reorganisation that there can, ultimately, be no place for fee-paying in schools coming wholly into a comprehensive system. We are aware of the advantages that many schools see in the payment of fees: we mentioned them briefly in the previous chapter and consider them more fully in the next chapter where we explain, in paragraphs 248 to 254, why we are convinced that fee-paying and comprehensive education are incompatible.[1] Here we need only point out that to permit the payment of fees to play any part in selection would clearly threaten the aims of reorganisation outlined in paragraph 199.

204. We must make our position clear on the question of "creaming". It has often been said to us that even the most selective direct grant schools recruit so small a proportion of the most able pupils in their large catchment areas that they have a negligible influence on the numbers of talented children entering comprehensive schools. This is sometimes, but by no means always, true—as we shall show later in this Chapter. But to defend the retention of selective direct grant schools on these grounds is to neglect the national character of the reorganisation in which we are engaged. If maintained grammar schools are being reorganised all over the country under policies strongly pressed by the central government—and they are—it is indefensible for that government to preserve and support other grammar schools, having similar aims and functions. The maintained grammar schools are as selective, as well-staffed and as successful as most direct grant schools. The two groups of schools cannot justifiably be treated

---

[1] But see paragraphs 231 to 233.

9

differently in this respect. The creaming effects of the direct grant schools cannot be considered in isolation from the broader questions of selection and segregation throughout secondary education.

205. But the creation of a wholly comprehensive system of secondary schools cannot eliminate the tendency of schools which have a better reputation to attract more able pupils than other schools in their neighbourhood. There will always be some schools that are better than others. Where these differences arise from remediable handicaps in the recruitment of staff or pupils, in scarcities of resources or poor leadership, then remedies must be sought. Where they arise only from the fact that some schools advance more strongly than others, in a system in which admission procedures are as fair as possible, no school is severely handicapped and all are encouraged to develop as far and as fast as possible, there is no cause for concern. We have never suggested that all schools should, or could, be the same.

206. We have sometimes been told that the creaming effect of direct grant schools would be eliminated if the system of direct grants were simply abolished. But for the most successful and prestigious schools this may well prove untrue. Large schools like Manchester, Bradford and Bristol Grammar Schools—and some smaller schools also—could dispense with their grants and become wholly independent if they wished. They would suffer some decline in the ability of their pupils but they would still recruit many of the ablest children in their areas. We foresee the possibility of some schools going independent as a result of our own proposals; correspondingly, we do not suppose that these proposals can completely eliminate the creaming problem.

207. It may be that those who have advocated abolition of direct grant intend that the schools should simply be nationalised or municipalised: few of them have been explicit on this point. The possibility of a compulsory "municipalisation" of independent boarding schools was discussed in the Commission's First Report. That Report concluded that public opinion would not accept the abolition of independent schools, that the local education authorities were not disposed to take on the task of running them, and that the resources compulsorily acquired could not be readily used for new purposes. The direct grant schools are also to a large extent independent, and similar considerations apply to them. Their participation in the movement towards comprehensive education must be willing if it is to be effective.

208. We now consider the ways in which these schools can participate. These will be briefly summarised, and some notes of general guidance follow. We envisage the following possibilities. They should be read in conjunction with the aims listed in paragraph 199.

(a) An all-through comprehensive school (providing for the age range from 11 or 12 to 18);

(b) one component of a tiered system, within which some schools will provide for the lower secondary stage (to the age of 13 or 14) and others for the upper secondary stage;

(c) a "mushroom" type of school, receiving pupils at the lower secondary stage (i.e. at the age 11, 12, 13 or 14) on a non-selective basis, and further pupils at the age of about 16;

(d) a junior or sixth form college, receiving pupils at the age of about 16;

(e) a comprehensive school for the age range 11 or 12 to 16;

(f) a school providing for special needs; for example, a choir school or a music school;

(g) a school meeting boarding needs.

Five of us believe that there should be one further possibility for a small number of schools—that of remaining a highly selective grammar school. This proposal is not related specifically to direct grant schools: if highly selective schools are to be retained they may in future be found just as often among the maintained or independent schools. We discuss the arguments for and against this proposal in Chapter 14 of our Report and therefore say no more about it here.

209. All-through comprehensive schools have been the pattern most generally favoured in the past by local education authorities. The main problem for direct grant schools contemplating this role is that good opportunities at sixth form level can be combined with economical staffing only if the school is large. The Department of Education and Science and many local education authorities say the minimum size should be six forms of entry; that is to say, about 1,000 pupils if the age of entry is eleven. In deprived neighbourhoods—and, some would say, in many other places—schools must be larger still. There are few direct grant or independent day schools of this size. If they are to adopt this pattern most would need large extensions.

210. It is, moreover, plain that in many parts of the country the 11-18 school housed in one set of buildings will not be attainable for many years—nor is it necessarily or in all circumstances the best form of organisation. For these two reasons the arrangements identified above as (b), (c), (d) and (e) have much to commend them, and experience of their working within the maintained sector is now becoming available. Neither now nor in the future can detailed national blue-prints be offered for the development of comprehensive schools of these types. Their form should depend upon local circumstances. Transitional and temporary arrangements will sometimes have to be accepted as the only way forward from the present selective system. We have tried, in paragraph 199, to identify the general principles which should govern the evolution of a comprehensive system and believe that the detailed interpretation of these principles must be left to the local education authorities, the schools themselves and the Government of the day. Questions of emphasis and of timing will be of central importance: most of us, for example, would expect and hope that a school or college confining its intake to students at 16+ would not seek indefinitely to limit its purposes and curriculum to providing for a relatively narrow academic band. The evolution of any of the present direct grant schools which adopt the relatively untried role of junior or sixth form college should generally follow the patterns that emerge throughout the maintained sector.

211. All of the arrangements outlined in 208 will operate most fruitfully where close and effective local co-operation exists. For example, two or more 11-18 schools will sometimes be able to develop wider opportunities at sixth form level by combining to offer a joint programme of studies: not all schools need to offer all courses, and an exchange of some pupils at 16+ should not be resisted where this is in their interest. Similarly, where pupils are transferred from one school to

another at the ages of 14 or 16, strenuous efforts must be made to guarantee a reasonable continuity of curriculum. In some cases, this can be achieved through informal consultation and agreement between all the schools concerned. In others, it will be better to create stronger machinery to bind together a partnership of several schools to improve the opportunities they offer and make them more widely available. Federations of schools, in which resources are pooled and responsibilities shared may be designed to have weak or strong links binding their component parts together. Some of us hope that the 1970's will see an extension of developments of this kind throughout the secondary system, believing that there are good opportunities here for making progress without unreasonably large demands for new buildings. Such arrangements must reconcile the needs of an educational system (which must, increasingly, be large) and the needs of pupils and teachers in working communities (which should, wherever possible, be relatively small).

212. It would be a mistake to lay down precise conditions for schemes of reorganisation. Good schemes must be based upon a thorough study of the needs of pupils and the resources of schools throughout an area in which there will generally be many schools. Much will depend upon developments within the national system (the re-definition of sixth form curricula, for example), upon the particular objectives assigned to each element within the local system (whether, for example, a sixth form college should temporarily confine its work to the traditional 'A' level courses), upon the social composition of local areas and the pupils recruited from them, upon the strength of the links between different schools in the same area, and upon the number and variety of optional subjects to be offered to pupils at any age. But we would expect any school, operating in fairly typical circumstances and expecting to be largely self-sufficient in terms of staff or daily organisation, to take at least six forms of entry each year, if it is to be fully effective within a comprehensive system. A sixth form college or junior college working independently should recruit over 200 students a year if it is to use teachers and equipment economically.

213. Schools catering for special needs and those meeting boarding needs (sometimes they will do both) should accept children with as wide a range of abilities as their size allows. Many of them will be too small to operate as fully comprehensive schools and for them we recommend an extension of the ability range, as envisaged in the Commission's First Report, to cater for all who can cope with a range of C.S.E. courses.

214. The present direct grant and independent schools must have time to adapt to their new roles. Often they will need new buildings, new facilities or new staff. Some of the existing teaching staff may have to accept new roles or new posts. Where this happens staff should be protected by the same sort of safeguards for salaries and conditions of service that apply generally to staff in maintained schools which are being reorganised. It will take more than ten years to complete reorganisation, though we hope many schools will move more quickly than that. The first step must be a commitment to one of the long-term goals we have outlined, in agreement with the local authority, followed by movement along the road towards that goal as far and as fast as circumstances permit. Thus a school aiming to become an all-through comprehensive but too small to do so right away might progressively widen the range of ability of the

pupils it admits. A school wishing to become a sixth form college might raise the age of admission in stages if that could be fitted into the local system; or it might, as a first step, become a mushroom school.

215. Difficult though they may sound, similar steps towards reorganisation are being successfully taken by the maintained grammar schools. To place these proposals in a more realistic context and to illustrate the opportunities and the difficulties they present, we conclude this Chapter with a brief examination of some of the local situations we have studied.

Some Examples

216. Every area presents different problems. In Bristol, for example, the education authority has been working towards a pattern of 11-18 comprehensive schools for many years. Every secondary school built since 1950 could be fitted into this pattern. By now, four out of five children go to comprehensive schools. But much of the centre of the City has yet to be reorganised. Here stand most of Bristol's independent and direct grant schools, along with maintained schools, some of which—pending reorganisation—have had little investment put into them.

217. The extensions required to convert direct grant schools in Bristol to all-through comprehensives would in some cases be very substantial. There would not be enough children to fill all the new places, and some of the schools have little space in which to expand. Thus to participate in reorganisation the schools must either be grouped in consortia with other direct grant schools or with maintained schools, or some form of tiering arrangement must be made, with a break at age 13 or 14 or at age 16. Whatever the solution, it is bound to call for a drastic reappraisal of plans on the part of the authority and on the part of the schools. The further an education authority goes in developing a comprehensive system without incorporating direct grant schools in its plans, the harder it usually becomes to fit these schools into the system.

218. Most direct grant schools draw pupils from the areas of several education authorities. Sometimes they take fewer pupils from the authority in whose area they stand than from neighbouring authorities. In Newcastle, for example, there is at present 'a surplus of secondary school places owing to a declining school population. If denominational preferences are not taken into account, the authority could for the time being readily manage without the 700 or so places they use at direct grant schools. But the Northumberland education authority would have to build or extend several of its own schools if deprived of the 900 places they take up in the Newcastle direct grant schools. Thus if the Newcastle direct grant schools were extended, their places could only be filled if they or the maintained schools of Newcastle took substantial numbers of pupils from Northumberland. The implementation of the recommendations of the Royal Commission on Local Government would change the situation. But meanwhile the plans and needs of both authorities must be taken into account before deciding what part the schools can play in a comprehensive system.

219. Occasionally schools are willing to participate, but the local education authority is opposed to comprehensive reorganisation. In Rutland, for example, the authority have refused to send in plans for reorganisation. Oakham School has suggested that it should become a co-educational junior college, taking all

pupils in the County who wish to stay on beyond the statutory leaving age, using for this expansion the premises of the newly-built but only half-filled girls' grammar school. They proposed to retain a separate and more selective boarding wing for boys aged 11 to 16, and already provide places for many sons of servicemen who need boarding education. There are many snags to the proposal, which the authority have pointed out, and much negotiation would be needed before a satisfactory plan could be agreed. Yet in this case a direct grant school is clearly willing to play a part in a comprehensive system but is unable to do so while the authority declines to contemplate reorganisation. Since Oakham School provides the only grammar education available for boys in the County, the authority must make some arrangement with it if its own schools are ever to be reorganised.

220. In some places the denominational schools face particularly intractable problems. In Manchester there are 28 Roman Catholic secondary schools, 5 of them direct grant and 23 maintained. Between them they serve five different dioceses and at least as many different local education authorities, each with different comprehensive plans. This group of schools, recently completed at great cost, was designed to fit into the tripartite system of 1944 (a warning to all educational planners). Thus most of the schools are no larger than three forms of entry, and they are scattered all over the city. The distances between them rule out grouping as split-premises comprehensive schools. Some form of tiering must presumably be adopted in the end, but that will call for considerable expenditure on adaptations and extensions—expenditure which cannot readily be met by direct grant schools, already heavily burdened by debt, if they cannot in future charge fees.

221. We have mentioned the problem of creaming and the view that the numbers of children at direct grant schools are so small that they have little effect on comprehensive schools. While this is often true, there are many contrary examples. Oakham School is the only grammar school for boys in its County. The Bedford direct grant schools take more than half the children selected by the education authority for grammar education in their area. Even where the proportion of pupils who go to direct grant schools is much smaller, it often represents a high proportion of the ablest pupils and thus a large share of those remaining at school to age seventeen or eighteen. For example the figures in Appendix 8 show that in Manchester only 5 per cent of the boys for whom the authority was financially responsible in 1966 went to direct grant schools, but these accounted for all the 11 boys with Verbal Reasoning Quotients over 140 and 62 per cent of the 72 boys with V.R.Q.s over 130. Taking the average for authorities for which figures were obtained, the direct grant schools took 91 per cent of all boys with V.R.Q.s of 140 and over, and 67 per cent of those with V.R.Q.s over 130. Actual numbers in any one area may be comparatively small. Nevertheless the loss of even small numbers of pupils of this calibre (all of them potential sixth formers) must have an effect on comprehensive schools in the area. In several places where 11+ selection tests have been abandoned we found that some primary schools still feel compelled to coach children for the selection tests used by direct grant schools. We were even told of independent infant schools coaching children aged six and seven to pass the selection tests of the junior schools attached to direct grant schools. The direct grant schools do not intend that such things should happen, but their present place in the system compels them to select pupils in some way or other and the rest follows.

222. In some areas it will be impossible to carry through comprehensive reorganisation or to achieve the benefits reorganisation can bring if the direct grant schools continue in their present role. Every area and school presents different problems of reorganisation, and each will call for patient negotiation between people determined both to extend the educational opportunities of all children, and to make constructive use of the urgently needed strengths which good schools can bring to this task.

Points of Disagreement

223. The foregoing Chapter 7 lays down certain principles on which the Commission's proposals are to be based. Our purpose in this note is to record and explain our disagreement with some of these principles and consequently with proposals that derive from them.

Our terms of reference as a Commission appear to be explicit. We were enjoined to advise on "the most effective method or methods by which direct grant grammar schools in England and Wales and the grant-aided schools in Scotland can participate in the movement towards comprehensive reorganisation, and to review the principle of central government grant to these schools". Upon analysis these terms are much more elastic than some would have us believe and do admit of considerable differences of emphasis and interpretation. We believe the emphasis put upon them by the Commission is misconstrued in two respects:

> *(i) too much attention has been focused on the theory of the comprehensive organisation of secondary education and too little on the direct grant grammar schools themselves and the part they can play in the movement towards reorganisation;*
> *(ii) too little attention has been given to the reality behind that very word "towards", and too little account taken of the inevitably gradual process by which alone successful reorganisation can be achieved.*

224. One result has been that the Report underestimates the importance of the first steps already taken by agreement between schools and local authorities. These may do no more than propose a gradual widening of the academic range of admissions to direct grant grammar schools, but given time and good-will on both sides, may lead on to more radical changes later. We believe that encouragement of this sensible and gradual approach should be written into our Report.

225. A second result of emphasising the theory rather than the schools has been a failure to recognise how far the 178 direct grant schools are working in accordance with most of the aims of comprehensive reorganisation as set out in paragraph 199. The evidence we have had shows that these schools do encourage more children to stay on longer at school; that they do offer a valuable opportunity to clever boys and girls from poor or culturally deprived homes for the full development of their abilities; that they are not "one class establishments", that they encourage rather than depress "the expectations and drive of children and their teachers" and that, because they transcend local boundaries and admit children from wide catchment areas, they do not suffer under the social limitations of many "neighbourhood" schools.

226. It follows that we are as anxious as our colleagues to ensure that these schools shall continue to co-operate with the State system through the local education authorities, as many of them have been doing since the Education Act of 1902. For this reason we would disagree with the limited list of roles in paragraph 208 and would propose one important addition.

120

Additional roles for direct grant schools

227. *It is conceded, elsewhere in our Report, that many of the direct grant schools, however willing, are too small to take on fully comprehensive tasks in the near future. Therefore, the way for some may be to shorten the school life for the individual child in order to widen opportunities for many. This seems to us to be a proper educational aim which could be undertaken by a number of direct grant schools and one which has been commended to us in some of the evidence received from the schools themselves. At the same time we have declared in the Report that we have no wish to see academic standards in the schools impaired, although we hope that opportunities for pupils entering the sixth form will become more varied. "But" we say "encouragement to excel, in varied ways, must be as keen as ever". Hence, to procure this diversification and maintain this encouragement we would add another role to those listed in paragraph 208, which retains an element of selection, although at a later age than eleven. The new role proposed would be, "Schools catering for the ages 14-18. Their intake would represent that proportion of the total ability range agreed between the governors and one or more local authorities". For this addition we would advance the following reasons:*

(i) *By postponing selection until 14 (if secondary transfer continues at 11) no child would be in attendance at one school for less than 3 years.*

(ii) *By postponing selection until 14 the errors attributed to selection at 11 would in large measure be avoided. Every child would have had 9 years of comprehensive education, comparable to the period spent in comprehensive schools under several Continental systems.*

(iii) *By curtailing from 7 to 4 years the period spent in a particular school the academic range could be widened without an increase in numbers and without costly investment in new buildings.*

(iv) *A change of school at 16, on the other hand, may very well increase the number leaving their education at the minimum age rather than persuading more to stay on.*

(v) *The exclusion of the younger children from the secondary school community may make possible the more "mature relationship between pupils and staff" often seen as one of the advantages of the sixth form college.*

(vi) *The 4th and 5th years of a secondary school, as well as the 6th and 7th, need the services of highly qualified teachers, while specialist teachers themselves can more effectively serve the needs of their pupils if they know something of them for 4 years rather than 2.*

(vii) *In paragraph 3 of Circular 10/65 the possibility of this kind of school is envisaged in number 4 of the "forms of comprehensive organisation" there set down. It speaks of a "senior school catering for those who expect to stay at school well beyond the compulsory age". It is true that this is one of the schemes "acceptable as interim solutions", but since evidence we have received has shown that in some areas it has taken twenty-five years to develop a system of secondary schools based upon the provisions of the Education Act of 1944, it may well be as long before comprehensive reorganisation is complete. We would maintain that schools reaching this kind of agreement with a local education authority as to their future role, would certainly be participating in the "movement towards comprehensive reorganisation". (see also paragraph 280.)*

228. We are also among those who would wish to see some direct grant schools given the opportunity to experiment with the creation of schools for highly gifted children. We recognise that there are a number of maintained and independent schools which could also serve in this way. We are therefore included with those mentioned in paragraph 375 who "wish to preserve and develop a small number of highly selective schools", although for reasons given below we would wish them to retain a fee-paying element. We would, however, take a further step towards bringing the first of such schools into existence by including this proposal as an additional role to those listed in paragraph 208 which would be open to direct grant schools.

Fee Paying and Assisted Places.

229. If we hold different views from other members of the Commission about the new roles to be offered, we also find ourselves in disagreement with our colleagues over fee-paying. In paragraph 185 the majority view is thus stated: "our third conclusion is that no fees should be charged for places in day schools which depend mainly on central or local government for their finance". Before dealing with our objections to this we would deal with a more general point.

230. The Commission has been invited to comment on "the principle of central grant to these schools". In our view there is no necessary or logical connection between recommending new contracts for direct grant schools and changing their administration. In fact, we believe that there are strong reasons for altering the Direct Grant Regulations as little as possible. Nevertheless we do regard the setting up of this Commission as an opportunity for improving the Regulations in certain respects, since in the main the system has proved its efficiency over so many years. There have been two criticisms of the present Regulations from the schools themselves. The first is that the total remission of fees to pupils holding free or reserved places means that many parents who could well afford to do so make no direct contribution to the cost of their children's secondary education; the second is that the scale of fee remissions does not apply to boarding pupils. These are two improvements that could easily be introduced through the medium of our Report.

231. For these reasons we would wish to see a Scheme whereby in the new direct grant schools an element of fee-paying is retained, one which would nevertheless ensure the principle that no child should be debarred from entry because his or her parents are unable to pay the fees. This points to a system of schools in which all pupils are assisted according to parental income. Under this, the parents of every child admitted to a direct grant school would pay either no fee, the full fee or some amount in between, according to their income assessed against a scale of remissions approved by the central authority. If this scale were subject to constant review and were generously drawn, justice would be done to rich and poor alike.

232. Our reasons for this proposal are these:

(i) No one has suggested that it is illogical to have free selective schools and fee-charging selective schools, nor is it if these same schools become comprehensive.

(ii) The abolition of fees involves, at least potentially, an increase of control by the administrative authority. Throughout our Report we argue for the greatest possible freedom of decision for the governors, heads and staffs of all schools. At present 22 per cent of tuition costs in direct

grant schools are met by parental contributions through fees. This proportion of the total revenue may seem insignificant and yet it makes a very important contribution to the well-being of the school. It enables an institution to be its own institution, and therefore to be organised for the especial benefit of those who are actually members of it. We believe there is a direct connection between how a school is administered and the quality of the education it can provide.

(iii) It is a strength to the schools to have the support of parents who are making a direct contribution to their children's education. It is an example and a symbol of the increased participation in the day to day progress of their children by parents, and indeed by the whole family, in the venture of education that we would wish to see encouraged.

(iv) The abolition of fees in direct grant schools would widen the cleavage between them and the independent sector which must demand full and often heavy fees, when the concern of the Commission is with the integration of our educational system and not with its fragmentation.

(v) The overwhelming evidence from the schools themselves (see Appendix 6, Section 2, answers to Question 16) is that the presence of a fee-paying element ensures a wider social spread and that graded fees do not militate against the admission of children from poor homes, nor, according to the evidence, is there any difference in treatment by the staff of those who pay fees and those who do not.

(vi) We are concerned elsewhere in our Report (Chapter 9) with the provision for capital expenditure under Scheme A and again, in Chapter 13, with the cost of our proposals. A system of schools in which all their pupils are assisted is relevant to both these sections. If fees in direct grant schools are abolished other means must be found for the extinction of existing debts and for the provision of capital for future development. Hitherto, the direct grant schools have been able to service their capital debts and to provide new buildings by a combination of endowments, appeals to parents and former pupils and a capital element within fees charged to parents and to local education authorities. They could, we believe, go on doing so if they are not required to change too rapidly and drastically, and provided that a reasonable proportion of the permitted fee may be charged to capital expenditure. In Chapter 13 the cost of the various recommendations made in the Report is calculated on various hypotheses as to what direct grant schools are likely to do if and when these recommendations are implemented. The retention of fees under a scheme for assisting all their pupils according to parental income may well persuade some direct grant schools to remain in association with the State system. This will mean that no extra capital will have to be found to provide places at maintained schools for those pupils sponsored at direct grant schools by local education authorities. Furthermore, it cannot be denied that the fees contributed by parents of children in these schools must increase the national resources for secondary education that will be available in the years of scarcity that lie ahead.

(vii) The description in Chapter 9 under Scheme A of the constitution and functions of the School Grants Committee shows certain similarities with the University Grants Committee. Under the latter's administration and through the agency of the local education

authorities a system of graded fees for all seems to work satisfactorily and there is no reason why it should not in the group of secondary schools we are concerned with.

(viii) The purpose of the Commission is to secure the greatest measure of co-operation from schools within its terms of reference, including the independent day schools. The abolition of fees, together with the proviso that outstanding debts will normally remain the responsibility of the schools themselves, would make it certain that few of the independent day schools would participate in the movement towards comprehensive reorganisation. The retention of fees under a system of assisted places might persuade some to join in, as we would all wish them to do.

These are some of the reasons why we recommend to the Secretary of State for Education and Science the consideration of a system of assisted places in the new direct grant schools rather than the abolition of fees. At the same time we are convinced that this assistance should come from a central authority as proposed under Scheme A, and not locally.

The Practical Application of a Scheme under which all Pupils are Assisted

233. Two questions about such a Scheme must be answered: first, how would it work in with local education authorities which charge no fees, and second, why would parents choose to pay fees when other secondary schools were offering free places for the same kind of education?

(i) The ex-direct grant schools and the local education authorities

Suppose a direct grant school were in a position to take on a role of becoming an 11-18 comprehensive school. The minimum size (in a favourable area) would be six forms of entry. By agreement the governors would offer to one or to a number of local education authorities a total of 50 per cent of these places, and would fill the others themselves. The authorities might allocate their places to candidates from particular zones whose parents wished them to go to the school in question; the governors' "residuary" places might be filled by pupils from other areas. The central authority (the Department of Education and Science or the School Grants Committee) would approve the total fee to be charged and publish an agreed scale of remissions according to parental income, which would be reviewed at least every three years. The local authorities might offer "reserved" places either on the basis that parents should pay their proportion of the fees direct to the school, or the local authority might meet the cost of the parental contribution, so that the pupils they sent would pay no fees at all. The balance of the fees payable by either parents or the local authorities would be made up by a deficiency grant from the central authority to the governors of the school. The governors and the local authorities would also have to agree on criteria for the admission of pupils. These could be based on the following:

(a) That parents had chosen this particular school, (b) that the intake should correspond to the bands of ability represented in the primary schools of the area, (c) that the heads of contributory primary schools should supply full reports on candidates and recommendations as to the courses they should follow, (d) that both the governors and the local authorities should be represented at any interviews of candidates for both governors' and local authority places.

(ii) Parental Choice.

We would wish to re-assert the agreed principle of parental choice. Parents might choose a school in which they were called upon to contribute towards the fees because they wanted a single-sex school, a denominational school, a school with which they had family connections, a school which offered certain courses or particular activities they desired for their children, or because they knew and liked the people directly concerned with the conduct of it.

234. Paragraph 2 of Circular 10/65 declared "It is important that new schemes build on the foundation of present achievements and preserve what is best in existing schools". We believe that the suggestions we have made will help to do this where the direct grant schools are concerned. The proposals of our Report must ensure that as few schools as possible shall be driven to revert to complete independence: this would constitute a real loss. They must, therefore, take full account of the "inevitability of gradualness" where all real progress is concerned. They must recognise the value of agreements already reached between local education authorities and direct grant schools to broaden the academic range of admissions and must allow such agreements to become the basis of future reorganisation where they meet local needs. They must also be prepared to admit the retention at any rate for some time to come, of an element of academic selection in our secondary system of education. To say that only independent schools may remain selective is to put an unnecessary obstacle in the way of the progress of many able boys and girls. They must also make possible the continuation of schools which in their organisation combine private enterprise with public provision. If our proposals are so framed they will lead more schools to participate in the movement towards comprehensive reorganisation; if not, progress will be retarded and divisiveness increased. It is for these reasons that we have recorded these points of disagreement and have made alternative suggestions.

235 To summarise these proposals:

(i) Certain direct grant schools should become schools catering for the age range 14-18 whose intake would represent that proportion of the whole ability range agreed between the governors and one or more local authorities. An element of academic selection must and should continue in the secondary system for a number of years, as otherwise opportunities will be denied in certain areas to children from poor or culturally deprived homes.

(ii) In paragraph 185 we read "Our third conclusion is that no fees should be charged for places in day schools which depend mainly on central or local government for their finance". For this we would substitute "Our third conclusion is that in direct grant schools entering into new contracts with one or more local education authorities, graded fees should be charged to all pupils". Places would be offered by the governors or through local education authorities. The amount payable by parents or local education authorities would be calculated according to a scale of remissions against parental income which should be generous and kept continuously under review. The deficiency in income resulting from these remissions would be made up by annual (or termly) grants from the central authority". Naturally such conditions would also apply to independent day schools which were prepared to participate.

(iii) Fuller recognition should be accorded to schemes already negotiated or under discussion between local education authorities and the governors direct grant schools. We would encourage both authorities and schools to build on the basis of these proposals where they envisage a widening of the ability range of children admitted to the schools at any age, or provide for other practical participation by the schools in the movement towards comprehensive reorganisation.

With the reservations set out in this addendum to Chapter 7, we support Scheme A, as described in Chapter 9, and are opposed to Scheme B.

RALPH ALLISON
ROBIN WOODS

CHAPTER .8

The Direct Grant System

236. Having explained our approach to the first half of our terms of reference—the participation of schools in the movement towards comprehensive reorganisation—we turn to consider the second half—the principle of central government grant to schools. We start by presenting the case for the present direct grant system, and then reappraise these arguments in the light of the changes now taking place in secondary education. We conclude that the system of direct grant cannot be continued in its present form and that a different relationship between the schools and the State is needed. We hope the schools will adopt new roles, of the kind outlined in the previous chapter, for which they will need a different form of financial support. We shall discuss how they can be given this support in the next chapter.

The Strengths of the System

237. The direct grant grammar schools are independent schools which have freely entered an agreement to provide services for the State; they are selective, and they charge fees to parents for some of their pupils. This is not the only basis on which schools might be given grants by the central government. But the arguments we have heard for the present system of direct grant are based on a commitment to these features of the system and on firm convictions about their value. The case presented to us can be briefly summarised.

(a) The schools working under this system are good. They have good and devoted teachers, and a long tradition of high academic attainment which sets a standard for the regions they serve—regions which often extend well beyond the education authorities in whose territories they stand. It would be educationally destructive and socially divisive to compel these schools to choose between taking on new work over a broader academic range for which they are not fitted, or becoming wholly independent and serving only those who can afford the higher fees they would then have to charge.

(b) The system of direct grants has enabled these independent schools to play a major part in the education of the nation. Integrated with the maintained schools, on lines much like those already proposed in the Commission's First Report for independent boarding schools, these schools have become particularly stimulating and lively places and they provide for all children, regardless of their parents' incomes, a route to the whole array of higher education and all the opportunities which that confers.

(c) Recruitment procedures which are academically selective but socially unconstrained have enabled these schools to serve all classes. Like any selective school, their social composition is biassed towards the upper end of the social scale, but, it is claimed, they are as socially mixed and undivisive as any grammar school can be. In this respect, too, they are said

127

to be a model of the social objectives the Commission was asked to bear in mind.

(d) It is argued that the payment of fees establishes a healthy sense of mutual responsibility between the schools and the parents and children they serve, encouraging all concerned to give of their best. It saves the taxpayers' money by securing a contribution from fee-payers to the national system of education, and by enabling the schools to raise, from appeals and their endowments, a continuing flow of investment in new buildings and capital equipment. Far from being obsolete, this system of mixed public and private financing should in future be more widely extended.

(e) Independence, it is said, confers control of the school and all its resources on those best equipped for the task—their governing bodies, heads and staffs, who are able to deploy resources in the most effective ways, to experiment, to seize opportunities, take risks and assume full responsibility for the consequences.

(f) The schools take pupils from several different local education authorities and it would be wrong to tie them administratively to one authority. They value their special link with central government as well as their close relationship with the various local education authorities they serve. This unique blend of freedom and responsibility provides a point of reference and comparison with maintained schools from which all benefit.

(g) Between the maintained schools which are said to be growing increasingly uniform and the independent schools from which the maintained schools diverge more sharply as comprehensive reorganisation proceeds, the direct grant schools offer an administrative solution which combines the best in both systems, adds variety to them and extends the choices open to parents. Parents whose children go to direct grant schools are exercising a choice which they are glad to make, often at some sacrifice to themselves, and they should not be deprived of this right.

(h) It would be surprising if the direct grant system had survived so long without needing some amendment. It was put to us that the arrangements for remission of tuition fees should be extended to cover boarding as well as day places in those schools which offer a boarding education; the income scales used to determine parental contributions should be more generous to parents with modest incomes, and all places in the schools should be subject to these scales—not only the residuary places. On this basis all capable of paying fees would contribute, but no-one would be debarred by poverty from entry to the schools. But the basic principles of central grant to schools remain sound—indeed, they are more valuable than ever. The system should be strengthened and extended to more schools, and the threats now hanging over it should be unequivocally rejected.

238. This, in brief, is the case for the present system as it was presented to us. Viewed from the standpoint of an independent school which has entered into the commitment that direct grant entails—at a time, perhaps, when direct grant schools offered the main avenue to an academic education for working class families in their region—it is a convincing case. The schools *do* offer a more demanding education and produce a higher standard of achievement than the

generality of independent schools. They *are* socially more mixed and less divisive than most independent schools; their pupils and their staff both move more freely and frequently across the boundaries which divide the State system from the private system. And, as we showed in Chapter 4, they achieve these things economically, with expenditure and staffing ratios no higher than those of the maintained grammar schools.

Reappraisal

239. But that is not the standpoint from which our own assessment of the system must begin. We have to consider the needs of all children, and the role of the schools within the rapidly changing national pattern of secondary education. We shall reappraise the argument from that point of view.

240. Much (though not all) of the case for the direct grant schools is a case for the selective grammar school—no different from the case for maintained grammar schools. This we have already dealt with in the previous chapter. We return in our final chapter to consider whether there is a case for retaining a few of the most highly selective grammar schools. A minority of us think there is. But we all agree that such a case is entirely independent of any argument for the direct grant system. If there are to be a few highly selective schools, it is just as appropriate to look for them among schools which are at present maintained or independent as among the present direct grant schools. If they are to select only the most able children of all, such schools should be entirely free, and hence they could not be administered under the present direct grant procedure.

241. It is often said that the direct grant schools achieve outstandingly good academic results. In fact, that cannot be expected of all of them because some take pupils with less ability than those in a maintained grammar school and do not claim that kind of academic distinction for themselves. But some do achieve outstandingly good academic results. So, for that matter, do many maintained grammar schools. In all schools the achievements of the pupils as a whole depend to a great extent on their intelligence and home backgrounds, and pupils of comparable intelligence and social background in maintained grammar schools seem to perform as well as their counterparts in direct grant schools.

242. Assessing academic achievement is always difficult. No one should rely too much on examinations as a measure of attainment, but there is some evidence, presented in Appendix 5, that pupils in some of the most highly selective schools do less well in public examinations than might be expected. This observation applies both to maintained and direct grant schools. It casts doubt on the claim that highly selective schools are outstandingly successful in producing the best academic results, as measured at the age of 18.

243. The direct grant schools have many excellent and devoted teachers. But we have found no evidence to show that they recruit and retain more or better staff than other schools of their kind. Assessment of the quality of teachers is as difficult as assessment of their pupils and we do not assume that an honours degree, or its class, provides a complete or reliable measure. But the figures presented in Table 21* do not support the contention that these schools, as a group, contain a unique resource of specialist sixth form teachers. Although there will be individual variations, on average both the boys' and the girls' direct

---

* See page 78

10

grant grammar schools have smaller proportions of graduates on their staffs than the maintained grammar schools, smaller proportions with first or second class honours degrees, and similar proportions with first class honours. Such evidence as we could discover about the turnover of staff in grammar schools becoming comprehensive does not show that there is a greater loss of teachers during this phase than at other times in the life of a school. It is uncertainty, rather than purposeful change, which disturbs morale. Small-scale studies of the aspirations and expectations of graduates in training for the teaching profession do not suggest that they are specially attracted to direct grant schools. Teachers intent on working with large sixth form groups can find opportunities in large comprehensive schools as attractive as any. The size of a school's sixth form depends not only on the proportion of pupils staying on to the sixth but also on the numbers from whom this proportion is recruited. In short, that part of the case for the direct grant system which rests on the arguments for selective grammar education is no better and no worse than the case for grammar schools in general: it cannot be an argument for the present direct grant system.

244. Arguments based on the value of fee-paying are more germane to the problem since their mixture of free places and fee-paying is a feature of the direct grant schools which distinguishes them from other schools. These arguments take three main forms bearing, first, on the motivation of all concerned with the schools, second, on the savings to public funds which may result and, third, on the independence and freedom of action of the schools. Clearly there is no direct relationship between achievement and the payment of fees. Fee-payers in general achieve poorer results than free place holders, but that is because they tend to be less able. We accept that a school with fee-payers in it is likely to be strengthened by keenly motivated parents and children. But we are not convinced that their interest in education would necessarily decline if they paid no fees. There is no evidence that it declines when fee-payers in the direct grant junior schools win free places in their upper schools—or that it increases when children from maintained junior schools enter direct grant schools as fee-payers. It may well be that parents who pay fees, and their children, could (even if they ceased to pay fees) make a most valuable contribution in drive and initiative to some of the maintained schools now deprived of their presence. Although some of our witnesses and respondents implied that teachers show greater concern for children whose parents pay fees, we are convinced that staff of the schools we visited were right when they told us that they generally neither knew nor cared which of their pupils were fee-payers.

245. The second leg of the fee-paying argument is much more complicated. As we explain in Chapter 13, the financial implications for public funds of abolishing fees in the direct grant schools depend on a series of questions to which the answers can only be guessed. How many direct grant schools will enter a comprehensive system and charge no fees? How many will become wholly independent and charge fees that cover their full economic costs? How many parents who might otherwise pay fees for a place in the present direct grant grammar schools will in future use free schools in a comprehensive system? How many will instead pay the full economic cost to use independent schools? If some of the present direct grant schools become wholly independent, will that produce an equivalent increase in the number of pupils in independent schools, or will a large share of their pupils be recruited from weaker independent schools

which must decline or close as a result? No one can answer these questions with confidence. If—to take one extreme set of assumptions—all the direct grant grammar schools went wholly independent, all their places were henceforth taken by fee-payers, and other independent schools lost no pupils, then the State would save a sum of about £15·7 million a year, amounting to about one per cent of its current expenditure on education. If—to take an opposite set of extreme assumptions—all the direct grant schools henceforth were maintained at public expense, charged no tuition fees and filled all their places, and there was no increase in the numbers at independent schools, then the State would have to find an additional £5·8 million a year, amounting to less than 0·5 per cent of its current expenditure on education. The outcome can only be guessed, but it is clear that it will not make a major impact on educational finance. At its most expensive for the State, the increase in annual public expenditure would be about one-sixteenth of the estimated increase in current expenditure on education between the year 1967-68 and the year 1968-69.

246. Whether there are savings or losses to public funds in capital expenditure depends on similar considerations. The direct grant schools spent £27 million on new buildings and equipment between 1950 and 1968, raised partly from private sources and partly from public funds through revenue income. If they had been independent schools, public funds would not have had to meet the share of revenue financed capital expenditure coming from local education authorities and the Department of Education and Science. If they had been maintained schools, the fees paid by parents would have been lost and there might have been reductions in the £6 millions (approximately) raised from appeals and donations: but the £3·5 millions (approximately) which came from school funds and sales of assets might still have been available. Either way, the savings or losses incurred would be very small in comparison with the national budget for capital expenditure on education.

247. The third leg of the argument for retaining fees depends on two assumptions: (a) that the direct grant schools have under present arrangements the independence and freedom of action they want and need, and (b) that these attributes would be lost if fee-paying was abandoned. The independence derived from charging fees depends on the willingness of parents to pay them, otherwise financial constraints may restrict the schools' liberty more severely than control by a public body. In the case of the direct grant schools it has to be remembered that their freedom of action is already limited by the Direct Grant Schools Regulations and the central Department's control of fees. When public money is involved there must be some safeguards to see that it is spent wisely and in accordance with public policy. The schools in general accept the Department's restraints as reasonable. The recommendations we make in Chapter 10 would preserve the essential elements of freedom inherent in the present system. They should be incorporated in instruments and articles of government. We do not believe that fees are an essential safeguard of these rights, though many of the schools do indeed see them in that light. We want to extend these freedoms as far as possible to all schools. To link them with the payment of fees may defeat that aim.

248. These arguments apply, whatever the educational role of the schools. But the introduction of comprehensive education raises new questions. Is it possible to have a mixture of fee-paying and free places within such a system? In a comprehensive school where all ability ranges are represented, it would be

difficult to distinguish those who should pay fees from those who are entitled to enter without charge. This has led some of our witnesses to suggest that all pupils at direct grant schools entering comprehensive systems should be liable to pay fees in accordance with an income scale.

249. This proposal leads to other difficulties. Schools adopting the comprehensive roles listed in paragraph 208 would be working in close collaboration with much larger numbers of maintained schools in which there are no fee-payers. If a small minority of schools charges fees, even scaled according to parental income, many parents—particularly from the working class—would be deterred from seeking places in these schools. That would encourage social selection and segregation. This process can be seen already within the present direct grant schools. Table 23 of Appendix 6, Section 3, shows that 75 per cent of the fee-payers and 50 per cent of the free place holders come from professional or managerial families. Conversely, 15 per cent of the fee-payers and 36 per cent of free place holders come from families of manual workers.

250. The children most likely to suffer from this tendency towards social segregation are those whose opportunities most urgently need to be extended. Local education authorities, teachers and others who have given evidence to us are convinced that fee-paying inevitably tends to discriminate against such children. They have pointed out that this is a problem which cannot be solved by generous income tests ensuring that no fees are asked of poorer families. Many people are unwilling to submit to means tests, or fear that the contribution they are assessed to pay at the outset of a child's school career will escalate out of their reach before his schooling ends. Others are reluctant to ask for remission of fees, under the mistaken impression that they are seeking some form of charitable help. Others are so accustomed to free education that they do not regard a school with fee-payers as coming within their aspirations: they would not apply for a place there. Since parents cannot be compelled to pay fees, such children would have to go elsewhere. In many places that would be inconvenient, and in some it would be much worse: equivalent schools might be a long way off. Everywhere it would tend to strengthen the tendencies to social segregation already apparent in most of the direct grant and independent schools. Because of the correlation between social background and academic achievement, a socially segregated school of this kind would tend to cater for children with higher academic aspirations. It would not have a comprehensive intake. The retention of fee-payers is thus incompatible with the aims of reorganisation which we outlined in paragraph 199. Nor is it in line with the schools' own expressed desire to be completely open to pupils from every kind of home—particularly the less well-off.

251. Even if some way could be found to resolve these problems, there would be difficulties over the recruitment of fee-paying pupils. Parents pay fees because they believe their children thereby get a better education, or greater opportunities, or superior facilities or some other feature which cannot be obtained free. They believe selective direct grant schools offer many of these advantages. Good schools will remain good schools in a reorganised system, but the curriculum and academic opportunities they offer would no longer differ fundamentally from those of other schools which charge no fees. Parents would therefore become increasingly reluctant to pay fees which would be regarded as a tax, arbitrarily levied on children in some schools, rather than the price to be paid for special opportunities. Meanwhile the schools, if they charged an economic fee, would

not be able to compete successfully for fee-payers with academically selective and socially segregated independent day schools unless they retained some of their academically or socially selective character.

252. Finally, fee-paying would make practical difficulties in arriving at a comprehensive role for direct grant schools. To play an effective part within a comprehensive system, schools must work in close co-operation with others in that system. A sixth form college or "mushroom" school must collaborate with the schools that feed it; the two parts of a two-tier system must work closely together; small comprehensive schools combining in a consortium to offer a wide range of sixth form opportunities must co-ordinate their efforts. In all these cases, pupils must be able to move from one school to another smoothly and easily with the minimum of disturbance. If some of the schools charge fees, that would impede the smooth flow. Many parents will not pay fees for something which is available in other schools free, and in a comprehensive system incorporating fee-charging schools their children's opportunities would therefore be restricted.

253. The only two direct grant schools which have agreed to accept a comprehensive intake and play their full part in a comprehensive system have also agreed that virtually all pupils should have free places paid for by local education authorities. We believe no other decision was realistically open to them.

254. We conclude that arguments for fee-paying within the selective system do not withstand close analysis. The introduction of comprehensive reorganisation rules them out completely, for the aims of reorganisation are not compatible with charging fees.[1] Schools which have an intake that is comprehensive in ability and social composition are unlikely to attract fee-payers. Schools excluding those reluctant to pay fees will not be comprehensive, and the attempt to retain such schools will restrict the opportunities open to children. The retention of fee-paying will prolong the uncertainty over the future of the direct grant schools which has troubled them for so long.

255. Arguments based on the social mix achieved in the schools are equally complex because they depend on assumptions about what will happen in future if the present direct grant arrangements are changed. They depend, in fact, on the same set of hypothetical questions to be considered when assessing the economic effects of fee-paying. Only two things can be said with confidence. The first is that we must choose between arguments based on social mix and arguments based on savings to public funds: they cannot both be true. The choice depends on the kind of school which middle class children in direct grant schools would have attended had there been no direct grant system. If the direct grant system brings many middle class children who would otherwise be in wholly independent schools into schools where they work alongside working class children, then it achieves a degree of social mix at the price of paying all, or a substantial proportion of, the fees for parents who would otherwise pay full fees in independent schools. In direct grant schools in 1966-67, even those who paid "full" fees met only 58[2] per cent approximately of the costs of educating

---

[1] Two members disagree. Their reasons are set out in "Points of Disagreement" following Chapter 7, paragraphs 229 to 233.

[2] The figure would be higher after the capitation grant was reduced in August, 1968.

their children and thus gained an average "subsidy" of £76[1] a year. Social mix is thus promoted, but there is a cost, not a saving, to public funds. But if the direct grant system detaches middle-class children from maintained schools which have a social composition more representative of the nation at large, then it frustrates social mix but imposes on residuary place holders whose parents' incomes are high enough to secure no remission of fees a "tax" amounting on average to 58[2] per cent of the costs of educating them, or £105[2] a year. There is thus a saving to public funds, but social mix is reduced. The second thing that can be said with confidence is that the roles we proposed in the previous chapter for direct grant schools entering a comprehensive system would bring a wider range of social classes into them than most of them now have. If "social mix" were our chief objective, the present system clearly could not take us far towards it.

256. Arguments based on the variety the schools contribute to the educational system and the additional choices they offer to parents can be interpreted in several ways. They are nearly all single-sex schools. As co-education spreads in the maintained schools and, more slowly, in the independent schools, this characteristic of the direct grant schools may come to be specially valued by parents who prefer it. But that would scarcely constitute a case for retaining direct grant finance: there are simpler ways of preserving the option of single-sex education. No other educational characteristics distinguish these schools, as a group, from other schools. It is often said that they form a "bridge" or link between the independent and maintained systems, but the significance of this bridge depends—as we have shown—on who uses it and in which direction they are proceeding. It could be said that they do act as a link in that although they are independent of local education authority control they share many points of common interest with maintained schools and this softens the abrupt distinction that might otherwise be seen between independence and the State system. Some of those who stress the variety offered by the schools mean only that they should remain selective grammar schools when the maintained grammar schools disappear: that they should "participate" in the movement towards comprehensive reorganisation by abstaining from it. Whether this view be right or wrong, it is clear that there is nothing sufficiently distinctive about this group of selective schools to justify treatment which differs from that applied to other selective schools.

257. More generally it may be argued that the schools, being partly exposed through their fee-payers to the market, survive by giving parents what they want, and this element of choice is valuable in its own right. We wish to extend the maximum range and the highest quality of educational choices to all children and their parents. Grammar schools are undoubtedly popular with those whose children get to them, but surveys we have seen show that the secondary modern school—to which four-fifths of the population used to go—is clearly the least popular form of secondary education.[3] The satisfaction of the minority entails the disappointment of the majority. Good comprehensive education offers all children a wider range of choices. It can permit choices between schools—and no-one who has visited many comprehensive schools would assert that they are

---

[1] The figure would be lower after the capitation grant was reduced in August, 1968.

[2] This would be higher after the capitation grant was reduced in August, 1968.

[3] E.g. *New Society*, "Education and Opinion" 26th October, 1967.

all the same—but more important are the choices it offers *within* schools which enable children to take up, mix or abandon a wider variety of subjects, to a much later age, than the old tripartite system permitted. We are well aware that all comprehensive schools do not yet attain this ideal. Our aim must be that they should—and that will not be achieved unless the whole system of secondary education is planned for that purpose.

258. This brings us to the last argument in the case for direct grant: the value of independence. We recognise the importance of this feature of the schools and the excellent use that many have made of it. We also recognise the many advantages that a good local authority can offer its schools through technical, advisory, in-service training, bulk-buying and other services. But any governing body and head of a school who are worth their salt will naturally want to preserve as much freedom of action as they can, and will be apprehensive of any step that ties them more closely to government, central or local. There are some local education authorities whose practice gives schools good reason for anxiety. There are others who give their schools as much freedom as any direct grant head and his governors could want. These authorities demonstrate that fee-paying is not the only guarantee of reasonable independence, just as struggling independent schools unable to do what they want through lack of funds show that fee-paying does not always guarantee freedom of action. If the direct grant schools came whole-heartedly into a comprehensive system on terms that were acceptable to them and to the local authorities, there would be more authorities of the kind we applaud and fewer of the kind we deprecate. How can we preserve the essential features of the independence of direct grant schools, and extend to all schools the freedom of action which the best authorities already afford? These questions pose some of the most difficult problems we have had to consider. We turn to them and to the question whether the schools should be financed by local authorities or a central body in the next two chapters.

Conclusion

259. We have presented the case for the present direct grant system. It is passionately argued by the schools which work under this system. These arguments must be sympathetically understood by anyone making proposals for their future. From the standpoint of those who originally entered the arrangements under which these grants were paid, the arguments are convincing. But much of the case for the system now amounts to a defence of the selective grammar school. If it is a good case, it must apply to all grammar schools. If it is not, it cannot justify the continuation of direct grant. Other parts of the case were convincing at a time when these schools provided, in many places, the only opportunity for working class children to take their education as far as they could go, and the only setting in which middle-class and working-class children could learn together. There are scarcely any places left where this is true. Circumstances have changed. Grammar schools of the traditional kind cannot be combined with a comprehensive system of education: we must choose which we want. Fee-paying is not compatible with comprehensive education. But the vigour and independence of direct grant schools must be preserved under new arrangements. We conclude that the present direct grant system must be brought to an end as soon as a new contract can be worked out for the schools. If this system of educational finance is now obsolete, that does not exclude the

possibility of setting up other systems giving the schools a direct grant from the central government. Neither does it amount to any disparagement of the schools themselves. They do very well the work they have been asked to do. New kinds of work, calling for a different agreement with the State, are now needed. We have no doubt the schools will fill these new roles equally well. In the next chapter we discuss how they can be enabled to do this.

CHAPTER 9

A New Settlement

260. In Chapter 7 we concluded that schools which want to play their part within the national framework that serves children throughout the country, and to secure the continuing flow of public funds which enables them to do that, must enter a comprehensive system of education in which no fees would be charged to parents of their pupils.[1] In Chapter 8 we concluded that the direct grant schools would have to make new financial arrangements with the State. In this Chapter we consider how these schools can be enabled to take on new roles and how their work should be financed.

261. These are our main conclusions. Negotiations between the schools and the local education authorities about the new roles which the schools are to assume within widely varying local systems of education should begin as soon as possible. The central government, which has been responsible for making grants to the schools and for determining the new policies in which they are now being asked to play their part, must help the local authorities and the schools to reach agreement and act as final arbiter of these agreements. Since direct grant schools will in future have no fee-payers, their approved current costs must be met from public funds. Those which have incurred debts, with the approval of the Government, to equip themselves for roles which they are now asked to change must be helped to repay those debts because they restrict their capacity to play a part in new policies. Upon these principles we are agreed.

262. We differ about the best means of applying them. Some of us are convinced that the difficult and delicate developments upon which the schools are to embark can reach a constructive conclusion only if the independence of the schools is assured by preserving their direct link with the central government and the central source of funds which expresses this relationship. They therefore propose arrangements which would preserve this relationship, adapt it to meet new needs, and retain a central source of finance. Others of us are convinced that local systems of education cannot develop effectively, and the schools cannot play a constructive part within these systems, unless the local authorities are responsible for maintaining the schools on which they rely for the performance of their statutory duties. They therefore propose that schools participating in the movement towards comprehensive reorganisation should adopt one of the forms of maintained status already available. Finally, certain of our members, while preferring one or other of these arrangements, are convinced that each could provide a framework which would enable the schools to participate in reorganisation and, provided that aim is achieved, they would be content with either.

263. Although there is this general consensus among us, and although we agree on many of the steps necessary to ensure the effective functioning of our

---

[1] These conclusions were subject to reservations by two of our members (at the end of Chapter 7).

proposals, we have decided, for the sake of clarity, to present them as two separate schemes.

Scheme A—"Full Grant" Status

264. Those supporting this scheme[1] believe that there is value to the national system of education in the diversity provided by having a group of schools which combine self-government with central control of finance, and that our proposals flow naturally and directly from the conclusions reached in the previous chapters.

265. We accept the assurance given us by the schools that they are anxious to continue to play their full part in a national system of education; we support their legitimate desire to preserve the kind of independence they have enjoyed in the past (indeed, we wish to see it extended to all schools, as is argued in Chapter 10); and, while being convinced that participation in the national system means accepting the functions required of schools in Chapter 7, we appreciate the financial and organisational difficulties the direct grant schools will face in doing so. We believe that the scheme outlined below, by taking all these factors into account, offers the schools a real opportunity to help meet the country's educational needs in the 1970s and beyond.

266. If proposals for participation are to have any chance of willing acceptance by the schools, they must be based on the following premises: (a) a central form of grant, guaranteeing both the national status and the individual freedom desired by the schools; (b) negotiations about participation which take full account of very different local needs, the varying pace of reorganisation in different areas, and the differing, but often considerable, periods of time that will be necessary for adjustment; (c) realism and generosity about capital needs. It is essential to remove the principal obstacle to participation—namely, the inability of the schools to finance their conversion to an entirely new role. Schools must receive up to 100 per cent assistance with approved debts, conversion costs, and future building.

267. Once the Government accepts these principles, the Secretary of State will announce the plans for putting them into effect through a centrally financed School Grants Committee. This body, we believe, will enable participation to take place more easily. We give our reasons for its establishment, together with an outline of its functions and composition, in the following paragraphs. Many of the considerations we adduce would apply with equal force to any form of central grant and its administration.

268. The direct grant schools have rightly pointed out that in order to carry on effectively, they must have stability and an end to the present uncertainty about their future. We agree. For this reason local education authority control of the schools is not appropriate. It is fairly certain that big changes will follow from the Report of the Royal Commission on Local Government. These are likely to take a long time and to involve a period of uncertainty and upheaval. It is not possible to see how the delicate and complex guidance needed to enable the schools to participate can be given by local education authorities against this background. Nor is it possible to predict with confidence the eventual shape of

---

[1] Proposed by Mr. Allison, Mother Angela Mary Reidy, Dr. Bliss, Mr. McGowan, Miss Wilks, the Dean of Windsor and Mr. Young. "We" used in paragraphs 264 to 282 refers to these members only.

educational administration. Provided, however, that the central authority has the ultimate say in policy and that the local authority knows what educational provision it can count on, there is no reason why there should not be more than one method of enabling governors, heads and staffs to run their schools. The direct grant system is one such method; our own scheme puts forward another. Furthermore, while the fears and suspicions of the governors and heads of direct grant schools about coming under the control of local education authorities may often be misplaced, they exist. The new approach to the government of maintained schools which is recommended in Chapter 10 will not develop overnight. The present direct grant schools will therefore need to be convinced that the changes are actually taking place before they will consider coming within the control of local authorities.

269. There are two further reasons for suggesting the establishment of a School Grants Committee. First, the central authorities in England and Wales, as in Scotland, will always have to place pupils in, and provide funds for, a number of regional or national schools. They will need some national agency for negotiating with these schools, for administering grants or fee payments, and for supervising the work to be done. In the Commission's First Report it was recommended that such an agency be set up for boarding education only; its functions could be extended to include the functions suggested below, particularly since many of the direct grant schools offer boarding facilities. Secondly, such a body is likely to be trusted by the schools and would give the new system a fresh start uncomplicated by any vestigial remains of the existing arrangements.

270. What would the Grants Committee be and how would it operate? Essentially it would be a body set up to help the three parties involved to bring about the participation of the schools in a national system as expeditiously and as smoothly as possible. Responsible to the Secretary of State, and representing both the public interest and the interests of authorities and schools, it would exercise the following main functions:

(a) Stimulate, guide and assess negotiations between education authorities and schools. Advise the Secretary of State of situations where it would be unrealistic for negotiations to be continued, as soon as this becomes clear, ensuring that no unreasonable delays occur. Review the progress made by individual schools towards participation through regular reports from the schools.

(b) In consultation with the governing body, assess the financial needs of each participating school, taking into account such endowment and other income as is expected in the forthcoming year. Give grants to governing bodies on the basis of approved estimates of expenditure (both recurrent and capital), ensuring that one school does not benefit at the expense of another and that expenditure is generally in line with that of maintained schools.

(c) Advise the schools on capital projects and the Secretary of State on building priorities in different local situations within the framework of central government policies for secondary education and overall central control of capital expenditure. Settle the schools' approved debts, meet the capital costs of conversion to a comprehensive role and make grants for further building in the future, taking account of any existing resources the schools may have.

(d) Receive financial contributions from central and local sources when the appropriate level of capitation payments has been determined. The guiding principles for financing the schools would be:

    (i) that no authority should gain or lose financially by having day pupils in their area attend these schools instead of locally maintained schools,

    (ii) that the staffing ratios, equipment, supplies and other resources of the schools should be generally comparable to those of maintained schools with similar functions, adjusted as appropriate to the particular circumstances of each school.

(e) Supervise the allocation of boarding places, administer the payments to be made to boarding schools from public funds (see Chapter 12) and carry out the other functions which were envisaged for the Boarding Schools Corporation in the First Report.

(f) Advise on the development of other regional or national schools, should the need arise.

271. The Committee ought to be constituted to represent the main interests participating. We do not feel this is the place to be specific about numbers, though we are clear that no one group should have a simple majority. The Committee might include:

an independent chairman;
"overlapping" member(s) with a similar Committee for Scotland;
local education authority representatives;
school representatives (governors, heads and teaching staff);
representative(s) of other educational interests, e.g. universities;
persons nominated for the "public interest", e.g. "lay" people, and representatives from employers and employees in commerce and industry;
assessors from the Department of Education and Science should be attached
to the Committee.

272. This is how we envisage the process of participation: in stage one there would be negotiations about the future of the school, dealing with its role, administration, and finance; in stage two the school would assume "full grant" status and the plans agreed in stage one would be put into practice. We take these in turn.

273. Stage one—negotiations. As has been said in Chapter 7, schools willing to play their full part within the national system and to retain the support of public funds must adopt comprehensive roles. The roles open to any particular school will depend on the needs and resources of the local situation. The role actually adopted by a school can only be determined by negotiations with the local education and, in some cases, church authorities. No school can decide unilaterally what its place and function should be in the local provision of education; equally, the local authorities, who are responsible for the needs of the whole area and must rightly have a large say in how former direct grant schools should fit into their comprehensive system, should nevertheless not be free unilaterally to reject schools who wish to participate, nor to select forms of participation which run counter to nationally agreed policies for reorganisation. The country has a responsibility and an interest in seeing that, wherever participation is at all possible, the resources of direct grant schools are not lost to the nation or misused through unreasonable decisions by local education

authorities. No direct grant school should be deprived, when short-term or long-term plans are being drawn up, of the possibility of playing any role deemed suitable for a similar maintained school. The negotiations between schools and authorities will have to include decisions about the numbers of pupils to be admitted and the procedures for admission; the areas and authorities from which pupils will come and the implications of the scheme for other schools in the area; the building programmes called for and the phases and timing of the whole scheme. There will have to be safeguards for teachers similar to those which protect the interests of teachers in the maintained schools that are being reorganised. The Secretary of State will explain to the negotiating parties the criteria he will apply when deciding whether to approve schemes of participation. If agreement is difficult to reach the local education authorities or the school can ask him to arbitrate. The School Grants Committee will have an invaluable part to play as convener, assessor and guide during the negotiations, particularly in situations where more than one local authority is involved.

274. Besides these important negotiations with local authorities, there are questions to be decided by the Secretary of State with the advice of the School Grants Committee: the composition of governing bodies and the Committee's relationship to them; the settlement of debts; the handling of endowments and endowment schemes, the cost and financing of the building programmes agreed upon with the local education authority. To make participation possible, approved debts and the cost of the building work mentioned above will have to be met in full from public funds. We consider the question of future capital expenditure on buildings in the next paragraph. Both the amount of the debts to be met and the costs of conversion schemes will require the approval of the School Grants Committee and the central government. In general, debts approved for grant will be those being met from fee income with the approval of the Department of Education and Science. We see two alternative methods of meeting debts and capital costs; indeed, one of them may be thought suitable for existing debts and the other for future debts. Either they can be extinguished by capital grants paid through the School Grants Committee; or they can be treated as loans, the servicing of which will become part of the running expenses of the school and be taken into account in determining the level of capitation payments. However they are dealt with, the principle is clear that if the Government asks the school to change its role, it must be prepared to bear the cost of the change.

275. We have recommended in paragraphs 266 and 270(c) that future capital expenditure beyond conversion costs should be eligible for up to 100 per cent grant depending on the other resources of the schools. It may be thought that this proposal cannot be considered in isolation from the situation of the voluntary aided schools. For it is arguable that since voluntary aided schools are required to meet 20 per cent of their capital costs, full grant schools should do so too, particularly if their debts and conversions costs have already been met. To do otherwise, it may be said, is to create an anomaly which would be unjust to the voluntary aided schools. Against this it must be pointed out that not only is "full grant" status a new concept and different from voluntary aided status, but the majority of the present direct grant schools simply will not be in a position to pay 20 per cent of future capital costs once they have lost their fee income. To expect them to give up the latter and at the same time to meet a 20 per cent share of these costs is, in the majority of cases, to ask the impossible.

The direct grant schools have for the past twenty-five years met the major part of the costs of their capital developments in accordance with their obligations under the Direct Grant Schools Regulations and to fulfil their functions as selective grammar schools. Under our proposals they are being asked to participate in the national system of education in a wholly new way and without the help of any income from fees (whether for residuary, reserved or free places), with complete independence as the only alternative open to them. The voluntary aided schools, on the other hand, have had a large proportion of their capital expenditure met from public funds during this same period, and in any case they deliberately made the choice of voluntary aided status in preference to other possibilities, knowing the obligations that choice involved. It may well be that the time has come for a review of the financial arrangements that now apply to the voluntary aided schools. We should not regret this; although we have not been asked to make recommendations regarding the voluntary aided schools, we are aware that the same problem does not arise for the Scottish Committee since denominational schools in Scotland do not contribute to capital costs. Furthermore, we cannot but bear in mind the logic of the argument of Chapter 10 for greater freedom for governing bodies and heads of secondary schools in the maintained sector. For we hope that the proposals in that chapter will secure for all schools the kind of freedom now secured for voluntary aided schools through their particular form of government. Since their share of approved capital costs is in part a recognition of this very freedom, the securing of such freedom for all schools might reasonably be expected to remove the need to exact a "price" for it from a particular group of schools.

276. The current regulations for the governing bodies of direct grant schools allow a welcome degree of flexibility in their composition. We believe that direct grant schools which are willing to adopt "full grant" status should operate under similarly flexible regulations regarding their governing bodies, bearing in mind what we say on this matter in Chapter 10. Regulation 7 of the "Direct Grant Schools Regulations, 1959" distinguishes two ways in principle of constituting a body of governors.[1] These are already well understood by direct grant schools, and both ways have been found by local authorities and schools alike to work well and to their mutual satisfaction. This being so, they may provide a pointer to a way by which the composition of governing bodies of "full grant" schools could be determined.

277. We have explained in paragraph 265 that flexibility will be needed in the timing of negotiations. This said, we believe that it should be possible to complete them within four years. In a few special situations, where local plans or unusual complications warrant it, the central government should be able to extend the negotiating period, on the advice of the School Grants Committee. We would not expect such an extension to go beyond seven years from the starting date for negotiations. Participation in comprehensive reorganisation is likely to become more difficult the longer it is delayed.

278. Some schools will decide not to participate and will choose independence; in some situations negotiations will fail. But at whatever point, and for whatever

---

[1] *Either* a third of the governors appointed by the local authority (as in Regulation 7 (1)(a)) *or* a majority of the governors "representative" governors (as in Regulation 7 (1)(b)); this would imply a majority of non-Foundation governors but not a majority from any *one* education authority, for "representative" has a wider connotation (cf. Regulation 7 (2)(a) and (b) and our own suggestions in paragraph 312).

reason, participation is found to be impossible, it will be for the central government, after considering the advice of the School Grants Committee, to decide what is to be done. Where a school decides to go independent, where after negotiation it cannot agree to a role which it might reasonably be expected to fulfil, or where the local education authority cannot reasonably make use of the school's participation, the present direct grant will be phased out, but in such a way as to protect fully the interests of all existing pupils and parents. Where a school would like to participate and proposes ways of doing so which the local education authorities refuse to accept, arbitration by the Secretary of State will be required. He cannot compel local education authorities to accept the help of a school if they are determined not to use it, but local authorities depend so heavily on the central government—in planning their building programmes, for instance—that the Secretary of State's advice about the participation of schools is bound to be seriously considered.

279. We now turn to stage two—entry into "full grant" status. On successfully completing negotiations and receiving approval from the Secretary of State for the proposed participation scheme, the school will relinquish its direct grant status and assume the new status of a "full grant" school. The appointed date for this should be as early as possible after the end of the negotiations. At this point all fees will cease; even the fee-paying parents of existing pupils will no longer pay fees, since we think there will be difficulties enough to be faced by the schools on the way to adopting their new comprehensive roles without sharpening differences between the old and new intakes by the retention of fees for a diminishing number of pupils. Grants covering the full running costs of the school will be paid through the School Grants Committee. Parents' rights in such matters as travel and maintenance allowances will be the same as those of parents of pupils in maintained schools.

280. The school will now be committed to participation, according to the role agreed with the local education authorities and as a full member of the group of schools in the area. The process of converting the school to its new role will, of course, take time, in accordance with the programme of development decided upon with the local education authorities: extension and adaptation of buildings, as well as new resources and equipment, will be required; new staff will have to be recruited; and the new, unselected entry will begin to be admitted in accordance with the agreements made. In some cases, for example where there are unavoidable delays in building programmes, or where the rest of the reorganisation plans of the local education authorities make it necessary, a school may even continue for a limited period to accept a "grammar school" or "extended" intake, if the participation agreement necessitates some delay in introducing a "comprehensive" intake.

281. Whatever the nature of the interim period of a school's transition from its present selective role to its new comprehensive role, the School Grants Committee and the Department of Education and Science should be fully apprised of progress. We suggest that regular reports should be submitted to the Committee by participating schools from the time when they assume "full grant" status until the process of transition is completed.

282. We may sum up our proposals by stating the principles on which we envisage a "full grant" school operating.

(a) It will fulfil a comprehensive role within the system approved for its area, working in close co-operation with the local education authority or authorities in the provision of education for that area.

(b) There will be no fee-paying[1] , and grants for current and capital costs will be met through the School Grants Committee.

(c) The governing body and head will be fully responsible for the administration of the school, combining independence of government with full participation in the national system of education.

Scheme B–Locally Maintained Status

283. Other members of the Commission[2] propose a different scheme. If the agreements which will be reached between local authorities and the present direct grant schools are to work well, and if the resources available for education are to be distributed fairly and efficiently between schools for the benefit of all children, then we believe the local authority must dispose of all the public money involved, and take responsibility for former direct grant schools which have entered into arrangements with it, as it does for existing maintained schools. We recognise that some people are dissatisfied, whether justifiably or not, with the ways in which some local education authorites wield their powers. We are not altogether satisfied on this score ourselves. But such problems, where they exist, can affect schools of all kinds, not only those that were previously direct grant schools. These problems must therefore be tackled on behalf of all schools through agencies which are democratically accountable to the public for education—the central and local education authorities. We are not convinced that a new central agency will make them any easier to solve.

284. Under the existing direct grant system there is the difficulty that the schools are under an obligation to a third party, the Department of Education and Science, and this may stand in the way of effective participation of the schools in local comprehensive systems. This difficulty would remain under any system by which a small proportion of schools were financed from a central source (whatever its name) and not from the local authority. If expenditure on a given school is determined by a central authority, difficulty, friction, and suspicions of unfairness are likely to recur.

285. We have been told that one reason for continuing a central system is that many of the schools have large catchment areas which extend beyond the boundaries of the local authorities in which they stand. The proposals of the Maud Commission, if adopted, will change this position substantially. The reorganisation of maintained secondary schools is already requiring the planning and redeployment of resources, particularly for sixth form teaching, over larger areas than hitherto. The difficulties which arise are not insoluble and not confined to schools in the present direct grant system.

286. The important questions of the rights and duties of governing bodies and of teachers in relation to local authorities are discussed in Chapter 10. The codes of practice called for there will apply to *all* schools. These codes are more likely to be adopted if some of the schools best placed to assert their freedom are

---

[1] But see "Points of Disagreement" following Chapter 7.

[2] Mr. Arnold-Forster, Dr. Faulkner, Dame Anne Godwin, Mr. Hill, Alderman Hutty, Mr. Marsh, Councillor Taylor and Professor Williams. "We" used in paragraphs 283 to 293 refers to these members only.

administered by local education authorities. If there were very great differences in the powers and responsibilities of governing bodies and teachers between ex-direct grant schools and other schools playing their part in the authority's arrangements, it is doubtful whether the full grant system proposed by our colleagues would itself work very happily.

287. The movement towards comprehensive reorganisation can proceed only as quickly as local authorities and the central government will and can make it proceed. We must take into account the administrative, financial and political realities. We cannot prescribe precisely what steps will be taken by 178 schools financed under the present direct grant system. There will be many consequences which cannot be foreseen and which will have to be dealt with as they arise. Our proposals are therefore designed to leave considerable latitude both in timing and in matters of substance to the Secretary of State, the local authorities and the schools.

288. This is how our proposals would work. The Secretary of State would announce his intention to discontinue the direct grant system, and lay down a period of two to three years during which negotiations would proceed between schools and local authorities about what roles the school may play. Some schools may decide immediately or during the negotiating period that they wish to go independent; they would agree with the Department of Education and Science upon the date at which they became independent and direct grant stopped. In that case pupils receiving free places should continue to do so until they complete their school course. Similarly the position of pupils holding residuary places should be protected by continuing the capitation, sixth form and remitted fees grants attributable to them until they complete their course. Schools participating in reorganisation schemes would assume a maintained status agreed between them and an appropriate local authority and approved by the Secretary of State. Most, we assume, would become voluntary aided schools, but others might become voluntary controlled, or county schools. If they wish to become voluntary aided schools the Secretary of State would, as usual, need to be assured that they are able to meet the normal financial obligations of voluntary aided schools (subject to the special provisions we recommend on existing debts and capital expenditure on building necessary for participation in comprehensive reorganisation). Before reaching such agreements, the schools and the local authorities would have to be satisfied about arrangements for admission of pupils, the age, sex, and ability ranges to be covered, the size of the school, the consequential requirements for buildings, staff and equipment, the rights and responsibilities of governing bodies, heads and staff, and other matters. If progress on some aspect of the scheme of reorganisation—the building programme or the recruitment of staff, for example—is later delayed, then the school must be entitled by the agreement made at the start to reconsider the pace at which other aspects of reorganisation proceed—the extension of the ability range or modifications of the age range, for example. Local authorities and governing bodies will both recognise that reorganisation cannot be conducted responsibly on any other terms.

289. So long as negotiations with a given school continue with hopes of a constructive outcome, direct grant would continue to be paid. In a case in which the school and the local authority fail to agree about the terms on which the school can play its part, the Secretary of State would have to arbitrate, and would generally expect to bring discussions to a conclusion within the 2-3 year

period (allowing for extensions in exceptional cases). In some cases, the prospect has to be faced that despite a school's willingness to participate, neither the authority nor the Secretary of State can see any way in which it reasonably can do so. In such cases, there will in the end be no alternative to the school either going independent or closing. A more frequent difficulty might be that a school was willing to participate and proposed a reasonable way of doing this, but the authority were not—or not yet—willing or able to find it a place in a comprehensive scheme. This might be because the authority's plans for reorganisation had not yet reached a point where the school could be accommodated, or because the authority refused to make such plans.[1] In either case the Secretary of State would investigate the local situation and give a ruling. If the school was rejected because the authority were rejecting reorganisation, and the Secretary of State had not taken, or was not using, powers to require reorganisation, then there might be a case for the temporary continuation of direct grant for such a school. But if reorganisation had not yet reached a point where the school could begin to play its part in a comprehensive scheme, then the school might become a voluntary aided grammar school for the time being, once a firm agreement had been reached about the way in which it would eventually participate in reorganisation. Clearly the Secretary of State cannot allow local education authorities to take on the maintenance of additional grammar schools unless their eventual place in comprehensive schemes has first been agreed.

290. As soon as a school began to take its first pupils under the new arrangements, the payment of direct grant would stop, together with private fee-paying. The school would become a maintained school. The obligations to existing pupils would be honoured, and fee-paying parents would henceforth receive the uncovenanted benefit of free places. That is what normally happens when schools assume maintained status.

291. The approved debts of a direct grant school which joins a comprehensive scheme will be either extinguished or taken over—by central government if the school becomes voluntary aided, by the local authority if it becomes voluntary controlled. The school's resources will be taken into account when the central government determines the debts to be approved, but in suitable cases a 100 per cent payment for debt will be made. In general, the debts to be met will be those already being met from fee income with the approval of the Department of Education and Science. In the event of a school becoming a county rather than a voluntary school, the local authority would acquire the school's land and buildings at district valuer's valuation, and that should enable the governors to pay off any outstanding debts. It may be said that our proposals about debts create an anomaly in relation to existing voluntary aided schools, since some ex-direct grant schools will have had their debts wholly assumed by the Government while existing voluntary aided schools will retain theirs. But existing voluntary aided schools have had the benefit of assistance with capital expenditure (recently at the rate of 80 per cent) while the direct grant schools have had to finance their capital expenditure on the assumption that the direct grant system would continue in the form in which it was when they joined it. Our proposals offer the fairest solution that we can find for the difficulties that some of them will face when direct grants end.

---

[1] If the Education Bill presented to Parliament on the 4th February, 1970 becomes law this situation should no longer arise.

292. But this difference between the past financial experiences of direct grant schools and of existing voluntary aided schools cannot justify differing treatment in the future. If a direct grant school becomes a voluntary aided school it must be treated like other such schools in future, which would mean (under present arrangements) that it would be entitled to an 80 per cent grant towards approved capital expenditure. Its own contribution towards capital expenditure is regarded as the symbol and price of the greater independence enjoyed by a voluntary aided school. We recognise, however, that there may be some schools which, having equipped themselves to play the educational role once expected of them, are now required to play another which calls for capital expenditures which they would find extraordinarily difficult to make. The ex-direct grant schools would be in no different situation in face of these difficulties than some of the present voluntary aided schools. Although we have not been asked to make recommendations about existing voluntary aided schools we must point out the questions which our own proposals pose in that sector. We think that for any voluntary aided school, whether it had previously been a direct grant school or not, which finds itself unable to participate effectively in reorganisation for lack of the necessary capital resources the possibility of a special capital grant for this purpose must be considered.

293. We cannot anticipate every difficulty which may arise from the ending of the present direct grant system, and our proposals deliberately leave a good deal to be decided in the light of experience. Nevertheless, the aim of our proposals is clear, and the proposals themselves are workable. They would enable all schools capable of playing their part in reorganisation, and willing to do so, to contribute to a comprehensive system of education.

Junior Schools

294. Two out of three direct grant schools have junior or lower schools for children of primary school age. They operate much like independent preparatory schools. Some of the independent schools willing to enter reorganisation schemes may have similar preparatory departments. Scheme A would apply only to secondary schools. The choices open to junior schools under either Scheme A or Scheme B would therefore be: (a) to close, thus making their buildings available for any expansion required to enable the secondary school to participate in reorganisation; or (b) to become an independent primary school; or (c) to become a maintained primary school. If they chose the second or third of these possibilities, it would have to be made clear in the arrangements for reorganisation that pupils from the primary school would have no privileged rights of entry to the secondary school. The opportunities taken for using the lower or preparatory schools' buildings for expansion of the secondary school would also be one of the factors to be considered before making grants to help with the capital costs of reorganisation.

Conclusion

295. The differences between these two schemes, important though they are, should not conceal the extent of our agreement. The aim of all of us is to enable as many direct grant schools as possible to participate as soon as possible in the movement towards comprehensive reorganisation. Those which cannot or will

not do this are free to become wholly independent. The schools and the local education authorities must negotiate agreements with each other which enable schools to make their best contributions to widely varying local systems of education. Before concluding such agreements, all concerned should reach clear understandings about the future roles of schools, the resources required to adopt them, and the rights and responsibilities of governors, heads, teaching staff and local authorities. The salary and status of teachers affected by reorganisation should be protected on the same terms as those applying to teachers in maintained schools. The central government must help the authorities and the schools to reach agreements which accord with national policies and the resources available to implement them. In the event of disagreement or uncertainty, the Secretary of State must be the final arbiter. Many of the direct grant schools cannot participate promptly and effectively in reorganisation unless they are given help in meeting the capital costs involved. Since they will take no more fee-payers, the State must meet and approve their current costs. The volume of resources they will need to perform their new roles should be the same as that available to maintained schools already doing similar work: we do not wish to create a privileged sector of secondary education. On all these basic principles we agree.

296. We approach the task of putting these principles into practice from two points of view. Some of us, believing that our proposals will not be acceptable to the schools unless their independence is explicitly protected, are convinced that their direct link with the central government must be retained. Grants for the schools must therefore be centrally administered by a body appointed to assist in carrying through the whole transformation required, and to advise all the parties concerned. Some of us, believing that the success of comprehensive reorganisation will call for continuous and careful planning by democratically accountable local authorities responsible for the education of children through-out their areas, are convinced that schools participating in this reorganisation should adopt a locally maintained status of the kind already available. The differing contexts in which we perceive these problems have led us to propose different routes towards essentially similar objectives.

297. Some of us[1] are convinced that each of these schemes could be effective and regard the choice between them as a pragmatic one to be decided in the light of the policies of the Government of the day and the response made by the schools and the local authorities to our proposals. Would a centrally financed scheme enable many more schools to participate willingly in reorganisation than a locally financed scheme? Would it alienate the local education authorities whose collaboration will be equally essential for success? Will the Government set up the central authority recommended in the Commission's First Report to develop a national system of boarding education—an authority which could also be asked to take on the task discussed in this Chapter? This group believes that final decisions must depend on the answers to these questions.

---

[1] Lord Annan, Professor Donnison, Dr. Judge and Mr. Waddilove.

CHAPTER 10

Government of Schools

298. We hope the proposals made in the previous chapter will enable many direct grant schools to participate with the maintained schools in the reorganisation of secondary education. In the next chapter we show how independent day schools can be enabled to play a similar part. We have said that before entering such schemes the schools would first have to be assured about the rights and responsibilities of their governors, heads and staff. What form of government would they have? What would be the composition of their governing body? What powers would the governors and head have, and what controls would be exercised by local and central government? These are the questions we deal with in this Chapter.

299. What we say applies to all maintained secondary schools—county and voluntary—as well as to the schools in our terms of reference. There must be some differences. The rights which can reasonably be expected by the governors of a school built from foundation funds, owned by them but used as part of the State system, cannot be the same in every respect as those which ought to be given to the governors of a school built and financed entirely from public funds. But all schools doing similar work on a similar scale should have the same sort of autonomy that we recommend for former direct grant schools. We are not alone in asking for more freedom and responsibility for the maintained secondary schools. A growing body of people connected with schools take the same view. The Royal Commission on Local Government recommended in its Report that "... the sphere of action open to managers and governors of schools and colleges should be widened".[1] The Association of Education Committees in its evidence to the Royal Commission said "... we believe it is imperative that there should be a governing body for a school or group of schools as may be found convenient, and that such governing bodies should have substantial powers".

Responsibilities of Central and Local Government

300. Democratically elected bodies must determine the general direction of educational development and the main policies to be followed in the public system of education. The evolution of local systems of education calls for better planning and closer co-ordination than ever before. Where public money is spent, those responsible for it must have the authority and the information to account for their actions to the representatives of the electorate. Democracy entails control, at both national and local levels.

301. The central government must determine the priorities for expenditure between different educational sectors and different areas—for the allocation of capital between primary and secondary schools, and the concentration of

---

[1] Cmnd. 4040, paragraph 318, H.M.S.O. 1969.

resources on educational priority areas, for example. It must ensure that different parts of the country get their fair share of available teachers. It must ensure that nationally agreed policies—for the reorganisation of secondary education, for example—are effectively carried out.

302. Local education authorities must control their total annual expenditure and play a large part in determining the priority to be given to major building projects. Since the number of teachers available is limited, they must decide how many of them may work in each school. Basic salary scales in schools participating in reorganisation schemes must be those applicable to all maintained schools, and the authorities must decide for each school the total number or value of special allowances and posts of responsibility. They must decide the minimum educational qualifications and standards for teaching posts. They must agree with the governors of a school on the part which the school will play within the educational system of the area and on the arrangements for the admission of its pupils. Without powers such as these, local authorities cannot carry out their duties under the Education Acts effectively or economically. They cannot reorganise their secondary schools into a satisfactory comprehensive system. They cannot be sure that public money is being spent wisely, and scarce resources shared fairly among the schools in their areas. We have said in Chapter 7 that few of the schools in our terms of reference are large enough to become comprehensives covering the age range from 11 to 18 without major expansion. Many, therefore, are likely to take part in tiering schemes and other arrangements which will call for the closest co-operation with other schools—co-operation which must be carefully and sympathetically planned with the education authorities.

Existing Controls

303. Any school which wishes to be supported from public funds will have to accept such controls—many of them already familiar to the direct grant schools. The level of their expenditure is already largely controlled by the Secretary of State through the requirement that he approve fees. This in turn largely determines the overall staffing complement. They cannot erect new buildings or carry out alterations of existing buildings without the Secretary of State's approval. There are regulations about the admission of pupils, about religious worship and instruction in the school and withdrawal from it, about the number, qualifications and minimum salaries of teachers, and about the composition of the governing body. In all these fields, the direct grant schools already accept that they do not have complete independence of action. A school which is at present a direct grant school and which is willing to take up the kind of role we have outlined will not, under our proposals, lose any of the essential freedoms it already possesses.

Responsibilities of the School

304. Within the general framework of public control, we think that the governors and the head should be left to run the school. The central and local authorities' legitimate financial concern is to ensure that the schools' overall expenditure is kept within approved limits and that they get good value for the money they spend. The first can be achieved by the approval of estimates of current expenditure and small items of capital expenditure which leave the

school to decide on the order of priority between the various calls on their resources provided they keep within these estimates. The school should be able to carry forward unspent money from one annual budget to the next. The second aim, value for money, is as likely to be achieved by giving the schools responsibility, together with clear advice, as by insisting on prior approval for every detail of expenditure. The schools will in any case be accountable through the usual audit of their accounts.

305. We have explained that schools participating in comprehensive reorganis- ation will negotiate with the education authorities their place within the educational system of the area—the age range they will cater for, the way they will fit into the authorities' comprehensive schemes, and the timing and transitional arrangements for this. Arrangements for the admission of pupils must satisfy a number of potentially conflicting criteria: parental choice, the desirability of social mix, maintaining a balanced intake so far as academic ability is concerned, and providing a proper range of courses at sixth form level. The situation will vary from school to school. Skilful drawing of catchment areas will help but over-rigid adherence to them must be avoided. We particularly hope that the practice of the most liberal authorities will be adopted when deciding on policies for the admission of pupils from neighbouring authorities: adminis- trative boundaries should not restrict parental choice to an unreasonable extent. It is beyond the scope of this Report to go into all the details of arrangements for admitting pupils: the important principle is that they should be agreed and that the Department of Education and Science should arbitrate where there is disagreement.

306. The school should be responsible for advertising for staff and appointing them, provided it keeps within the total establishment approved by the authority and observes minimum specifications about educational qualifications. (There may also have to be arrangements for ensuring that authorities can find appointments for teachers whose schools have been closed or reorganised.) Sometimes it will be important to appoint someone quickly: if advertisements must first be approved by the authority disastrous delays may result. A new member of staff has to fit in with the other members of the teaching team and with the head, both personally and professionally. Thus the school, and the head in particular, should have the main say in deciding who should be appointed. This is not always the way in which maintained schools work at present.

307. The heads and their teaching staff are professionals. Their knowledge, experience and status cannot be fully used unless it is acknowledged and respected. The school must be given freedom in professional matters. It should not be necessary for teaching staff and heads, as now happens under some authorities, to seek permission from the local education authority to attend an educational conference or course. This sort of decision should be left to the head in the light of the overall needs of the school. Similarly, decisions about educational visits by school parties should be decided by the school within the resources available for such purposes.

308. The choice of equipment, books and supplies ought to be the school's. Very considerable economies may be achieved by bulk purchasing and the school may be expected to use central purchasing arrangements where it would be clearly uneconomic and less effective not to do so. Subject to this, the school should be able to buy what, when and how it likes within the budget available to

it. In too many cases, authorities require schools to seek approval for their purchases or to purchase only through the authority. In too many cases, maintained schools do not get the equipment they want but substitutes which are not necessarily cheaper.

309. The repair and maintenance of buildings and grounds involve large expenditures annually and require expert management. It must be for the authority to define the main lines of policy to be followed in respect of maintained schools and to make any necessary large scale arrangements with contractors or with specially appointed staff. Nevertheless if frustration and delay are to be avoided, the head must be given sufficient discretionary powers to deal promptly with local emergencies and to give instructions for urgent repairs. Within this framework, heads and their staff should be given a great deal of say over such things as the design of new buildings and modifications, the timing of operations, the choosing of colour schemes, and the layout of grounds.

310. Maintained schools vary enormously in the degree of independence they have. Some heads and governors clearly feel they have all the freedom they need to run their schools. Equally plainly others do not. We think that the mixture of freedom, responsibility and control we outline above would give maintained schools the essential freedom which the direct grant schools have at present. The direct grant schools which became maintained schools on these terms would gain advantages through belonging to a larger organisation. Professional advice freely available, use of in-service training facilities, access to expensive equipment shared by several schools, extra sports facilities, economies through bulk purchasing enabling more to be achieved at the same cost—these can be gained through having the support of a group with resources of money, facilities and expertise.

311. Direct grant school heads and governors are used to running their schools with a minimum of control by the Department of Education and Science. If they are to be attracted to a form of maintained status they will want reassurance that local education authorities will give them the same responsibility. We believe that they are right and that the sort of freedom we have described should be available to all maintained secondary schools.

The Governing Body

312. With adequate powers and responsibilities it should be possible to attract governors of high calibre and standing. They will be badly needed if the recommendations of the Royal Commission on Local Government are acted upon, for education authorities will become larger and more remote from their schools. Every secondary school should have its own governing body. The relationships of the governing body with the head and staff of a school on the one hand and the local education authority on the other are subtly changed when that governing body is composed of people who are not only of high ability but are directly associated with the school and dedicated to it. The governing body should include representatives of parents of the pupils in the school. It should take formal steps to ensure that representatives of the teachers are properly associated with it, for example through executive sub-committees, in the process of discussion and decision. Some of us would wish to go further and recommend that representatives of teachers, being themselves serving teachers in the school, should be full members of the governing body. Governors of maintained schools must clearly include representatives of the local authority—

not necessarily those who have given the longest political service nor, in all cases, members of the Education Committee. Other interests from which representatives could be drawn are local establishments of higher or further education (a university, colleges of education, technical colleges and colleges of further education), trade unions and employers, district councils and the primary or middle schools from which pupils come. Some people should be appointed who have wide experience in education but represent no organisation or interest at all. In the case of voluntary schools any extension of the interests represented must be arranged by agreement between the authority and the foundation in ways which avoid upsetting the proportions of local authority and foundation governors laid down in the Education Act of 1944.

Responsibilities of the Head

313. The division of responsibilities between the head and the governors must be flexible to suit the needs of different personalities, capabilities and local circumstances. But there are certain fixed points. The head (often in co-operation with the heads of other schools) must decide on academic matters—on what is taught and how it is taught—being guided by his teaching staff, current educational thinking, the advice of H.M. Inspectors and the local education authority's professional advisers. He should be responsible for the appointment and deployment of staff within the establishment approved by the authority, taking advantage of the advice and expertise available to him among local education authority officers, governors and his senior staff. He must be responsible for discipline in the school and have the power to suspend pupils, subject to some provision for appeals. Many other powers and duties should normally be delegated to the head by the governors, subject to their general oversight. He should have the right to attend throughout every meeting of his governors unless excluded for good reasons.

Full Grant Schools

314. The proposals of this Chapter relate to all maintained secondary schools. They would thus apply as they now stand to any school at present receiving direct grant which became (for instance under Scheme B) a locally maintained school. If the alternative scheme proposed in this Report were adopted (Scheme A) and schools now receiving direct grant were administered through a School Grants Committee, the proposals of the present Chapter would also apply in principle, though their application would differ in practice. The schools would have to co-operate equally closely with local authorities in determining their place within a local comprehensive system. Policies for the admission of pupils, the age range to be covered, links with other schools, the phasing and timing of integration—every aspect of the function of the schools—would be agreed with the authorities concerned. But within the context of this agreement the schools would be accountable for the use of their resources to the School Grants Committee. We hope they would also be given the opportunity of using the local authority's technical, advisory, bulk purchasing and other services.

Conclusion

315. Direct grant schools coming into either of the schemes proposed in Chapter 9 will need new instruments and articles of government. We have set out

the principles on which these documents should be based. But, under our central and local scheme alike, some of the most important features of the relationships between authorities, governors and heads cannot be embodied in a legal document. They depend on mutual trust and respect. The law cannot create a harmonious partnership but it can create circumstances which will foster good relationships. We think our proposals will help to achieve that.

316. The schools in our terms of reference which participate in reorganisation schemes will have the opportunity of discussing the responsibilities and powers of their governors and heads with the authorities before entering a new contract, and the right to appeal to the Secretary of State who should act as final arbiter of these agreements if they are dissatisfied with the terms they are offered. We hope they will make good use of these opportunities to maintain their essential freedoms. These are freedoms to which every school should be entitled. We therefore recommend that the Secretary of State should issue to local education authorities a memorandum of guidance on the government of schools, incorporating the principles outlined in this Chapter. If such a memorandum were issued as soon as possible it would be a helpful preliminary to negotiation with the present direct grant schools. More important still, we suggest that the authorities review their procedures, attitudes and day to day practices and consider whether they accord with the general principles set out in this Chapter.

CHAPTER 11

Independent Day Schools

317. We turn now to the wholly independent day schools. We shall concentrate on the secondary schools. That is not because the primary schools are unimportant but because the primary schools have recently been considered by the Central Advisory Councils for Education,[1] and the work they do depends so heavily on the needs of the independent secondary schools that it is now more important to clarify the role of the latter.

318. The secondary schools, as we showed in Chapter 5, are an exceedingly varied group, including small schools with a local clientele and an uncertain future, a few larger schools with academic standards unsurpassed anywhere in the country, a number of denominational schools, some schools which cater for those with special talents, and many other types. Some have long had close relationships with the State system, taking children nominated and paid for by the local authorities; many have no such links. Some offer boarding as well as day education; most do not. In short, they defy generalisation.

319. Our recommendations about the policies which the Government should adopt towards these schools are derived from principles upon which we are unanimous. The rights of voluntary bodies to provide, and of parents to pay for, private education that is recognised by the State as efficient should not be abridged by law. Independent schools should wherever possible be encouraged to participate in the reorganisation of secondary education in the ways proposed for direct grant schools in Chapters 7 and 9. It follows that the purchase of places in independent schools must not be used to perpetuate academic selection or to frustrate comprehensive reorganisation. Local education authorities should be allowed to use places in independent schools to meet special needs which would otherwise remain unsatisfied; but independent schools wishing to confine their partnership with the maintained schools to the provision of places for abler pupils only should not be supported by public funds.

320. These recommendations are linked to each other and to the argument of our previous chapters. We want as far as possible to avoid the division of secondary education into academically and socially distinctive sectors and therefore we recommend that the proposals made in Chapter 9 for direct grant schools should also apply to independent schools. An independent sector will remain. We believe that only compulsion would prevent its continuation and we have rejected this alternative. But if local education authorities were to take up places at independent schools on an academically selective basis, comprehensive reorganisation would be hindered and there would be less incentive for independent and direct grant schools to enter into the full partnership which we regard as essential. It is for these reasons that we propose that local authorities should take up places at independent schools solely in order to meet special needs that

---

[1] "Children and their Primary Schools" H.M.S.O. 1967. "Primary Education in Wales" H.M.S.O. 1967.

the full grant or maintained schoo███ ███ ███ld be drawn up for meeting those needs within th███ ███ ███sible, either by building new schools or by en███ ███ ███to become full grant or maintained schools.

Present Prospects for the Schoo███

321. As we showed in Chapt███ ███ ███le have for many years been losing grou███ ███ ███numerical terms. But that does not mean███ ███ ███nction. The numbers of schools which are ███ ███ ███ers of pupils in them, have not greatly c███ ███ ███in the best known of the independen███ ███ ███they must compete both with the in███ ███ ███maintained day schools, the independe███ ███ ███their standing must continually improve t███ ███ ███Some are clearly capable of meeting this challe███

322. The future of the indepe███ ███ ███e forecast: it depends on too many unpredictable███ ███ ███exposed to growing competition from the maintaine███ ███ ███oosing between the two systems will no longer be deterred by anxieties that their children may find themselves in one of those secondary modern schools which can offer only scant opportunities for an education extending beyond the minimum school leaving age. But others who would only be satisfied with a selective grammar school may prefer to pay for places at independent schools rather than rely on comprehensive education. The balance between these conflicting influences will depend largely on the conviction with which reorganisation is carried through, and the resources put into the reorganised system. The continually rising costs of education may persuade more parents to use maintained or full grant schools free of charge. Changes in the tax treatment of income and wealth devoted in various ways to the payment of school fees, and demands by the State for a growing contribution from students and their parents to the costs of higher education—all these are possibilities which could increase the economic pressures on independent schools. Social influences must also be considered: changes in the size of families, apparently operating in different directions in different social classes; changes in the academic standards demanded of education for girls, and in attitudes to co-education; changes in the distribution of real, post-tax incomes, and in class distinctions and social relationships—these and other factors will play a part in the story.

323. Our guess—and it can be no better than a guess—is that under present arrangements the independent schools' contribution to secondary education will continue to fall, both in the proportion of the age group educated in these schools, and—even more sharply, as the numbers of pupils staying at maintained schools beyond the age of 15 increase—in the proportion of the whole secondary system that remains under independent management. The number of recognised schools may not change for a long time to come. If no action is taken on the Commission's First Report, boarding schools may lose ground to day schools, and the less famous boarding schools may increasingly meet the special needs of children who for various reasons require a boarding education. The most famous independent schools will continue to thrive, and places in the strongest day schools in a few of the biggest cities will be in particularly keen demand. If we

are right, this prospect may encourage the more successful independent day schools, like some of the strongest direct grant schools they resemble, to choose independence at all costs, reluctantly shedding such links as they may have with the maintained schools. But, if our guesses about the future are right, they should first reflect that independent schools will never again be so prominent in the whole system of secondary education, or be in a position to contribute so much to it. As a group, they are dwindling in numbers and in influence. If they are to participate in the development of the national system, now is the time.

What the Schools Can Offer

324. The schools discussed in the Commission's First Report provide boarding education which is only available on a small scale within the maintained system. "Boarding need" constitutes a humanly acceptable and administratively feasible criterion for choosing the pupils to go to them and, although the schools could not meet the country's entire potential needs for boarding education, they could go a long way towards achieving that—and in ways that would probably be more effective and would certainly be more economical than the creation of a complete national system of maintained boarding schools. The independent day schools are in a different position: what most of them provide is already offered by the local education authorities. To bring assisted pupils into schools which still have fee-payers is a sound arrangement for boarding schools because they can cater more satisfactorily for children in need of boarding if they have other children as well. But such an arrangement for day schools cannot be reconciled with the aims of a comprehensive system as we explain in Chapter 8. Thus independent day schools cannot be integrated with the maintained schools on a footing similar to that we proposed for boarding schools—that is to say, with a proportion of assisted places. Some, we hope, will become full grant or maintained schools. Some will provide special services not available in these schools. And the help of some will be needed to alleviate shortages of places in maintained schools.

OUR PROPOSALS

Participation

325. A number of independent day schools already have a close relationship with the maintained sector and offer substantial proportions of their places to pupils paid for by local education authorities. They are much like direct grant schools. Others might be prepared to enter into a closer relationship if the terms on which they could do so were favourable. All independent secondary schools should be invited to participate in comprehensive schemes on terms similar to those we propose for direct grant schools. The only difference we propose is that any debts they may be carrying should not be met from public funds unless the schools become voluntary controlled schools.[1] The reasons which led us to suggest that the direct grant schools' debts should be eligible for grant from public funds do not apply to the independent schools. Where, however, the

---

[1] If the school becomes a voluntary controlled school approved loan charges may be met by the local education authority as part of the cost of maintaining the school.

Secretary of State regarded it as particularly desirable that the offer of an independent school to take on full grant or voluntary aided status should be accepted, and the school's capital resources were insufficient to meet its debts in the absence of fee income, we should not be opposed to the balance of the debts being met from public funds. Whether a particular independent school can play a part in the comprehensive plans of its local education authority and just what that part should be must depend on that authority's needs and be subject to the Secretary of State's approval. Independent schools can be given no prescriptive rights in this respect. For some, as for some of the maintained schools, participation will be precluded by their small size and lack of resources, or the plans already made for maintained schools may make the role proposed by the school impracticable, or there may be a temporary surplus of maintained school places. Nevertheless we are confident that, with good will on both sides, most of those who wish to participate could fulfil a useful role within the authorities' plans.

326. Many of the independent schools have preparatory schools or departments and there are many other preparatory schools not linked with particular secondary schools. It is already open to these to apply to become voluntary schools, either controlled or aided. If the proportion of all children who attend independent secondary schools continues to decline, if the maintained primary schools continue to improve and competition for grammar school places becomes a thing of the past, the independent primary schools may well find that voluntary status becomes a more attractive proposition. We would not wish to make full grant status (under Scheme A of Chapter 9) available to primary schools. The considerations which led to that proposal do not apply to primary schools and administrative difficulties would arise if too many schools were to come into the scheme.

327. In Chapter 14, a minority of us propose that there should be a small number of super-selective schools, financed on a full grant basis. This role would be open not only to direct grant and maintained schools but also to independent schools which were prepared to give up charging fees[1]. The Government will have to reach final decisions on this proposal as soon as possible. If it decides to keep and develop such super-selective schools it should state which independent schools it considers could fulfil such a role. If this is not done promptly, it will be difficult for some at least of the schools to enter into negotiations about comprehensive reorganisation with any real sense of purpose.

Schools Remaining Independent

328. Some independent schools will be unwilling or unable to enter into the close partnership with the State entailed in full grant or maintained status. For them there should henceforth be a clearer and nationally agreed policy so that they may know where they stand and what help the State may ask of them.

329. At present, local education authorities have a duty under Section 6 of the Education Act, 1953, to pay the whole of the fees of children attending independent schools who are receiving an education suitable to their age, ability and aptitude which cannot be provided in a maintained school because of a shortage of places. The authorities also have the power to assist (in accordance

---

[1] But see paragraphs 229 to 233.

with a parental income scale) with the fees of children attending independent schools under Section 81(b) of the Education Act, 1944. The Act provides that such arrangements should be subject to the approval of the Secretary of State for Education and Science. In practice, since 1959 when general grant was introduced, the Secretary of State has given a blanket approval to all such arrangements and no longer requires authorities' arrangements to be submitted to him. Authorities interpret the legal requirements and use their discretionary powers in different ways and we believe clearer and more uniform principles should be applied by all authorities. The simplest way to ensure this would be for the Secretary of State to set out clear guidelines for local authorities. If authorities wish to make additional arrangements which depart from these guidelines, they should submit them for his approval. We are not suggesting that individual cases should be referred to him; only that the general lines of policy should be agreed.

330. We think these are the principles which should be observed:

(i) The fees of pupils attending schools not recognised as efficient should not be paid in full or in part by authorities.

(ii) Where a child's aptitude requires a particular kind of educational provision not available in an accessible maintained school or college of further education, the authority should pay the full fees. We think however that the Secretary of State and the local authority organisations should together investigate the interpretation to be put on this requirement to see that a more uniform policy is adopted. It seems to us unsatisfactory, for example, that a child who excels at ballet may in one area have his or her fees at a ballet school paid by the local education authority, whereas in another assistance may be related to parental income, and in another the authority may refuse to give any assistance.

(iii) Where there are not enough places in full grant or maintained schools to meet the needs of children whose parents want them to go to these schools, the local education authority must be able to take up places at independent schools which are willing to co-operate in this respect. But the Secretary of State should require the authority to make plans which will render this expedient unnecessary, either through reaching agreement with an independent school that it should take its place in the local educational system as a full grant or maintained school, or through building more maintained school places. If the latter course is necessary the Secretary of State should allow for these places when approving future building programmes. How soon this can be achieved will depend on the resources the Government can devote to the purpose.

(iv) Local education authorities should retain their present powers to enable pupils to attend independent denominational schools, provided places are not available in accessible maintained denominational schools, and provided the progress of comprehensive reorganisation is not hindered.

(v) Local education authorities should continue to have discretion to assist with the fees of children, already at independent schools, whose fees had in the past been paid by parents but whose financial circumstances have so changed that unless assisted their education would be disrupted.

(vi) Local education authorities provide special educational treatment for children requiring it. We have no wish to interfere with these arrangements and nothing we say should be taken as applying to such pupils. In addition there may be children, without disabilities serious enough to be classed as requiring special educational treatment, who for physical or psychological reasons would especially benefit from education at particular independent schools rather than the maintained schools available to them. In such cases, authorities should continue to have discretion to assist with their fees, taking account of parental income.

331. Pupils already holding free or assisted places in independent schools must not have their careers disrupted, and should complete their schooling on the terms already offered to them. The principles set out above should therefore apply to pupils not yet receiving financial help.

332. There are wide variations in the income scales now used for assisted places in day schools. Policy and practice should be more uniform so that parents can more readily discover their rights. We suggest that the Secretary of State and the local authority organisations should study this question and recommend a suitable standard income scale for determining parental contributions where assistance is given to day pupils at independent schools.

333. These proposals would lead to some tightening of the constraints imposed by the central government on some local education authorities in their dealings with independent schools—though they would also extend the use that other authorities make of these schools. We should justify any new restriction to be imposed on democratically elected local authorities. The arguments are partly educational and partly economic.

334. We explained in Chapter 7 that the reorganisation of secondary education now in progress must improve and extend the opportunities of all children and postpone to as late an age as possible the point at which irrevocable decisions are made about their future. This calls not simply for the creation of a new kind of school, labelled "comprehensive", but for the reorganisation of a whole system in ways which differentiate wisely between children's needs and aptitudes within schools but avoid the segregation of children by ability, aspiration or social class between different kinds of school or distinct departments of schools. All this will be impossible to achieve if pupils are selected for some schools partly because of the ability or willingness of their parents to pay fees. The evidence we have seen[1] of the social and intellectual segregation of children which results from the assistance of pupils at independent day schools suggests that such arrangements are as liable to frustrate comprehensive reorganisation and to impoverish the maintained schools as are the arrangements made for sending children to direct grant schools. It would be unfair and inconsistent to treat the two categories of school differently, and it would deter schools from entering the new arrangements we propose to enable them to participate in reorganisation if public money was still to be spent on pupils attending socially or intellectually selective independent schools.

335. Local education authorities which now send children to independent schools sometimes have places in their own schools available at a marginal cost well below the fees paid at independent schools. For example, sixth form pupils can often be found a place in existing groups without extra staff, accommodation or major items of equipment. Those authorities without sufficient places

---

[1] E.g. the study of the inter-relationship between the State school system and private schools in Middlesex submitted to us as evidence by Miss R. Saran in 1967.

in their own schools may make short-run savings by using independent schools, but the course of action we propose would soon prove more economical for them. How soon these savings would be achieved cannot be exactly forecast, but the following estimates show that it need not take long.

336. There are at the moment some 19,000 fully assisted and 2,000 partly assisted day pupils in independent schools.[1] About 60 per cent of each are in Catholic schools, and our proposals will not have any significant financial effect on the costs of educating these children. Of the remaining pupils in non-Catholic independent schools, some 7,000 are fully assisted. We cannot say with certainty how many of the pupils paid for by local education authorities would under our proposals still go to independent schools if their parents paid full fees. If 2,000 did, it would provide a saving of approximately £400,000 a year at an estimated average annual fee of £200. There are far fewer partly assisted pupils, and their numbers are unlikely to change sufficiently to make an appreciable financial difference. There might thus be 5,000 pupils, whose fees would have been paid in full at independent schools under the present arrangements, who would in future be accommodated in maintained schools. The difference in current costs for such pupils in maintained schools would be small; but some capital expenditure would be necessary to accommodate them. At the most, if new places had to be provided for all of them, capital expenditure of about £2·5 million would be needed. The annual repayments on a loan of this size over twenty years would be £274,000. In practice, places could be found for a number of the pupils without new building. Moreover, under our proposals some of the independent schools would become full grant or maintained schools, and this would reduce the amount of new building required to provide maintained school places. Thus the capital expenditure attributable to a reduction in the take-up of free places at independent schools (something under £2·5 million) might be recovered by savings on current expenditure (of perhaps £400,000 a year) in a comparatively short period of time.

Conclusion

337. Our proposals may at first appear severe to independent day schools which have been prepared to offer many of their places to children whose fees are paid by the local education authorities. But we hope that schools with the most important contribution to make will find these proposals offer them a way of entering the comprehensive system and playing a valuable part in it. Those which prefer to remain wholly independent succeed in doing this only by offering something which differs—in the eyes of parents, at least—from the education offered by maintained schools. Where their distinctive contribution is of a kind that is needed and cannot be provided through the full grant or maintained schools, we hope the local authorities will make full use of it. Where it is not, there can in the longer run be no case for continued public expenditure on places at these schools.

---

[1] See Volume II, Appendix 6, Section 4.

12

CHAPTER 12

Direct Grant Boarding Schools

338. We have presented our proposals for the direct grant and independent day schools but have still to consider the direct grant boarding schools. There are 63 direct grant schools with some boarding pupils. Some have only a few boarders and are akin to the day schools. For the purposes of our proposals we distinguish between the schools with less than a quarter of their pupils boarding, which we shall regard as day schools, and those with a quarter or more. There are 33 direct grant schools with some boarders but with less than a quarter of the pupils in their upper schools boarding. They contain 2,260 boarding places—accommodation which the country can ill afford to lose. However, they are mainly day schools, operating in a local context, and we therefore apply to them the proposals we make in Chapter 9 for day schools. In this Chapter, we are mainly concerned with the 30 schools (23 for boys and 7 for girls) in which at least a quarter of the pupils in the upper schools are boarders. These are the schools we mean when we refer in this Chapter to boarding schools. Between them they provide 6,427 boarding places (making a total of 8,687 boarders in direct grant schools as a whole).

339. The possibilities open to a direct grant boarding school will depend upon whether the proposals in the Commission's First Report are adopted, and whether Scheme A or Scheme B of the present Report is adopted. If the First Report's recommendations about independent boarding schools are implemented, suitable arrangements will be available for the integration of boarding schools at present receiving direct grant, whether they go independent or not. If those recommendations are not implemented, no special arrangements will be available for schools which go independent. But for schools that do not go independent, suitable arrangements will be available if either Scheme A or Scheme B of the present Report is adopted. These possibilities are spelled out in detail in paragraph 355.

Need and Provision

340. In Chapter 7 of the Commission's First Report it was estimated that there would be a need for boarding education, coupled with a demand for it from parents, for about 63,000 children in 1970 and about 80,000 children in 1980. Dr. Lambert's Research Unit into Boarding Education, using different methods, arrived at similar totals.

341. In 1967 there were 152,000 boarders in schools in England and Wales. Of these, 35,500 were wholly or partly assisted by public funds: 19,000 in independent schools recognised as efficient, 11,000 in maintained schools, 4,000 in direct grant schools, and 1,500 in unrecognised schools. This in brief outline is the statistical picture of boarding education presented in greater detail in the First Report.

342. Thus from their relatively slender resources the direct grant schools are already making a major contribution to meeting the country's boarding needs. Although they provide only some 6 per cent of the country's boarding places, they provide more than 11 per cent of the assisted boarding places. About 45 per cent of their boarders are assisted and therefore have some officially recognised need for boarding education. These schools have thus gone a long way towards the sort of integration proposed in the First Report.

343. Can they go further still? There are limits to what they can do. The number of places they can offer now and for the foreseeable future is fairly small. Most of them are relatively small grammar schools and therefore unable to cover the whole range of ability for which boarding education is needed. It is more difficult for boarding schools than for day schools to expand or change their age range. They can best meet boarding needs if the proportion of their boarders in need of this form of education (i.e. need as defined in paragraphs 156 and 157 of the First Report) does not exceed about two-thirds of all boarders.[1] In fully maintained boarding schools, 30 per cent of the pupils have no officially recognised need for boarding education, and this policy was endorsed in the First Report which said that "filling all boarding places in maintained and direct grant boarding schools with pupils in need" would be "educationally unsound".[2]

The Recommendations of the First Report

344. The First Report proposed that wholly independent boarding schools capable of playing a part in meeting the country's boarding needs should as soon as possible make at least half their places available to children from maintained schools who need boarding education. A Boarding Schools Corporation would be responsible for setting up and administering this scheme with the help of the local education authorities and the independent boarding schools. Most schools should admit children from a wider range of abilities than they now take. A few are large enough to become comprehensive, and most of the rest should extend the ability range of their intake to include pupils of an ability level corresponding with that required for courses leading to the Certificate of Secondary Education. It was also suggested that for schools wishing to enter the maintained system a new form of nationally aided status, supported by the central government, should be considered.

345. For Britain as a whole, these proposals would in time provide 47,000 places in independent schools to meet boarding needs (45,000 in England and Wales). About 38,000 of these would be in secondary schools. Children taking these places would have free tuition, but their parents would pay a boarding fee according to an income scale which would be similar at the lower levels of income to that used for university education but more severe at the upper end of the scale.

346. Alongside this potential contribution from independent schools there are the 11,000 places in maintained boarding schools. All pupils in these schools

---

[1] The proportion of children in need of boarding education who can effectively be helped in a given school depends greatly on the different types of need represented. This suggested guide cannot be regarded as more than a very rough rule of thumb.

[2] The First Report, paragraph 214

receive free tuition. If the local education authority consider pupils cannot get an education suited to their age, ability and aptitude except by boarding they also receive free board and lodging. Boarding fees based on various income scales devised by the authorities are payable by the parents of all the other boarding pupils in the schools. Authorities vary in their intepretation of this distinction and there are many boarders in maintained schools whose parents pay fees according to an income scale although they fall into the categories of need outlined in the First Report.

OUR PROPOSALS

Integrated Independent Schools

347. If the scheme proposed in the First Report is implemented, it will be open to a direct grant boarding school to become an integrated independent school of the kind recommended in that Report. At least half its boarders would be selected on grounds of boarding need. These children would be drawn from the wider range of ability proposed in that Report, would get free tuition and pay a boarding fee which would depend on their parents' incomes. The school's fees would be paid by the Boarding Schools Corporation (or School Grants Committee) which would recover these payments from parents and local authorities. The authorities would contribute under one of the two pooling arrangements proposed in the First Report. Other boarding pupils would pay fees in the normal way without assistance. The arrangements for taking day pupils paid for by the local education authority would be worked out between the authority and the school and be subject to approval by the Secretary of State. These arrangements would be considered by the Boarding Schools Corporation (or School Grants Committee) and taken into account when assessing the schools' proposals for integration.

348. Many of the direct grant and independent boarding schools have day places. If the schools become integrated independent schools, the arrangements for filling these places would have to be taken into account when schemes of integration are approved. To ensure that the purposes of integration envisaged in the First Report are not frustrated, local education authorities should be encouraged to take up day places at these schools. These places should, if possible, be filled by pupils drawn from at least as broad a social and intellectual range as the assisted boarding pupils.

Full Grant Schools

349. The First Report recommended that serious consideration be given to a form of national aided status for boarding schools. Those of us who support Scheme A in Chapter 9 see full grant status as the natural development of that original concept—modified, and spelled out in much greater detail. The First Report's Boarding Schools Corporation would become the School Grants Committee and take on the functions outlined in Chapter 9. At least a half but (unless the school decided to go further) not more than two-thirds of their boarding pupils would then be selected on grounds of boarding need as defined in the First Report. The day pupils in these boarding schools would be selected under arrangements that accord with local needs for secondary education as explained in Chapter 9. Boarding pupils should so far as possible be drawn from a similar intellectual and social range.

350. As in the locally maintained schools, tuition would be free for all pupils. For pupils who can only get a suitable education by boarding, no parental contribution would be required. But the parents of other pupils would contribute according to the income scale proposed in the First Report. The cost of the schools would be met by the School Grants Committee (taking foundation income into account). The Committee would recover its costs in respect of boarding pupils from local education authorities by means of one of the two pooling systems proposed in the First Report for pupils at integrated independent schools.

351. The pooling of local authority contributions under this scheme is a departure from the present procedures under which each authority contributes only for pupils drawn from its own area, except for pupils classed as not belonging to the area of any particular authority. This departure is justified because boarding needs are unevenly distributed across the country (being particularly heavy in sparsely populated areas and in areas with a mobile population, for example) and because the payment for many children (e.g. those who cannot be allocated to any particular authority or those whose parents move after they have started at boarding school) must in any case be pooled. The First Report explained why a special system is needed for the scheme proposed for independent boarding schools. Our proposals for direct grant schools should not lead to the creation of yet another system for financing boarding education.

Locally Maintained Status

352. There are already 151 maintained schools with boarding pupils. It should be open to direct grant schools with boarders to apply for maintained status—such as voluntary aided or voluntary controlled status—under the terms of Scheme B described in Chapter 9, and those of us who favour Scheme B believe this to be the best solution for these schools. Their boarding sections would operate like those of other schools of this kind; the maintaining authority should offer places in these schools to children from other authorities. Under the present arrangements, tuition is free for all pupils. No boarding fees are charged for children with officially recognised boarding needs but all other children are charged boarding fees according to the authority's parental income scale.

353. We do not propose any change in the framework of these arrangements. However, local education authorities should standardise the exceedingly varied procedures they now use for determining boarding fees at their schools and we consider that the income scale used for determining contributions from parents should be nationally uniform. The criteria for distinguishing between pupils whose need for boarding education is sufficiently clear to call for no parental contribution and those for whom a contribution is required should also be standardised. The details of the policies for the admission of pupils should be negotiated between local authorities and the schools, but the underlying principles should be the same throughout the country so that parents should have equal rights wherever they live and may know those rights with greater certainty.

Mainly Day Schools

354. There remain the thirty-three direct grant schools whose boarders amount to less than 25 per cent of their total numbers. These should be treated as day schools. By this we mean that the future role and status of each school should be

determined within the framework set out in Chapters 7 and 9. If the proposal set out in Scheme A is accepted, all boarding pupils in full grant schools would receive free tuition; the School Grants Committee would pay the boarding fees of those who could not get a suitable education without boarding, and would assess the parental contribution to the boarding fees of other pupils by an income scale. The pupils would be selected on the basis outlined in paragraph 349. If, on the other hand, a school were to become a locally maintained school, the local education authority would normally maintain the boarding as well as the teaching accommodation and the arrangements for admission of pupils to boarding places would be broadly the same as for other maintained schools with boarding places which we have described above.

Conclusion

355. The range of possibilities available under the various assumptions we have mentioned may be drawn together as follows. For a school which decides to go independent, there would be, if the First Report were implemented, the option of becoming an "integrated" school within the terms of that Report. If the First Report is not implemented, there will of course be no such option, and a school going independent will find its own way in the market. For a school which does not go independent, a national aided status would be available if the First Report is implemented, or if Scheme A of the present Report is adopted. The First Report suggested such a status for schools wishing to enter the maintained system, and Scheme A of the present Report offers something that comes to the same thing (see paragraph 349). If, lastly, the First Report is not implemented, and Scheme B of the present Report is adopted, then the status available for a school not going independent will be that of a locally maintained boarding school, as described in paragraph 352, with its recruitment from outside the area of the maintaining authority secured by inter-authority arrangements.

CHAPTER 13

The Cost of Our Recommendations

356. How much will our proposals cost? This is an unusually difficult question, partly because the outcome will depend upon the response of individual schools to our recommendations, and partly because we are concerned not only with the abolition of fee-paying but with the adaptation of the schools for a comprehensive role.

357. It will help to distinguish at the outset the different aspects of cost with which we are concerned. First, what is the total cost to public funds of the proposals in this Report? Second, what effect will these changes have upon the total resources used for education—the economic cost? In a system which is partly financed from public funds and partly from fees, the economic cost may be very different from the cost to public funds. Throughout this Chapter we are concerned with the cost of *change*, not with the average sums of money at present spent on pupils in different types of school. These are described in some detail in Appendix 7.

The Cost to Public Funds

358. Some of the organisations which submitted evidence to the Commission argued that the direct grant schools saved public money. This argument suggests that to end the direct grant system will increase the cost to public funds. Others argued that the system involved an unnecessary subsidy to middle-class parents. This suggests that to end the system will result in a saving to public funds. In practice either result is possible, depending on the answers to two questions. First, how many schools will choose to become independent or close rather than participate as non-fee-charging schools in a comprehensive system? Second, how many parents will choose to pay fees at independent schools rather than send their children to the reorganised ex-direct grant schools? Since this immediately brings us into the realms of speculation it would be wise to consider first the theoretical limits of expenditure that could be involved. In the financial year 1969-70 the total tuition costs of the upper schools are estimated to amount to about £22 million. Of this, parents will meet about £5·2 million by paying fees. Under both the schemes outlined in Chapter 9 fee-paying would end. The running costs of the schools would have to be met jointly by the taxpayer and the ratepayer under either scheme. If *all* opted to become full grant institutions under Scheme A or *all* schools opted to become maintained schools under Scheme B, there would be an extra annual cost to public funds of about £5·2 million. On the boarding side, some parents would pay boarding fees according to means and others would not pay anything. Taking into account the fact that 4,259 boarders out of 8,687 are already being assisted from public funds it is estimated that the maximum additional annual expenditure would be £0·6 million. For former direct grant schools, tuition and boarding costs together

167

would therefore add a maximum of about £5·8 million a year to public expenditure if all the schools and parents participated.

359. But it was clear from replies which heads and governing bodies gave to our questionnaires and from visits we made to individual schools that some direct grant schools will not wish to abandon academic selection or fee-paying, and that they could and would become independent schools rather than do so.

360. If a direct grant school becomes independent and manages to fill roughly the same number of places, there will have been a net increase in the independent sector, unless its pupils are drawn from other independent schools. If the independent sector is enlarged by the numbers of former direct grant places brought into it, then the burden on public funds will have been correspondingly reduced. In order to arrive at a more realistic estimate of cost it is therefore necessary to make some assessment of how many schools might want and be able to become independent, and the net increase in the independent sector that would follow from their change of status. Whether or not a school has a real choice of becoming independent will depend on many factors, such as the reputation of the school, the present importance of parental fees as a source of income, the social class composition of the school, the size of the endowment funds backing the school, and the existence of other independent or potentially independent schools in the area. To guess at the numbers of schools which might become independent would be hazardous. The schools themselves will have to consider the question carefully and await the Government's decisions on our recommendations before they decide. We have therefore given in Table 30 four sets of estimates of cost or saving in current expenditure, on the assumptions that 75, 50, 25 or no schools go independent. These estimates are based on the costs of the particular schools thought most likely to go independent, taking account of the most relevant factors known to us.

361. Estimates of costs depend on other assumptions, in particular about the number of pupils who will go to the newly independent schools and the number who go to local authority schools. Some parents who would have sent their children to direct grant schools will not be able to afford to pay the full economic fees in independent schools. Many other parents will not want to do so. On the other hand, some parents who would have sent their children to a direct grant grammar school may prefer not to send them to a reorganised school if they can afford to pay fees. But if a direct grant school becomes independent it may attract pupils from other independent schools which may have to close or reduce in size. Some of these factors tend to cancel each other out. Since we are concerned to give an upper limit to the cost of our proposals, we have assumed that there would be no movement out of reorganised schools and have only considered the additional costs to local authorities of the net increase in pupils who might attend their schools. Where direct grant schools go independent, it was assumed that local authorities would have to provide extra places roughly equivalent to the number of children at present in the schools who do not have a father in a professional or managerial occupation. Where their own schools were too overcrowded the authorities would either be forced to purchase places at the former direct grant schools or other independent schools, or would in the longer term provide new places in maintained schools.

Table 30

The Estimated Current Costs to Public Funds

	£ million 1969 prices			
	Assuming that the following number of direct grant schools become independent:			
	None	*25*	*50*	*75*
Annual Costs				
1. Replacing parental fees in schools going maintained (tuition only).	5·2	3·9	3·0	2·1
2. Extra provision in maintained schools (see paragraph 361)	–	1·0	1·7	2·3
3. Additional cost of meeting boarding fees net of parental contributions and aid to central government employees.	0·6	0·5	0·4	0·4
Total costs	5·8	5·4	5·1	4·8
Annual Savings				
The present contribution of public funds to schools going independent.	–	2·8	4·6	6·3
Net annual cost	5·8	2·6	0·5	–
Net annual saving	–	–	–	1·5

Source: Department of Education and Science.

362. Table 30 shows the minimum annual cost to public funds on various assumptions. As this Table indicates, if 75 schools were to become independent the saving to public funds would more than balance the costs. If 50 schools did so, then the cost would still be relatively insignificant.

363. So far we have only considered the costs of ending fee-paying in direct grant schools. There are also the costs of going comprehensive. There should be no extra current expenditure: a local authority is not expected to spend more, per pupil, on teachers and equipment when it reorganises its secondary schools. Equally the cost per pupil in reorganised direct grant schools would not be expected to rise. But most of the schools will need adaptation or enlargement or both.

Capital Expenditure

364. Capital expenditure therefore presents a different problem. The range of costs which may be incurred in reorganising a direct grant grammar school of average size (about 660 pupils) can be illustrated from the following examples which assume that existing buildings are adequate for their existing use.

13

Reorganisation envisaged for grammar school of 660 pupils	Approximate capital cost of:	
	adaptation	enlargement
1. Extended by 400 places to become a 6 form-entry school for pupils aged 11-18	£25,000	£200,000
2. Extended by 240 places to become a 6 form-entry school for pupils aged 11-16	£25,000	£100,000
3. No change in number of pupils: school converted to 16+ sixth form college	£50,000 to £100,000	–
4. No change in number of pupils: age range reduced to 13-18	£50,000	–

The cost of adaptation and enlargement will obviously vary greatly according to the condition and circumstances of each school and such estimates can only be very approximate.

365. The first two examples involve enlargements which, under present policies, would be permitted only if there was a need for additional places in the area. But, as we explained in Chapter 2, the number of pupils in maintained secondary schools is expected to increase from 2·9 million to some 4·2 million during the next decade and there is no doubt that such needs will arise in most parts of the country. The cost of enlargement cannot be attributed to our proposals: if the school was not enlarged, the local education authority would have to provide places on a similar scale elsewhere. The last two examples, which involve no increase in numbers show costs attributable to adaptation for reorganisation. If we adopt a figure of £50,000 per school and assume that all 178 schools participate, about £9 million would be spent on adaptation alone. In practice many of the schools would have to be enlarged, and that might reduce the costs of adaptation.

366. Some of the schools will also need improvement to bring them up to the standards prescribed for maintained schools. It is impossible to estimate how much this will cost. Hitherto the money needed to improve direct grant schools has come partly from private donations. In future, more of this expenditure may have to be found from public funds. Although the sums involved may be considerable for individual schools, the total will be small in comparison with the costs of accommodating a growing secondary school population during the coming years.

367. If the schools participate fully in the maintained system either as full grant institutions or as locally maintained schools their buildings would remain the property of the governing body so no question of compensation is raised. But most of the schools have capital debts. We have recommended that approved debts being met from fees should be met by the Department of Education and Science, taking into account the foundation funds available to the school. These debts amount to over £6 million. The cost of servicing them has already been accounted for in the current costs shown in Table 30. If the debts are liquidated by a capital payment the cost to public funds would be higher in the short term, but lower in the long term. Loan charges met from fees and grants at present amount to about £0·7 million per annum for the schools as a whole.

Economic Cost

368. So far we have been discussing changes in the financing of the schools, not

changes in the value of the resources they employ. The latter should be small. The Department of Education and Science already controls the level of expenditure in the schools. This ensures that on average the current resources devoted to these schools are not very different from those devoted to maintained grammar schools. The position so far as capital expenditure is concerned is difficult to forecast but in general (and apart from the costs of adaptation to a comprehensive role discussed earlier) there is no reason to suppose that any additional call on resources would arise when a school assumes full grant or maintained status.

Independent Schools

369. Thus far we have confined our discussions to direct grant schools. We hope that our proposals will bring more independent schools into full grant or maintained status. That will impose further costs on public funds. How much? That will depend on how many schools choose to participate in this way, how many of their pupils are already being supported by local authorities and how their change of status affects other independent schools in the area. It is not possible to estimate the sums involved.

The School Grants Committee

370. If Scheme A is adopted, the School Grants Committee will incur some administrative costs. The withdrawal of the present direct grants will reduce administration costs in the Department of Education and Science. The additional costs which are neither balanced by this saving nor already taken into account in the First Report's estimates of the costs of the Boarding Schools Corporation will be small.

Summary

371. In brief, the effect of our recommendations depends on how many schools become independent, how many become full grant or maintained schools, and what happens to the pupils who would otherwise have attended them. At the most, public current expenditure on the present direct grant schools would be increased by some £5·8 million per year. The cost would be less than this if some schools became independent or closed. If more than 50 schools became independent the costs would nearly be cancelled out by savings. Capital costs cannot be predicted but the element attributable to the Commission's recommendations (i.e. the cost of adaptations) should not exceed about £9 million even if all schools became full grant or maintained comprehensive schools. Repayments on a loan of this size over a period of twenty years amount to less than £1 million per year. The costs of our proposals for independent schools are even harder to forecast. They are likely to be much smaller than those attributable to our proposals for direct grant schools. The total public expenditure on secondary education in England and Wales will be about £550 million in the year 1969-70. We are therefore discussing figures equivalent to about one per cent of this sum. It is clear that the financial effect of our proposals is small, when compared with the importance of the educational and social issues involved.

CHAPTER 14

Educating the Most Gifted

372. Some of those who presented evidence to us will find it odd that we should postpone to this last Chapter our discussion of the education of the most gifted children: this, they believed, was the chief function and glory of the schools in our remit and the main question we had to deal with. The education of the most gifted children does indeed present some of the most important, urgent and difficult problems we have had to consider. But the task is one in which schools of all kinds should—and do—play a part. Specially gifted children and teachers are to be found in every type of school. The direct grant grammar schools and many of the independent day schools do excellent work, but we have no convincing evidence that they achieve better results than other schools with similar pupils. Neither does this group of schools, taken as a whole, have better qualified teachers, better facilities or larger sixth forms than are to be found in maintained schools of similar academic type and standing. The education of the gifted poses important problems, but they are not problems which are being dealt with or can in future be resolved only by the schools in our terms of reference. These are our first conclusions.

373. We also agree that there should be a few schools—schools maintained by the State in the ways we have proposed, and independent schools used by local authorities for free place or assisted pupils—which specialise in teaching children particularly gifted in one or more of the arts, particularly in music or ballet. Outstanding performance in these fields calls for an early start and special teaching skills.

374. Most of us are convinced that children with exceptional gifts of a more general academic kind should be educated along with their less able contemporaries within a comprehensive system—both for their own sake, and for the sake of other children. There they will need better opportunities and more skilled teaching than some comprehensive schools are yet able to provide, and steps must be taken to give them what they need. Whatever system of education is adopted, however, we all agree that further research and experiment is required to ensure that the talents of the most gifted are not wasted. Too little is known about these difficult questions.

375. A minority of us wish to preserve and develop a small number of highly selective schools, covering the normal secondary age range and taking children from about the top two per cent of the ability range. These schools would be drawn from the maintained, direct grant and independent sectors. Henceforth none would take fee-payers. All would be maintained by the central government through the School Grants Committee first proposed by some of us in Chapter 9 of this Report. When we know more about the needs of the most gifted and have gained more experience of teaching them under different systems, these members of the Commission believe that either this experiment of "super-selective" schools should be extended to cover the whole country, or the schools should assume another role.

172

376. These are the main conclusions of this Chapter. They are explained more fully, with the evidence on which they rest, in the pages that follow.

Who Are the Gifted?

377. How can gifted children be enabled to develop their full potential? The first difficulty with which we were faced, was one of definition. What we were looking for were children capable of achieving great things after they leave school. Can such predictions be made? Subject examinations are affected by the child's home background and the success or failure of his previous teaching. Rating by teachers is also influenced by factors not directly related to a child's ability. Both are even less successful in predicting future academic achievements than intelligence tests. Yet these tests are only an uncertain and approximate measure of some aspects of a child's capabilities. Originality, creativity and flexibility of thought are aspects of ability not measured satisfactorily by conventional intelligence tests.

378. Even if methods could be devised to measure the many different facets of ability, we would then have to decide just what proportion of the population should be classed as gifted. Definitions range from 5 per cent to one half per cent or even less. In terms of I.Q. scores this would amount to a range from 125+ to 140+. For the purposes of this analysis we shall take pupils in the top two per cent of the ability range as those with whom we are particularly concerned. But it should be remembered that many who discuss the questions are concerned with the top half per cent or less.

379. At the extreme upper end of the ability range, testing becomes more than usually hazardous: indeed, the reliability of the tests decreases at both extremes of ability. For gifted eleven-year-olds special tests would be required, more like those normally used for 13 or 14-year-old children. These would not be the kind most children are used to and special coaching could distort the results.

380. Moreover, factors of interest, motivation and personality determine the degree to which that potential is realised and the manner and slant of the achievement. Many psychologists claim that beyond a minimum threshold level of intelligence, achievement increasingly becomes a function of interest and motivation. Thus, to ensure that all those who were likely to achieve highly in later life were included, one might have to cast the net so widely as to include a majority who would not be classed as gifted by anybody. Alternatively one might have to wait until the age of 15 or later, when other factors can be more clearly described.

381. Longitudinal studies of the careers of the gifted appear to bear out these conclusions. A monumental study of this kind has been carried out by Terman and his associates in America who have for over forty years followed the fortunes of 1,500 gifted Californian children identified by intelligence tests and other methods. A high I.Q. score did, indeed, seem to be required for high achievement, but the relationship between measured intelligence and achievement was far from perfect. For example, although more than 90 per cent of gifted boys and 86 per cent of gifted girls entered colleges, thirty per cent of them failed to graduate. Terman's sample yielded many eminent people whose names were included in such directories as "American Men of Science", but it also yielded many solid citizens who were in no way remarkable. Forty-five per cent entered the professions, twenty-two per cent the semi-professions and

business, and six per cent skilled manual and clerical occupations. Variations in achievement were related to character traits and dimensions of the children's social background and experience.

The Experience of Other Countries

382. Identification and selection techniques may improve. If so, we must next decide how best to educate the gifted children so selected. Should they be separated into schools concentrating on gifted children only, or should they be given special treatment within the general framework of comprehensive schools? We considered the experience of other countries.

383. Most European societies have had élite secondary schools, academically (and thus, to some extent, socially) selective, admitting around 20 per cent of the population between the ages of ten and twelve. Streaming within these schools created further differentiation and the gifted children collected in top streams of selective schools. The difference between their needs and those of other children in the teaching group was not considered large enough to create teaching problems. But they, or the less able children in selective schools, may not have been given the special attention they needed.

384. With widespread recognition of the disadvantages of selection and the introduction of comprehensive education has come an increasing awareness that the most gifted need exceptional and individual treatment. In Sweden, the country which has made more radical efforts to introduce comprehensive secondary education than any other in Western Europe, there is no attempt to segregate the gifted at an early age, but there is increasing differentiation of courses in the later stages of their school careers, and further education after school is designed to find and develop their special gifts. Attention is turning away from the structure of the educational system to the methods of instruction used within schools and classes. The hope is that by changing teaching methods, learning will become a more individual process.

385. In the U.S.S.R. and the U.S.A., basically comprehensive systems of education have provoked considerable thought about the needs of the exceptionally able. In Russia the standard educational unit is the neighbourhood-based 8-year comprehensive school (ending at about age 15 if no grades have been repeated). After the age of 15 there is provision for greater differentiation and specialisation. There are in addition some schools which give special attention to particular subjects—music, ballet, languages and mathematics—after the end of the first year of schooling. These still cater for the immediate neighbourhood before offering places on a wider basis: they are not highly selective academically. A few of the gifted are segregated into special highly selective schools, but that does not take place until the age of 15 or 16, after completion of the 8-year comprehensive school course. It applies only to children from rural areas who are exceptionally gifted in mathematics or physics; those successful in selection examinations go to the four University boarding schools in Moscow, Kiev, Leningrad and Novosibirsk. The U.S.S.R. still has a large rural population and their education must present special problems. Children gifted in other subjects, and all children in urban areas, pass through the normal post-comprehensive school provision.

386. American education is more decentralised and practices vary widely between states and within states. There are a few schools for the exceptionally

gifted in the United States. They include the Bronx High School of Science and the Brooklyn Technical High School in New York. These select the most able in mathematics and science of those who apply at the eighth grade, i.e. at about age 13. The High School of Performing Arts enrols students who have demonstrated particularly high aptitudes in dance and drama, combined with generally high scholastic ability and achievement. More common are various methods of special treatment within the normal system of schools. There has been a great deal of research on the merits and demerits of various schemes and the whole subject is hotly debated. There is no clear conclusion to be drawn from this research and the education of the gifted in the United States remains, even now, in an experimental stage. In general, expert opinion tends to favour special programmes for the gifted rather than the creation of special super-selective schools for them.

Our Own Proposals

387. Any school structure has its drawbacks. The conventional grammar school implies secondary modern schools and the suppression of talent that results from selection at 11. Even in grammar schools, taking some ten to twenty per cent of the ability range, the needs of the exceptionally gifted may be neglected. Small comprehensive schools, on the other hand, may not have the resources to offer their most able pupils what they need, and schools confined to a catchment area with severe social deprivations face special handicaps. A generally low standard of aspiration can be as "infectious" as a high one. In this country there is likely to be an increasing shortage of the most highly qualified teachers in mathematics and science subjects, and the greatest care must be taken to ensure that they are deployed to the best advantage. It is open to question whether they are best used in the teaching of the most able eleven and twelve-year-olds or whether they should concentrate on older children capable of taking their education beyond the minimum leaving age. Clearly they must not be wasted on teaching tiny groups of two or three children for 'A' level subjects. The Inner London Education Authority Report on Sixth Form Opportunities[1] pointed out various ways in which the resources needed at sixth form level can be more effectively deployed. Other authorities, which have not retained selective schools, will find it easier to organise the sixth forms of comprehensive schools without undue restriction on choice of subjects because their comprehensive schools will not be losing potential sixth formers to grammar schools. Nevertheless the advantages to be gained from co-operation between schools at sixth form levels should be explored in all areas.

388. We agree that there should be some schools which have a bias towards one or other of the arts, such as music or ballet. Some people are convinced that to produce outstanding performers in these fields it is necessary to start rigorous training young and this is most easily done in schools concentrating in this sphere yet at the same time providing a good general education. Some of these will be locally maintained schools serving more than one local authority. If the proposals made by some of us for full grant schools are adopted, these arrangements would be well suited for schools which would draw pupils from all over the country. A few independent day and boarding schools could also take

---

[1] "Sixth-Form Opportunities in Inner London", Report of a Working Party, December, 1968, I.L.E.A., 951.

on specialist roles of this kind, and local authorities would be able to send assisted pupils to them—as was proposed in the Commission's First Report[1] and in Chapter 11 of this Report.

389. The question remains whether the most academically gifted children should be educated in separate schools with others of similar ability. We agree that the evidence from research is not conclusive. The findings may be interpreted in different ways.

390. Most of us[2] conclude that the evidence, despite its weakness, suggests that academically gifted children are best taught in the various forms of comprehensive school now developing. But special arrangements must be made for them. Various programmes are possible. One is acceleration, either for individual children or for groups of children, which brings them to the point of entry to higher education a year earlier than most pupils, though the trend of opinion in recent years has moved firmly against schemes of this nature. Another is an enriched course which allows the gifted child to explore a subject in greater depth or breadth—it has been described as "getting ahead sideways". This can be achieved either within the normal class unit by individualised methods of teaching or through special arrangements and special classes. Pupils might be released from part of the normal course to attend lessons at a special centre catering for gifted children over a wider area. These lessons or seminars can provide a stimulation which carries over into the rest of the course. Similar classes or activities can be held out of normal school hours in the evening, on Saturdays or during the summer. We think segregation of gifted children into separate schools at an early age may create more problems than it solves. There is some evidence that the least able, relatively speaking, of the pupils at schools which cater for the very able do less well than they might have done in comprehensive schools.

391. It is extremely difficult to select children with predictive accuracy for a normal grammar school curriculum before the age of 15 or 16 and this in itself has already led to scepticism about the traditional tripartite system. The more selective schools become, the greater the difficulties of accurate selection.

392. The effect on other pupils must also be considered. To take away the brightest children from a comprehensive school is to deprive the children who remain of an invaluable source of stimulation. The deprivations felt by pupils excluded from super-selective schools may generate more militant opposition than traditional selection procedures: if children in the top two per cent of the ability range are to be selected instead of the top 20 per cent or so, the middle-class families most sensitive to educational hierarchies would mostly be

---

[1] First Report, paragraph 288.

[2] Lord Annan, Dr. Bliss, Professor Donnison, Dr. Faulkner, Dame Anne Godwin, Mr. Hill, Alderman Hutty, Dr. Judge, Mr. Marsh, Mother Angela Mary Reidy, Councillor Taylor, Mr. Waddilove, Professor Williams. The views expressed in paragraphs 390 to 393 are endorsed by these members of the Commission and "we" used in these paragraphs refers only to these members.

While agreeing with this majority view, Mr. Arnold-Forster considers that the whole Chapter is about a non-existent problem. In his view, the (comparatively few) witnesses who said that the education of exceptionally gifted children present urgent problems were unconvincing. Teachers now in schools can recognise and nurture genius more efficiently than systems for super-selection. These systems would have rejected Einstein and probably would have rejected Churchill.

among those excluded. The support many of them now evince for selection might not survive this experience.

393. More important still are the broader social implications of a selective system. Selection procedures for picking the ablest children at the age of eleven exert a distorting influence on the last years of primary education. Elite schools create and sustain social divisions which are no longer tolerable. Able children who go to such schools may fail to acquire the understanding and respect for their less able or fortunate contemporaries which a good comprehensive education can engender. Those excluded must tend to feel inferior, and not only in a purely intellectual sense. That is not the way to create the society we hope this country will become.

394. The remainder of us[1] take a different view. A few direct grant schools, as well as some independent and maintained schools, concentrate especially on the top two to three per cent of the ability range. (The large majority of selective schools of all types at present take a wider ability range than this.) We admire the work being done in these highly selective schools and believe that the children in them, especially the exceptionally able, get a better and deeper education and develop further and faster than they would in a neighbourhood comprehensive school. The future of the country depends greatly on our ability to bring out the best in these exceptional individuals. This can be most effectively and economically done at present by educating such children in schools specially designed for their needs. If they are dispersed through the comprehensive system—the system as it often is and will be, not as it might ideally become—they will tend to fall back and grow bored, to under-achieve and fail even to stimulate others in the way that is expected of them. They need competition from other pupils with like ability and the stimulation and guidance of able teachers if they are to develop their full potential. To achieve this economically, able pupils and teachers must both be concentrated in schools of a special kind.

395. We agree that the evidence is inconclusive and that further research should be done on the education of the gifted. The results of research and further practical experience may lead to the conclusion that super-selective schools are the best answer. While this remains possible it would be foolish to destroy those that already exist.

396. We see the social dangers of such a policy but think they can be overcome by inter-school and out-of-school activities, and by fostering a sensible attitude within each school. We suspect that there are as many dangers in giving able children special treatment within a comprehensive school—and special treatment they must have. We therefore favour keeping some of the best and most selective schools and developing them for the ablest two per cent of the children in their areas until such time as it can be established whether this way of catering for them is the best or not. If it is, then a system of such schools should be set up to cater for all areas. Larger towns will be able to support a day school. The rest of the country would have to be served by selective boarding schools or by attaching boarding wings to selective day schools. Some of these super-selective schools would be found among the present direct grant schools, others among

---

[1] Mr. Allison, Mr. McGowan, Miss Wilks, the Dean of Windsor, Mr. Young. The views expressed in paragraphs 394 to 397 are endorsed by these members of the Commission and "we" used in these paragraphs refers only to these members.

maintained or independent schools. The number of schools eventually needed would depend on the proportion of the ability range to be served and the efficiency with which they can be selected. In England and Wales, 2 per cent of the year group now amounts to around 13,000 pupils. However, substantial numbers of parents would probably not want their children to travel long distances or board at schools of this special kind. Others will prefer education in the local comprehensive school. Taking these factors into account we think that provision would need to be made for about half the children we are talking about i.e. between 6,000 and 7,000 children. If they enter secondary schools at the age of eleven and stay seven years, these children could be educated in some 40 to 50 schools of about 1,000 pupils each.

397. The full grant system proposed in Chapter 9 would be particularly suited for these schools. Clearly there must be no fee-payers in them if the ablest children are all to have the opportunity of entering them no matter what the incomes or aspirations of their parents. We hope the Government will reach decisions on these proposals and approach the schools which would be invited to adopt this super-selective role as soon as possible. Local education authorities cannot pursue the integration schemes planned for their own grammar schools, and direct grant and day independent schools cannot negotiate the new relationships most of them will have with the State system till the fate of these proposals and the schools they would affect are known.

398. Those of us who wish there to be for an experimental period a system of schools specially suited to the needs of the exceptionally able and those of us who think that such pupils can best be taught within a comprehensive system join in urging that more research and experiment be devoted to these problems. Whether gifted children should be segregated into separate schools or taught in comprehensive schools, at what ages selection for different purposes is justifiable, and what teaching methods can best develop ability to the full in schools of all kinds: these are vital questions which we must learn more about, whatever pattern of schools ultimately emerges from our present debates.

Acknowledgements

Our enquiry could not have been made unless a great many people had been willing to help us.

The governors and heads of schools and the officers of education authorities went to great trouble to answer our questionnaires. We visited education authorities and schools of all kinds—maintained, direct grant and independent—and were kindly received by members of the authorities and their officials, and by school governors, heads, staff and pupils. They showed us their schools, explained their work, and patiently answered our questions.

Officials of the Department of Education and Science and the Scottish Education Department did their utmost to find the information we needed.

Many people gave us evidence, and some of them met us to discuss the problems we were dealing with.

Throughout our work we relied heavily on the knowledge and guidance of Mr. Howard Glennerster of the London School of Economics and Political Science and Mr. Eric Hoyle of the Department of Education, Manchester University. Their task of conducting, summarising and interpreting research in an exceedingly complex field for a Commission grappling with urgent, practical problems demanded a rare blend of objectivity and commitment, detachment and realism.

Mr. Geoffrey Petter, H.M.I., Mr. Evan Morgan of the Department of Education and Science, and Mr. William McIndoe and Mr. John McClellan of the Scottish Education Department acted as assessors to the Commission. They attended many of our meetings, accompanied us on many of our visits to schools and education authorities, and gave us much helpful advice.

We made enquiries of the representatives of foreign Governments in London and many of them gave us information about education in their own countries. We visited Sweden and were hospitably received by many people there who went to great trouble on our behalf. Mr. Sven Elmgren, of the National Board of Education, deserves special thanks for the success of our visit.

Mr. Dan Neylan was the Commission's first secretary. The prompt and effective start we made on our work was largely due to him. His sudden and tragic death deprived us of an able officer and a personal friend. Our enquiry might have been disrupted and delayed, had it not been for Mr. Gordon Etheridge who had served the Commission since it was set up in 1966 and who took over the work and carried it forward without a moment's interruption. Mr. James Sinclair of the Scottish Education Department was secretary of our Scottish Committee. He and Mr. Etheridge had the difficult and delicate task of organising and harmonising both reports, and faithfully expressing the varied and sometimes conflicting views of twenty-six people. We are grateful for their unfailing devotion, wisdom and good humour.

179

We also want to thank the teams who worked with our secretaries in London and Edinburgh—particularly Mr. Robert Horne, the Commission's assistant secretary, Mr. David Stevenson, Mr. Robert Hostler, Mrs. Sue Sandifer, Mr. Roger Aylward, Miss Judy Slater, Mr. Val. Truscott and Miss Joyce Fisher.

No Commission could have received more generous help than we have been given by all who collaborated in our enquiry. We thank them all.

Signatures	*Chairman:*	DAVID DONNISON
	Vice-Chairman:	ANNAN
	Members:	C. RALPH ALLISON
		KATHLEEN BLISS
		T. EWAN FAULKNER
		ANNE GODWIN
		MARK ARNOLD-FORSTER
		WILLIAM S. HILL
		FRED H. HUTTY
		H. G. JUDGE
		R. M. MARSH
		BRUCE McGOWAN
		ANGELA MARY REIDY O.S.U.
		TOM TAYLOR
		LEWIS E. WADDILOVE
		JEAN R. F. WILKS
		BERNARD WILLIAMS
		ROBIN WOODS
		R. W. YOUNG

Secretary: G. ETHERIDGE

INDEX

Unless otherwise stated, references are to paragraph numbers. The Appendices in Volume II have not been indexed in detail but a few major references are included in this index. The introduction and summary of recommendations have not been indexed.

LIST OF APPENDICES WHICH WILL APPEAR IN VOLUME II

1. Method of working
2. List of direct grant schools and day public schools
3. Visits to schools and other institutions, and local education authorities
4. Evidence
5. The research reviewed—by Mr. Hoyle
6. The questionnaires and a survey of the replies
7. The finances of the direct grant schools—by Mr. Glennerster
8. Analysis of the V.R.Q. distribution of pupils in a sample of local education authorities
9. Direct grant—background papers
10. Local education authority schemes of transfer of pupils from primary to county secondary schools: two examples

The Scottish Report is published as Volume III.

Printed in England for Her Majesty's Stationery Office
by McCorquodale & Co. Ltd., London

Dd. 501578   K 80   2/70